M000280202

FOLLOWING IN THE FOOTSTEPS OF CHRIST

TRADITIONS OF CHRISTIAN SPIRITUALITY SERIES

At the Fountain of Elijah: The Carmelite Tradition
Wilfrid McGreal, o. carm.

Brides in the Desert: The Spirituality of the Beguines
Saskia Murk-Jansen

Contemplation and Compassion: The Victorine Tradition
Steven Chase

Eyes to See, Ears to Hear: An Introduction to Ignatian Spirituality
David Lonsdale

God's Lovers in an Age of Anxiety: The Medieval English Mystics
Joan M. Nuth

Heart Speaks to Heart: The Salesian Tradition
Wendy M. Wright

Journeys on the Edges: The Celtic Tradition
Thomas O'Loughlin

The Language of Silence: The Changing Face of Monastic Solitude
Peter-Damian Belisle, OSB Cam

Mysticism and Prophecy: The Dominican Tradition
Richard Woods, OP

Our Restless Heart: The Augustinian Tradition
Thomas F. Martin, OSA

The Poetic Imagination: An Anglican Spiritual Tradition
L. William Countryman

Poverty and Joy: The Franciscan Tradition
William J. Short, OFM

Prayer and Community: The Benedictine Tradition
Columba Stewart, OSB

Silence and Witness: The Quaker Tradition
Michael L. Birkel

Standing in God's Holy Fire: The Byzantine Spiritual Tradition
John Anthony McGuckin

Silence and Witness: The Quaker Tradition
Michael L. Birkel

The Spirit of Worship: The Liturgical Tradition
Susan J. White

The Way of Simplicity: The Cistercian Tradition
Esther de Waal

FOLLOWING IN THE FOOTSTEPS OF CHRIST

The Anabaptist Tradition

cf. p. 154? for title

C. ARNOLD SNYDER

SERIES EDITOR:
Philip Sheldrake

ORBIS BOOKS
Maryknoll, New York 10545

Founded in 1970, Orbis Books endeavors to publish works that enlighten the mind, nourish the spirit, and challenge the conscience. The publishing arm of the Maryknoll Fathers & Brothers, Orbis seeks to explore the global dimensions of the Christian faith and mission, to invite dialogue with diverse cultures and religious traditions, and to serve the cause of reconciliation and peace. The books published reflect the views of their authors and do not represent the official position of the Society. To learn more about Maryknoll and Orbis Books, please visit our website at www.maryknoll.org.

First published in Great Britian in 2004 by
Darton, Longman and Todd Ltd
1 Spencer Court
140-142 Wandsworth High Street
London SW18 4JJ
Great Britain

First published in the USA in 2004 by
Orbis Books
P.O. Box 308
Maryknoll, New York 10545-0308
U.S.A.

Orbis ISBN 1–57075–536–1

Library of Congress Cataloguing-in-Publication Data

Snyder, C. Arnold, 1946–
    Following in the footsteps of Christ : the Anabaptist Tradition / C. Arnold Snyder
        p. cm. – (Traditions of Christian spirituality)
Includes bibliographical references (p.   ).
    ISBN 1–57075–536–1
    1. Spiritual life—Anabaptists.   2. Anabaptists—Doctrines.   I. Title.
    II. Series.
        BX4931.3.S66   2004
        284′.3—dc22

                                                                    2003018597
                                                                    Rev.

For

Alan and Eleanor,

who know this story
and treasure its truth.

CONTENTS

ACKNOWLEDGEMENTS

This book first began to take shape in dialogue with students. Of these students, those in the Master of Theological Studies programme, Conrad Grebel University College, were particular witnesses to several iterations and not-so-successful attempts to organise the material. I am thankful to them for their engagement, enthusiasm and insights, as together we explored and tested different approaches to the story of Anabaptist spirituality.

I am thankful to the board and administration of Conrad Grebel University College for providing such a wonderful academic home where, in an atmosphere of true collegiality, questions such as these can be pursued and discussed among friends who care. Conrad Grebel generously made available the sabbatical time needed for the completion of the present manuscript. I am grateful to Philip Sheldrake and the able staff at Darton, Longman & Todd for the helpful editorial direction they provided in the more advanced stages of the work.

And finally, I must thank Alan and Eleanor Kreider. They have been an inspiration, an encouragement and a witness. Without their keen interest, support and counsel this book would not have been written or published. It is to them that the book is dedicated, with gratitude and affection.

C. Arnold Snyder
Kitchener, Ontario
February 2004

PREFACE TO THE SERIES

Nowadays, in the Western world, there is a widespread hunger for spirituality in all its forms. This is not confined to traditional religious people, let alone to regular churchgoers. The desire for resources to sustain the spiritual quest has led many people to seek wisdom in unfamiliar places. Some have turned to cultures other than their own. The fascination with Native American or Aboriginal Australian spiritualities is a case in point. Other people have been attracted by the religions of India and Tibet or the Jewish Kabbalah and Sufi mysticism. One problem is that, in comparison to other religions, Christianity is not always associated in people's minds with 'spirituality'. The exceptions are a few figures from the past who have achieved almost cult status such as Hildegard of Bingen or Meister Eckhart. This is a great pity, for Christianity East and West over two thousand years has given birth to an immense range of spiritual wisdom. Many traditions continue to be active today. Others that were forgotten are being rediscovered and reinterpreted.

It is a long time since an extended series of introductions to Christian spiritual traditions has been available in English. Given the present climate, it is an opportune moment for a new series which will help more people to be aware of the great spiritual riches available within the Christian traditions.

The overall purpose of the series is to make selected spiritual traditions available to a contemporary readership. The books seek to provide accurate and balanced historical and thematic treatments of their subjects. The authors are also conscious of the need to make connections with contemporary experience and values without being artificial or reducing a tradition to one dimension. The authors are well versed in reliable scholarship about the traditions they describe. However, their intention is that the books should be fresh in style and accessible to the general reader.

One problem that such a series inevitably faces is the word 'spirituality'. For example, it is increasingly used beyond religious circles and does not necessarily imply a faith tradition. Again, it could mean substantially different things for a Christian and a Buddhist. Within Christianity itself, the word in its modern sense is relatively recent. The reality that it stands for differs subtly in the different contexts of time and place. Historically, 'spirituality' covers a breadth of human experience and a wide range of values and practices.

No single definition of 'spirituality' has been imposed on the authors in this series. Yet, despite the breadth of the series there is a sense of a common core in the writers themselves and in the traditions they describe. All Christian spiritual traditions have their source in three things. First, while drawing on ordinary experience and even religious insights from elsewhere, Christian spiritualities are rooted in the Scriptures and particularly in the Gospels. Second, spiritual traditions are not derived from abstract theory but from attempts to live out gospel values in a positive yet critical way within specific historical and cultural contexts. Third, the experiences and insights of individuals and groups are not isolated but are related to the wider Christian tradition of beliefs, practices and community life. From a Christian perspective, spirituality is not just concerned with prayer or even with narrowly religious activities. It concerns the whole of human life, viewed in terms of a conscious relationship with God, in Jesus Christ, through the indwelling of the Holy Spirit and within a community of believers.

The series as a whole includes traditions that probably would not have appeared twenty years ago. The authors themselves have been encouraged to challenge, where appropriate, inaccurate assumptions about their particular tradition. While conscious of their own biases, authors have none the less sought to correct the imbalances of the past. Previous understandings of what is mainstream or 'orthodox' sometimes need to be questioned. People or practices that became marginal demand to be re-examined. Studies of spirituality in the past frequently underestimated or ignored the role of women. Sometimes the treatments of spiritual traditions were culturally one-sided because they were written from an uncritical Western European or North Atlantic perspective.

However, any series is necessarily selective. It cannot hope to do full justice to the extraordinary variety of Christian spiritual traditions. The principles of selection are inevitably open to question. I hope that an appropriate balance has been maintained between a sense of the likely readership on the one hand and the dangers of narrowness on the other. In the end, choices had to be made and the result is inevitably weighted in favour of traditions that have achieved 'classic' status or which seem to capture the contemporary imagination. Within these limits, I trust that the series will offer a reasonably balanced account of what the Christian spiritual tradition has to offer.

As editor of the series I would like to thank all the authors who agreed to contribute and for the stimulating conversations and correspondence that sometimes resulted. I am especially grateful for the high quality of their work which made my task so much easier. Editing such a series is a complex undertaking I have worked closely throughout with the editorial team of Darton, Longman and Todd and Robert Ellsberg of Orbis Books. I am immensely grateful to them for their friendly support and judicious advice. Without them this series would never have come together.

PHILIP SHELDRAKE
University of Durham

1 ANABAPTIST SPIRITUALITY IN HISTORIAL PERSPECTIVE

Writing a book describing Anabaptist spirituality immediately calls for a clarification of terms. What are we seeking to describe, and among what group of people, when we go in search of 'Anabaptist spirituality'?

SPIRITUALITY

The term 'spirituality' is one that everyone seems to understand – it carries a wealth of connotations. Nevertheless, spirituality is a word that is almost impossible to define precisely – its denotation is a matter of debate. In the Christian context, the word spirituality evokes a strongly interior, personal nuance, bringing to mind such words as grace, mystery, spirit, faith, prayer and contemplation. To some people, spirituality has to do almost exclusively with these interior 'things of the spirit'. For this reason it is important to clarify that in the Christian tradition the 'life of the spirit' has always been understood to extend beyond the 'inner-looking' activities of prayer, meditation and contemplation. What is explored in the volumes of this series is 'the whole of human life, viewed in terms of a conscious relationship with God, in Jesus Christ, through the indwelling of the Holy Spirit and within a community of believers,' as Philip Sheldrake explains.

The recognition that Christian spirituality embraces both the inner and the outer lives of Christians – that is, both their contemplative and their active lives – provides a particularly helpful beginning point for an exploration of Anabaptist spirituality. The visible features of the Anabaptist understanding of the faithful Christian life – the baptism of adults and living in faithful and active discipleship – are certainly best known and most easily recognised. However, they are only a part of the story. What is less well known, and what will occupy us particularly in this volume, is the spiritual understanding and practice that undergirded, nourished and defined the visible Anabaptist witness.

ANABAPTISM

Who were the Anabaptists? Answering this question properly would require its own historiographical volume. The definition and description of 'Anabaptism' has long been a contentious historical issue. In this book we will apply a simple historical definition in order to cut the Gordian knot: as we will use the term, an Anabaptist was anyone in the sixteenth century who practised the baptism of adult believers. Having provided this simple definition, however, we must immediately qualify it, for it both excludes some figures often associated with the baptising movement, and also includes more baptisers than is useful for a study of this kind.

Excluded from the Anabaptism we will be describing are some influential 'forerunners' who never came to practise adult baptism. Two of the most notable are Andreas Karlstadt and Thomas Müntzer, erstwhile followers of Luther whom historians have classified as 'radical reformers'. Readers who wish to explore the historical connections between these Reformation radicals and the beginnings of Anabaptism may do so in other available studies.[1] Attempting to include in our study *all* those who practised adult baptism in the sixteenth century casts too large a net for a book of this scope. The baptising movement was a spontaneous, decentralised, grassroots, underground movement of spiritual renewal and biblical reform, carried forward by 'common people' of no particular theological expertise. In its beginnings there were no governing church authorities, defining theologians or political patrons. The baptisers therefore were an unusually heterogeneous lot, especially in their first generation. Even a sympathetic contemporary observer like the spiritualist Sebastian Franck – who knew individual Anabaptists well – complained that 'almost no one agrees with anyone else in all matters'.[2]

One way of telling the Anabaptist story is to pursue these differences in some detail, as some social and intellectual historians have done.[3] While detailed studies have their place, we have chosen to describe the shape of the forest, rather than attempt to detail the features of its individual trees. We will be guided by the most common features visible in the spiritual teaching and practice of the baptising movement and trace how those features gave shape to the surviving baptising tradition beyond the sixteenth century. As often as possible, we will tell the story by utilising the testimonies, songs and writings of the Anabaptists themselves.

A BRIEF HISTORICAL SKETCH

Historians have traced the beginnings of three distinct baptising movements in sixteenth-century Europe, namely the Swiss, South German/Austrian, and North German/Dutch Anabaptist groups.

Swiss Anabaptism: the Swiss Brethren

In late January of 1525, in a small house near the cathedral in Zurich, Switzerland, a small group of people gathered to discuss what they considered to be a serious setback to the reform of the church. A contemporary source describes the basic issues they felt they were facing:

> In the fear of God they agreed that from God's Word one must first learn true faith, expressed in deeds of love, and on confession of this faith receive true Christian baptism

as a covenant of a good conscience with God, serving him from then on with a holy Christian life and remaining steadfast to the end, even in times of tribulation.[4]

Certain key words and themes appear in this testimony that we will see again and again in the testimonies of the baptising movement: fear of God, God's Word, true faith, deeds of love, confession of faith, baptism as a covenant, serving God, a holy life, steadfastness, and tribulation. The basic position was this: only adult baptism was biblical, and should be practised in response to a person's coming to 'true faith'. The results of this baptism would be visible in 'deeds of love' and a 'holy Christian life'.

But, in spite of the best efforts of this group of Christians to convince the Zurich city council that theirs was the correct biblical understanding and the apostolic practice, the council heeded Ulrich Zwingli's opinion instead, and decreed that all unbaptised infants must to be brought for baptism. Furthermore, any further 'agitation' related to baptism would not be tolerated, on pain of civil punishment.

Rather than accepting the judgement of the Zurich council, the participants in this small nocturnal meeting took a radical step: they baptised one another according to their understanding of the biblical order. The same source cited above, the Hutterite *Chronicle*, describes what happened:

> After the prayer, Georg Blaurock stood up and asked Conrad Grebel in the name of God to baptise him with true Christian baptism on his faith and recognition of the truth. With this request he knelt down, and Conrad baptised him . . . Then the others turned to Georg in their turn, asking him to baptise them, which he did. And so, in great fear of God, together they surrendered themselves to the Lord. They confirmed one another for the service of the Gospel and began to teach the faith and to keep it.[5]

This baptismal event is the first documented case of 'believer's baptism' in the sixteenth century.

The baptisers soon came to be called Anabaptists by their enemies, the name suggesting that they were 're-baptisers' who were performing an invalid second baptism, in spite of having received a perfectly valid infant baptism. The baptisers themselves insisted that they were not re-baptising, but receiving the only valid baptism there was. They rejected the name Anabaptist which, in any case, was intended as a condemnation and carried an ancient imperial penalty of death.[6] The baptisers usually referred to one another as 'brothers and sisters in the Lord'.

Among the leaders of this earliest baptising movement were Conrad Grebel, Felix Mantz, George Blaurock, Margret Hottinger, Balthasar Hubmaier and Michael Sattler. By 1530 none of these leaders was still alive. Of this group, only Conrad Grebel died a natural death; Mantz, Blaurock, Hottinger, Hubmaier and Sattler all met martyrs' deaths, two by drowning and three by being burned alive at the stake. A large number of the Swiss baptisers were forced to flee their homeland. Many fled to the East, and found refuge in the Moravian territories (today in the Czech Republic) which, at that time, remained fiercely independent under the governance of noble families, inclined by their Hussite background to welcome religious dissidents.

The baptisers who followed the teachings of this early movement soon were called 'Swiss Brethren' by baptisers elsewhere. Although some spiritualist emphases are visible in their original leaders, particularly in George Blaurock and Margret Hottinger, the Swiss Brethren were noted for their insistence on a visible and holy life of conformity with Christ. The 'Brotherly Union of Schleitheim', authored by the former Benedictine prior Michael Sattler, provided the Swiss Brethren with a simple constitution that required a disciplined life of discipleship, non-violence and truth-telling (the non-swearing of oaths).

By the seventeenth century the Swiss Brethren had had many contacts with Dutch Anabaptists, who in their turn had come to be called 'Mennists' or 'Mennonites' by their enemies.

Later in the seventeenth century, the Swiss Brethren came to call themselves 'Mennonites' as well, recognising their spiritual kinship with the Dutch brethren. At the end of the seventeenth century, the Swiss Brethren (or Swiss Mennonites) suffered through a bitter division and schism. A reforming Swiss Mennonite leader named Jacob Amman set out to introduce a more rigorous church discipline and practice. The result was a schism in 1693 that saw the Swiss Mennonites divide into 'Mennonite' and 'Amish' factions. Although a small number of Mennonites and Amish descendants managed to survive in Switzerland, Alsace and the Palatinate, the majority migrated to North America beginning early in the eighteenth century, where Mennonite and Amish groups have grown and flourished.

South German/Austrian Anabaptism

The South German baptising movement began early in 1526, appearing first in the free imperial cities of Nuremberg, Augsburg and Strasbourg. The historical record, fragmentary as it is, has provided no documentation of historical connections to the earlier Swiss movement, but there are striking similarities in doctrine and practice. The similarities suggest far more contact and communication between the Swiss and the South German Anabaptists than the documentation can prove. But there are also some well-marked differences between the two groups, and this points to different sources of inspiration as well. The South German Anabaptist movement was more obviously spiritualist in its early years than were the Swiss baptisers. Many of the early South German leaders had a high regard for the mystical writings of Johannes Tauler and the anonymous Taulerian *Theologia Deutsch*. The South German baptising movement also had strong apocalyptic elements that had been far more muted among the Swiss. Many of the early South German Anabaptists believed that they were living in the End Times, and that by reading the prophetic books of Scripture, they could figure out exactly when Jesus would return.

Two early leaders of this movement were Hans Denck and Hans Hut. Hans Denck was a baptising leader who particularly valued the mystical legacy of Johannes Tauler. He baptised Hans Hut in 1526, but Hut developed a different Anabaptist emphasis. Hut had been a follower of Thomas Müntzer, and remained convinced that Jesus was about to return to earth. Hut was a very successful Anabaptist missionary in South German lands. However, by the end of 1527, both Denck and Hut had died, Hans Denck of the plague and Hans Hut through martyrdom.

The early South German Anabaptist movement was richly diverse and fertile. From this milieu came the irenic Anabaptist leader and engineer Pilgram Marpeck, several prominent spiritualist Anabaptists, and Jacob Hutter, leader of the communitarian Hutterites. Of all the persons and movements that appeared in the 1520s and 30s, only the Hutterian Brethren (Hutterites) survived as an identifiable group beyond the sixteenth century. The distinctive Hutterian teaching is a community of goods (all things owned in common), a way of life still carried out in Hutterite colonies in North America. The distinctive spiritualist and apocalyptic emphases of the early South German movement came to play no significant role in defining Hutterian belief; rather, with the exception of their teaching on the community of goods, the Hutterites adopted an Anabaptism that closely resembled that of the Swiss Brethren, in many cases copying and preserving Swiss Brethren writings in their communities.

No original Hutterite communities survived in Europe. Although there were sporadic problems in Moravia in the sixteenth century, the Hutterian Brethren were mostly tolerated and flourished there from about 1550 to the end of the century, when re-Catholicisation began to be strictly applied by the Hapsburg crown through the agency of the Jesuits. By 1620 the Hutterites had been expelled from Moravia, but still maintained some colonies in Slovakia. By 1700, Hapsburg control of Slovakia had closed that precarious refuge as well. In 1770, after a sojourn through Romania, a very small group found refuge in the Ukraine. When the Russian crown threatened military conscription in 1870 it led to the migration of all Hutterites to North America (1874–79) where they have flourished and multiplied on the plains of the United States and the prairies of Canada.

North German/Dutch Anabaptism

The baptising movement that spread to northern Europe was begun and led by Melchior Hoffman, who became an Anabaptist in 1530 in Strasbourg. Hoffman, who had earlier promoted Lutheran reform in northern German lands, returned to the north in 1530 as an Anabaptist missionary. The movement he inspired (also called 'Melchiorite' Anabaptism) spread throughout North Germany and especially into the Netherlands where it shared with the Sacramentarians a rejection of the Roman Catholic sacraments. In its first phase (1530–33), Melchiorite Anabaptism was very apocalyptic (certain of Jesus' imminent return), but peaceful – expecting God's action to initiate the Last Days. By 1533 Melchior Hoffman had been arrested and Melchiorite Anabaptism entered a second phase (1533–35), under the leadership of the prophetic visionary Jan Matthijs. He was a baker from Haarlem, in the Netherlands, who became convinced that he was the prophet Enoch of the Last Days. Under his direction, the Melchiorite movement abandoned its passive waiting for Christ's imminent return and became more militant. Matthijs taught that the baptised saints of the Last Days were supposed to take the 'sword of righteousness' into their own hands, to prepare the way for the return of the Lord. Inspired by the prophecies of Matthijs and other visionaries, some Melchiorite Anabaptists took control of the city of Münster in Westphalia early in 1534, and held the city against a military siege until June 1535, when the city finally fell, most of its inhabitants slaughtered.

A third, more peaceful phase of Melchiorite Anabaptism gained strength after the fall of Münster. The followers of the

Anabaptist leader Obbe Philips had opposed the Münsterite enthusiasm, as had the prophetic spiritualist David Joris. This 'peaceful wing' worked to reorganise the northern baptising remnant after Münster. In 1536, a parish priest from Frisia named Menno Simons left the Catholic Church and became an Anabaptist, baptised into the movement by Obbe Philips. Menno soon emerged as a central pastoral leader of the chastened baptisers in the Netherlands and Northern Germany.

Menno was staunchly biblicist, uncompromisingly opposed to both spiritualistic, prophetic visionaries and apocalyptic militants. He wrote an impressive number of pastoral and apologetic tracts and miraculously avoided capture, in spite of the considerable price that had been placed on his head. He died in 1561 of old age. Those whom he pastored were soon called 'Mennists', and from this label we get the name 'Mennonite': followers of Menno Simons. Whereas the supporters of Münsterite apocalypticism faded from view after 1535, and the spiritualistic followers of David Joris went underground and also soon disappeared from view, the followers of Menno Simons established communities that have survived to the present day. The baptisers that remained in the Netherlands came to be known as the *Doopsgezinden* (baptism-minded), while Mennonite exiles from the Netherlands migrated along the Baltic, first to the Danzig area (by 1530), then in large numbers to New Russia at the invitation of Catherine the Great (1776). Three subsequent waves of migration (1870s, 1920s, 1945ff.) brought these 'Russian' Mennonites to Canada, the United States and several South American countries, especially to Paraguay and Brazil.

The first generation of baptisers in all regions of Europe included people who taught and practised some things later repudiated by the surviving tradition. Two particular early emphases – apocalypticism and radical spiritualism – were extremely significant elements of early Anabaptism. Hans Hut, Melchior Hoffman, Jan Mathijs and Bernhard Rothmann were important Anabaptist leaders who were convinced they were living in the Last Days. They set about gathering together and baptising the Bride who would welcome Christ back to earth. Many of their baptised converts continued on in Anabaptist communities, but failed apocalyptic prophecies bequeathed no permanent shape to the movement that survived. Likewise, some Anabaptists became radical spiritualists, such as the erstwhile baptising leaders Hans Bünderlin and Christian Entfelder, or the prophetic spiritualist David Joris. Although these spiritualisers were important historical figures at particular points of Anabaptist development, they also failed to imprint their emphasis on a 'purely spiritual' and invisible church on the surviving tradition of baptisers.

By excluding a detailing of the apocalyptic and radical spiritualist minority, our account of Anabaptist spirituality will take a longer, but narrower historical view of the baptising movement. We will deliberately allow the surviving traditions to inform our description of the shape and contours of sixteenth-century Anabaptist spirituality. This is not done to deny 'Anabaptist' status to the apocalyptic and spiritualist Anabaptists, or any other baptisers for that matter. There were a remarkable number of historical variants within the early baptising movement, but our purpose is not to be historically encyclopaedic. Rather, our narrative will describe the beliefs and practices of the broadest stream of sixteenth-century baptisers, whose spirituality subsequently gave shape to an 'Anabaptist tradition' that has survived to the present.

THE ANABAPTIST TRADITION: NEITHER CATHOLIC NOR PROTESTANT

When we take a longer view of Anabaptist origins and the subsequent development of the baptising movement, we can easily identify the basic 'shape' and movement of Anabaptist spirituality. These repeated patterns of belief and practice have continued to inform, shape and challenge the surviving Anabaptist tradition to this present day.

The baptising movement emerged in the context of the Reformation, and cannot be understood apart from Protestant reform. The baptisers all agreed with early Reformation criticisms levelled against the late medieval Roman Catholic Church – although the baptisers developed these critiques in their own unique way. The Anabaptists agreed with the evangelical (Protestant) Reformers, for example, that holy Scripture was the final authority in matters of belief and practice. The baptisers were anti-clerical, following the early Protestant critique of the power and authority of ordained clergy. The baptisers were uniformly anti-sacramental in a way that mirrored Ulrich Zwingli's view more closely than Luther's mature view. In sacramental matters, the Anabaptists insisted that visible church ordinances were signs, incapable of conveying spiritual power. Finally, the Anabaptists agreed with the Protestant Reformers that salvation was by faith through grace, and not the result of the reception of grace by sacramental means.

In spite of this undeniable Reformation parentage, however, the Anabaptists developed their own emphases and interpretations of both belief and practice that led them away from the mainline Reformation camps of Luther and Zwingli. In terms of the authority of Scripture, for example, Anabaptists insisted that the Holy Spirit had to be active in the interpretation of the letter. So, for example, a spiritually enlightened peasant would be a more reliable interpreter of Scripture than was a professor of biblical languages who lacked the Spirit. All the same, with the exception of a few prophetic spiritualists, the Anabaptists read and interpreted the text of the Bible itself in a decidedly practical, non-theological way, as will be seen in more detail below. The Anabaptists could not agree that political authorities had any right to decide matters of biblical interpretation or decree matters of faith or practice for the church, thus challenging the close church–state relationship that had been taken for granted by the Reformers. Once one moves past the apparent agreement of Anabaptists with the Reformers on the authority of Scripture, and asks how, and by whom, Scripture is to be interpreted, fundamental differences appear.

Likewise, the apparent agreement between Anabaptists and Reformers concerning salvation by faith faded quickly. The Anabaptists insisted that true, saving faith must be manifested by a holy life of obedience. Salvation, insisted all the Anabaptists, is not by faith *alone*, but by a faith that obeys. This 'obedience of faith' becomes possible, the Anabaptists maintained, by the power of the Holy Spirit who regenerates believers. If there is faith, the Anabaptists insisted, there will be a visibly holy life – not because human beings are innately good, but because they have yielded to the power of God, which power produces good works. Finally, the Anabaptists uniformly opposed the predestinarianism of both Martin Luther and John Calvin, and held that human beings are invited to faith, and are given the power (are 'freed') to respond in obedience or disobedience to God's call. Human free will means also that human response and responsibility are a part of the saving process, and not just God's action. The fact that regeneration by the power of God's Spirit is a gift of God's grace did not change the Anabaptist conclusion, that human beings must do their part and regeneration must be visible in works.

The Anabaptist interpretation of Reformation teachings led to a unique ecclesial expression, based on their reading and interpretation of Scripture. From the start, Anabaptist congregations in all places were marked by the baptism of adults, the mutual admonition and discipline of members, a memorial Lord's Supper, to be celebrated by those committed to a particular congregation by baptism and mutual discipline, and mutual aid (community sharing) among members of the church. The church, or the Body of Christ as the Anabaptists often called it, was thus a visible gathering of the saints in the world. By about 1540, the surviving Anabaptist groups had agreed further that true disciples of Christ would live without weapons and would not participate in warfare, and that disciples would likewise refuse to confirm the truth of their words with oaths, but would simply say Yes or No.

The baptising movement began with Reformation principles, but developed those principles in a unique manner.

Particularly galling to later Protestants was the importance the Anabaptists attached to the living of a new and holy life as a necessary correlative to faith. And so we read in the definitive Lutheran Confession, the Formula of Concord of 1580, that among the erroneous teachings of the Anabaptists is the requirement of renewal (*in der Erneurung/in renovatione*) in order to attain righteousness before God, a teaching that 'cannot be tolerated in the church'. Such a teaching was denounced by orthodox Lutheranism as 'nothing else than a new sort of monkery'.[7]

The accusation of 'monkery' was, as we shall see below, not entirely off the mark. In many important ways the Anabaptist movement retained spiritual ideals central to monasticism and late medieval piety, which the Protestant Reformers vigorously opposed. In particular, the Anabaptist understanding of reform expressed an undeniably ascetic and penitential understanding of the Christian life and of salvation. The Anabaptists likewise insisted upon a process of regeneration as a necessity for salvation, hearkening back to similar expressions in late medieval movements of renewal. In this connection, a marked Christocentrism shaped Anabaptist spirituality in ways that recall late medieval movements of devotion to Christ and a call to follow in his footsteps. The fusion of a late medieval structure of piety with Reformation principles gave a unique colour, shape and texture to Anabaptist church reform, marking it, to quote Walter Klaassen, as 'neither Catholic nor Protestant'[8] – or, as Sjouke Voolstra has suggested, 'both Catholic and Protestant'.[9]

The Anabaptists themselves recognised that they had no comfortable home either in Roman Catholicism or in Protestantism. The Hutterite *Chronicle* expressed the general Anabaptist view in the polemical terms common to the time:

> These two, Luther and Zwingli, exposed all the deception and villainy of the pope and brought it to the light of day as if they would strike everything to the ground with thunderbolts. But they put nothing better in its place. As

soon as they began to cling to worldly power and put their trust in human help, they were just as bad – like someone mending an old kettle and only making a bigger hole. They left behind a shameless people, whom they had taught to sin. To speak in a parable, they struck the jug from the pope's hand but kept the broken pieces in their own.[10]

With more historical perspective we can recognise now how much of both ascetic Catholic piety and Protestant reforming ideas the Anabaptists retained and uniquely shaped. By 1560, the surviving Anabaptist groups were clear about their status as neither one kind of church nor the other. They had settled the larger questions of how to interpret Scripture, and had outlined very specific 'rules of discipleship' for their members. The surviving Anabaptist traditions (the Swiss Brethren, Mennonites and Hutterites) came to agree on most crucial interpretive issues, with relatively minor differences. These mature Anabaptist 'traditions' have been handed on to succeeding generations.

2 THE HUMAN CONDITION: COMING TO A KNOWLEDGE OF THE TRUTH

Common to all the baptisers in the sixteenth century was the conviction that a truly Christian life must begin in a recognition of the truth about human existence and the path back to God. In this chapter we will explore the Anabaptist emphasis on 'coming to a knowledge of the truth', particularly as it relates to the call of God to individuals in their innermost beings. Throughout this chapter we will make occasional reference to selected late medieval devotional and edifying literature, in those cases where thematic and linguistic parallels seem significant. Although they were inspired by the Reformation call to be guided by 'Scripture alone', the Anabaptists, it will be plain, were not hacking out remarkable new trails in a spiritual wilderness. They traversed what already was a well-marked and well-known spiritual path.

FEAR OF GOD

Soetgen van den Houte was about forty years of age when she was arrested, tried and convicted for her Anabaptist faith in 1560. She was the mother of three children – David, Betgen and Tanneken – and a widow whose husband had been martyred for his faith in 1551. She wrote a final letter from her prison cell in Ghent, a testament of faith written for her children. Her testimony speaks with the intensity of a mother facing certain death for refusing to recant her most cherished beliefs, yet desiring to continue to care for her beloved children,

soon to be left with no earthly parents. 'My dear children,' she
wrote, 'since it pleases the Lord to take me out of this world, I
will leave you a memorial . . . I should like to write a jewel into
your heart, if it were possible, which is the word of truth, in
which I want to instruct you a little for the best with the Word
of the Lord.' What advice did she have for her children, to carry
them through a dangerous world? She begins in a manner
often seen in Anabaptist testimonies:

> In the first place, I admonished you, my most beloved,
> always to suffer yourself to be instructed by those who fear
> the Lord; then you will please God, and as long as you obey
> good admonition and instruction, and fear the Lord, He
> will be your Father and not leave you orphans. For David
> says: 'What man is he that feareth the Lord? Him shall he
> teach in the way that he shall choose.' Ps. 25:12. He also
> says: 'The eye of the Lord is upon them that fear him, upon
> them that hope in his mercy; to deliver their soul from
> death. The angel of the Lord encampeth round about them
> that fear him. O fear the Lord, ye his saints; there is no
> want to them that fear him; for the fear of the Lord is the
> beginning of wisdom.' Ps. 33:18, 19; 34:7, 9; 111:10.[1]

Fear the Lord and be instructed by those who also fear the
Lord, and you will no longer be orphans. Soetgen's confident
advice to her children is somewhat surprising to readers in
this century, striking us as negative in tone. But in fact, the
theme of 'fearing the Lord' runs consistently through
Anabaptist testimonies and writings, and points to a fundamental teaching.

When Joost de Tollenaer wrote his final testament from
prison in 1589 to his beloved 15-year-old daughter, he likewise
admonished her to 'fear God and keep His commandments'.

> My dear child Betgen, hear and understand my word,
> written to you in the name of the Lord, and let my speech
> enter into your heart, and receive it as a precious treasure
> of gold, that is, that you are from your very youth to learn

> to fear the Lord your God with all your heart, with all your soul, and with all your ability . . . For the fear of God is an overflowing fountain of eternal life, which quickens the heart and spirit, and creates a longing and desire to hear the words of God; for they strengthen the inner person in soul, spirit, and body.[2]

In the context of sixteenth-century Christianity, the ubiquitous Anabaptist call to 'fear God' was certainly not original. This biblical theme had been well developed by the preceding ascetic and pious movements within the Western church. A well-known instance is found in the Rule of St Benedict, where learning the 'fear of the Lord' (Ps. 34:12) is presented as one of the objectives of the vowed religious life and the first step in ascending the ladder of humility.[3] The Anabaptists, appealing as they did directly to Scripture, did not refer to church fathers or monastic rules, but rather buttressed their admonitions to fear God with numerous biblical passages brought together, in the manner of topical concordances, from all parts of the Bible – as the church fathers also had done. The 'topical' manner of organising, memorising and citing the Bible is evident not only in Anabaptist prison testimonies, such as the ones cited above, but also in the hymns the Anabaptists sang and the topical biblical concordances they compiled, printed and used. In the much-reprinted Swiss Brethren Concordance of 1540, for example, the very first topic of the 66 biblical topics collected is 'Fear of God'.[4]

Pointing to the 'fear of the Lord' as the fundamental attitude necessary to embark on the narrow way to salvation is rooted in a broader world-view, which the Anabaptists simply took for granted. God, the almighty creator of heaven, earth and of all things on the earth, is a living God who has promised salvation to those who repent, return to him and obey him. He also has promised judgement and condemnation for those who persist in unbelief and self-willed disobedience. Humanity, following Adam and Eve, has chosen and continues to choose to disobey, and so is on the road to perdition. But God in Christ has

reconciled humanity and promised salvation to those who
believe and obey.

At the heart of the Anabaptist world-view is a human
problem: self-willed human alienation from God, and a steadfast denial that there is any such problem. Equally disastrous,
they believed, were the humanly pleasing inventions that
purported to solve the problem of human alienation and
disobedience, but actually only made things worse. There is a
clearly marked way to salvation, back from the path to perdition, they believed, and that path back to God is clearly
described in both the Old and New Testaments – properly read
and understood. The 'fear of God' is the biblical door that
stands at the beginning of the path back to God because it
describes the necessary attitude and frame of mind needed to
get reality back into proper focus.

The Anabaptist world-view is not remarkable as such; it is
only remarkable because the baptisers took the biblical
description to heart, and drew from it the most serious life
consequences. Fearing the Lord means recognising God's
sovereign power and one's own negligible (and yet, destructive)
place in the greater scheme of things. Seeing things in this
light makes plain the urgent need to set out on the path of
salvation. Fear of God arises from an awareness of the actual
human condition of sin, complicity and powerlessness, and
expresses human dependence on God's grace and mercy.
Hubmaier had said, 'Such a miserable little thing is the person
who ponders and recognises himself,' pointing to the human
side of the equation. The correlative to the recognition of
human sin and impotence, however, is the recognition of God's
almighty power over human life and creation. Soetgen van den
Houte and Joost de Tollenaer each advised their children not
only to 'fear God', but also always to 'seek to be instructed by
the God-fearing'.[5] Anabaptist testimonies and writings
commonly refer to the pious, righteous believers as 'the God-
fearing'. Those who truly fear God are not only those who have
the right perspective and attitude, but are those who 'keep the
commandments' and live lives of obedience. Joost, who placed

the fear of God at the heart of his testament for Betgen, advised her to 'fear God from the heart; not as the world does, who profess that they know God but in works they deny Him'.[6]

Fear of the Lord lies at the beginning of the way of salvation because it requires a genuine humility, and results in unceasing prayer to God for grace. It will bear visible fruit; namely, a people who have experienced a genuine repentance and give evidence of a holy walk – a 'God-fearing' people. And so a Swiss Brethren hymn listed the fear of God as the first of the Holy Spirit's good gifts, and pointed to its fruits:

> The first gift . . .
> Is called the Fear of God,
> It is the beginning of all wisdom
> Which prepares the path to life for us.
>
> It trembles at the Word of God
> And enters through the narrow gate,
> It drives out sin and a godless life,
> Diligently watches and protects its house.[7]

GOD IS NO RESPECTER OF PERSONS

A corollary to the fear of God is a corresponding lack of fear of any created thing: to fear God is to fear no human. This attitude of fearlessness, when coupled with an absolute reliance on Scripture as the final authority in all matters of ultimate truth, made the political and religious authorities suspicious that rebellion and sedition were afoot. Here were common people, men and women, mostly uneducated, who presumed to speak to their social betters as if they all stood on the same plane before God. The fact was that, in the Anabaptist understanding, all human beings *did* stand on the same plane before God, namely, all were judged equally by Scripture, and all were equally in need of repentance and grace. God, they said, does not see social or political rank or status, but only the reality hidden in the human heart. God is no respecter of persons, they insisted again and again, citing their favourite Old and New Testament Scripture passages to that effect. A particularly favourite passage was taken from the book of Acts 10:34–35: 'Peter said: Now I hear the truth, that God does not respect persons, but in every nation whoever fears him and does right is acceptable to him.'[8] Whether consciously or not, the Anabaptists were here echoing sentiments that had already been voiced in the lay devotional piety of the Brethren of the Common Life.[9]

In 1536 in Rothenburg ob der Tauber, the Anabaptist prisoner Endres Keller composed a long testimony of faith in a cold dungeon, writing without aid of a Bible, citing Scripture entirely from memory. He wrote with some difficulty, since he had been tortured repeatedly on the rack, an experience which he said had almost completely ruined his ability to use his hands. He was emphatic about not 'respecting the person' when it came to hearing the truth:

> Believe me, even if an apostle were to rise from death or an angel were to come from heaven and would tell me what was not in harmony with the New Testament, I should not believe him. And if a poor herdsman, whom I had never seen, were to tell me the truth, I should believe him . . . For the secret of God is not in outward appearance of a person, whether he be king or emperor, prince or count, noble or common, burgher or farmer, herdsman or still lower, as you can find written everywhere. For David says in Psalm 25[:14]: 'The secret of the Lord is with them who fear him, and he will make his covenant known to them,' whether he be rich or poor, king or emperor, prince or count, herdsman or farmer.[10]

To fear God meant also to have confidence in God's Word and one's understanding of that Word. Many thousands of Anabaptist prisoners confronted expert questioning by learned pastors, both Catholic and Protestant, and demonstrated the scriptural foundations of their faith.

Elizabeth, who was arrested in 1549, was questioned by a

group of 'lords' who tested her on a variety of theological issues; she answered in the typical Anabaptist way, by citing Scripture passages. When she denied the real presence in the bread and the wine, citing Scripture to support her view, the noble lords accused her of speaking from a 'spirit of pride'. She answered, 'No, my lords, I speak with frankness.'[11] Fearing God had to do with obtaining the right perspective on the status of humankind in the face of God. The attitude that resulted was not timidity in the face of the powerful of the world, but rather fearlessness. God, they said, is no respecter of persons – a phrase that carried far more radical connotations in the structured social hierarchy of the sixteenth century than it does in our day. Those who fear God will know the truth, and will fear no human being. Fear of God gets priorities in order, even though the guardians of human structures of power may feel threatened by the truth.

REPENTANCE

It was a central Anabaptist truth that in the eyes of God, all human beings have sinned and will receive the same recompense. Menno Simons wrote in 1537:

> Hear God's irrevocable sentence and judgment as pronounced upon all who live after the flesh, no matter who it is, whether emperor or king, duke or earl, baron, knight or squire, noble or commoner, priest or monk, learned or unlearned, rich or poor, man or woman, bond or free. All who live after the flesh must forever remain under the just sentence and eternal wrath of God; otherwise the whole Scriptures are untrue.[12]

We hear in Menno's words again the clear conviction that 'God is no respecter of persons', but rather looks directly into all human hearts. What God sees there is human sin and rebellion. Menno is clear about what every human being must do:

> Take heed to the Word of the Lord and learn to know the
> true God . . . He will not save you nor forgive your sins nor
> show you His mercy and grace except according to His
> Word; namely, if you repent and if you believe, if you are
> born of Him; if you do what He has commanded and walk
> as He walks.[13]

In admonishing his readers to a 'true repentance', Menno
expressly opposes what he himself had observed as a Roman
Catholic parish priest just two years before. As examples of
the misplaced 'hope of the ungodly', he mentions infant
baptism, masses, matins, vespers, confessions, sacraments,
superstitious ceremonies and idolatries. All of these 'Romish
superstitions', Menno maintains, will not result in salvation.
Menno likewise opposes those who appeal to the Protestant
understanding of salvation by 'faith alone'. Where in the Bible
does it say, he asks, 'that an unbelieving, refractory, carnal man
without regeneration and true repentance was or can be saved,
simply because he boasts of faith and the death of
Christ . . .?'[14] Those who rely on 'human inventions' or 'faith
alone' and still remain unrepentant will perish in their sins,
Menno concludes, regardless of what status they hold in the eyes
of the world or what their outward church practices may be.

The fear of God and a heartfelt repentance describe
moments of self-recognition of the truth, but they are more
than simply one-time events – stages that one passes through
on the way to something else. Fear of God and repentance
describe fundamental attitudes that need to remain a constant
focus throughout one's earthly pilgrimage. One's aim in learning to fear God is to become a 'God-fearing person'. Likewise,
coming to repentance is not simply a one-time event that puts
away sin, once and for all. One must live a penitent life, for
temptation and the struggle with sin will continue. The
Anabaptists were confident that a penitent frame of mind, a
permanent rejection of sin, would keep them on the road to
salvation. Joost de Tollenaer wrote to his daughter, also named
Betgen:

Have God always before your eyes in all your ways, and seek to please Him with an upright heart; and God shall be with you, and have compassion upon your weakness, and look past your sin when it comes upon you unawares through ignorance or misapprehension. But presumptuous sinning and obstinacy are an abomination before the Lord, and He will not leave unpunished such as thus lightly esteem His words. Therefore take heed to yourself, that you be not a slave to sin.[15]

Anabaptist spirituality was imbued with a penitential air, from its beginnings in the recognition of the depth of sin, a heartfelt repentance, and throughout life's pilgrimage in the continuing struggle against sin.

CONTEMPTUS MUNDI

An Anabaptist hymn composed by Adam Reissner in the 1530s, and still sometimes sung by the Old Order Amish of North America, contains the stanza:

No one can come [to heaven]
Who does not renounce the whole world.
All creatures on earth
Must yield themselves entirely to Christ,
And offer up their bodies and lives to him.[16]

Repentance for one's life of sin is a renunciation of specific wrongs that have been committed. But there was a wider and deeper renunciation that informed Anabaptist spirituality from the start. The 'contempt for things of this world', expressed in the second line of the hymn stanza cited above, points to the profound polarity of the Anabaptist world-view. They were convinced that 'the world' and 'the flesh' stand in constant opposition to 'heaven' and 'the spirit'. By 'the world' they did not mean the creation as such which, they affirmed with biblical backing, God had originally created good and could still be used for good. They meant to indicate by the phrase that part of the good creation that had 'fallen' with Adam and Eve's disobedience, under Lucifer's prompting. 'The world' is all that pleases Satan and a fallen humanity, and displeases God; the world is all that has been corrupted by fallen, disobedient human nature; the world is the 'broad path' that will most certainly lead to perdition. The world and the flesh are the locus of self-will, pleasure, self-seeking and sin. 'All who live after the flesh must forever remain under the just sentence and eternal wrath of God,' wrote Menno Simons. If one is to be saved, there must be a profound turning away from 'the creatures' to the Creator, a turning away from 'the things of the flesh' to the 'things of the spirit'.

Anabaptist spirituality developed within the polar opposition between the 'things of heaven' and the 'things of the world', the 'things of the spirit' and the 'things of the flesh', and posed a basic choice. As Hans Denck said, 'all who truly fear God must renounce the world'.[17] It hardly needs demonstration that precisely this understanding had provided the framework for Christian piety for more than a millennium.[18]

Anabaptist spirituality was more than just incidentally similar to the 'world-renouncing' piety that had preceded it. It accepted the polar terms of reference of late medieval ascetic piety, and defined its spiritual path within those basic polarities. All the same, the Anabaptists reinterpreted *contemptus mundi* and framed its understanding in the biblical, anti-clerical and anti-sacramental terms common to the early Protestant Reformation. Jan Wouterss wrote this admonition in 1572, as he was awaiting execution.

> The saving grace of God teaches us to deny the ungodliness of this world, and its lusts and desires; as Paul says: 'And be not conformed to this world; but be ye transformed by the renewing of your mind, that is, after the mind of Christ.' Tit. 2:11; Rom. 12:2. If you do this, you will walk in the light, and not in darkness, wherein the world walks.[19]

In harmony with a deep stream of piety that preceded them, the Anabaptists held the conviction that the path to salvation lies in turning from the 'ungodliness of this world'. In fact, they conceived of life on this earth as a participation in a cosmic battle between God's forces of good, and Satan's forces of evil. The act of renouncing 'the devil, flesh, and the world' simply enflames those who serve the forces of darkness. Menno Simons wrote:

> The regenerate in turn have now become enemies of sin and the devil and have taken the field against all their enemies with the Author and finisher of their faith, under the banner of the crimson cross, armed with the armor of God, surrounded with angels of the Lord, and always watching with great solicitude lest they be overcome by their enemies who never slumber, but go about like roaring lions, seeking whom they may devour, hurt, and harm.[20]

The polar world of spirit and flesh, heaven and world, becomes particularly aggressive when the narrow path to salvation is chosen. The cloistered suffering of the 'temptations of the flesh' described by those dwelling in the monasteries or the communities of lay Brethren in the late Middle Ages took on a different actuality for the Anabaptists, who found themselves struggling against uniformly hostile church and political authorities in the midst of daily life. The Anabaptist 'denial of the world' only intensified and took on further nuances of meaning for the Anabaptists, as they experienced persecution for having attempted to be true to God's call in Christ.

SIN AND *GELASSENHEIT*: YIELDED ABANDONMENT

The Anabaptists believed, in continuity with many late medieval spiritual writers, that the sin that condemns is essentially a matter of the fallen human will, and is thus a human responsibility in the final analysis. Their focus therefore fell not on the theological issues surrounding original sin, but rather on the practical dimensions of sin, repentance and righteous living. Original sin is understood as an inherited *tendency* to choose or will evil. No human being can evade this inherited potentiality, which shows itself as soon as a person is actually able to choose either good or evil. Human beings inevitably choose evil, being prompted by 'the flesh'. But original sin is not a 'stain on the soul', worthy in itself of damnation, which can be removed only by a sacramental remedy. The Anabaptist view was that condemnable sin is sin that is freely and consciously chosen and consented to – sin that involves the conscious will.

This understanding of sin formed a central part of the Anabaptist understanding of the spiritual life – if sin involves the will, the remedy for sin also will involve the human will. Likewise, this understanding of sin contributed to a rejection of infant baptism, as we will see below, for infants do not yet have the capacity consciously to 'choose evil'.

The sin that is the focus of Anabaptist attention is willing what God does not will, as a long spiritual tradition within the Western church had often asserted. This means that the remedy for sin is not sacramental (a remedy for original sin), or even (as the Protestant theologians had it) in 'faith alone'. Rather the remedy for sin lies in learning obedience, learning to will what God wills, as the monastic tradition had long emphasised.[21] How is this to be done?

It is done, first, by the grace of God, but accepting God's grace will necessarily involve a fundamental readjustment of the human will and desire. Pilgram Marpeck wrote:

> It does not depend on our willing or running, but rather on the mercy of God and on His grace in and with Christ. He gives the will, He can also do and accomplish it in His own. We must simply in all of our actions stand idle ourselves, as dead in ourselves, if Christ is to live in us, which life and walk alone are pleasing to the Father.[22]

Human beings must 'yield themselves entirely to Christ', 'die' to themselves, 'abandon' themselves to the divine will *(sich gelassen)* if God is to work God's will through them. This abandonment is often, but not exclusively, indicated in Anabaptist testimonies and writings by the word *Gelassenheit*, translated variously as 'yieldedness', 'resignation' or 'abandonment'. What must be done, the Anabaptists insisted, is to 'give up' and 'stop striving' for one's own desires, accepting instead what God wishes to accomplish through one's life. *Gelassenheit* is, paradoxically, the 'doing' that is 'doing nothing' and is a theme that will run through all of Anabaptist spirituality as a central, directing theme. It is a theme that had dominated mystical and devotional writings in preceding centuries.[23]

Hans Denck, who was strongly influenced by Tauler and Taulerian writings such as the *Theologia Deutsch*, wrote in 1526:

> Whoever wishes to offer himself in the depths of his soul and in truth to the Lord, that is, whoever wishes to leave off his own will and to seek the will of God and has respect for the work of God, him the merciful Father will receive with great joy and take back regardless of how he had conducted himself hitherto . . . O that the whole world would come in this manner! The Lord would surely be wonderfully ready to favor them.[24]

'Yielding one's own will to God's will' thus stands at the very beginning of the Christian walk, as the Anabaptists understood it. The human will and wilful self-assertion are the greatest impediments to the presence of God. 'Leaving off one's will', conversely, opens the door to divine forgiveness and reconciliation with God.

Hans Hut, who died in prison in 1527, wrote: 'Whoever wants to rule with God must be ruled by God. Whoever wants to do God's will must set aside his own. Whoever wants to find something in God must lose as much in him[self].'[25] This last sentence has also been translated 'whoso will find somewhat in God must by so much lose himself',[26] an understanding that has close parallels in the mystical and spiritual writings of preceding centuries.[27] God's desire to enter into the hearts of human beings is prevented by humanity's insistence on doing their own will, rather than God's will. So it is that by the measure that human beings 'yield' and get out of God's way, by that same measure God will enter in and carry out his will. Maeyken de Corte, soon to be martyred, wrote from her prison cell in Antwerp in 1559, 'I notice that the less I make of myself, the more our mighty God works in me and the more he pours his mercy over me.'[28] The insistence that God will enter only in direct proportion to the degree of human 'abandonment' is something that shapes this spiritual path in unmistakable ways. The sincerity of one's desire for God's presence is tested by one's efforts to yield to God's will in all things. Salvation cannot be 'earned' apart from grace, but grace must be sincerely sought by the path of self-renunciation.

The understanding that sin is closely tied to the human will was a determining factor in shaping Anabaptist spirituality. It contributed to the continuing penitential character of Anabaptist spirituality. In the polar universe marked by heaven and the world, the spirit and the flesh, Satan is continually attacking those who have set out on the narrow way. Therefore, some sins can be expected to spring up 'unawares'. When they are detected, these sins need to be opposed, and not consented to; one must exercise one's will in active opposition to sin, and the outcome will be positive. *Ausbund* hymn 48, for example, states that 'nothing can be hurtful to us, unless we give our will to it'.[29] The Schleitheim Articles of 1527 institute the practice of fraternal discipline in those cases of baptised brothers and sisters who 'still somehow slip and fall into error and sin, being *inadvertently overtaken*'.[30] Such members – if their faith is true and their desire for 'yieldedness' sincere – will respond to admonition and confess their failing. They did not 'will' the sin, and so it does them no mortal harm. This attitude towards sin and its remedy is, not surprisingly, plainly visible in the preceding spiritual tradition.[31]

In the case of 'inadvertent sin', a believer is called again to repentance, to fall back again upon God's compassion and forgiveness, sometimes at the prompting or the admonition (discipline) of the community. In fact, it is the community that oversees the process of naming sin, calling for repentance, and re-accepting the repentant sinner back into the community, as we will see below. In the early stages of coming to the knowledge of the truth, believers are called to yield their wills to God's will in a deep inward process; after baptism, believers are called to 'yield' to the wisdom and discipline of the community, the Body of Christ on earth; and in all things believers are to accept what happens to them in 'the world' as matters ultimately in God's hands. The attitude of *Gelassenheit* thus applies to the profound inner 'yielding' to God that must take place in the heart, and the external 'yielding' that must take place in the daily life of the community and the world.

DISCIPLESHIP: SUFFERING WITH CHRIST

The Third Witness is Christ, who has himself said that his life is an example for us according to which we are to live and walk, everyone according to his measure, as Peter said: 'Christ has suffered for us and left us a likeness or an example that we should follow in his steps' (1 Peter 2[:21]). He continues: since Christ has suffered in the flesh for us, arm yourselves with the same mind, for whoever has suffered in the flesh has finished with sin so as to live for the rest of your earthly life no longer by human desires but by the will of God.[32]

These biblical words, remembered and written from prison in 1528 by Hans Schlaffer, point to the very heart and centre of Anabaptist spirituality: Jesus Christ. Jesus Christ not only died so that sinners might live, but also lived a life that was a 'likeness and example' for believers to follow. *Folge im nach*: Follow after him. These words were a constant Anabaptist refrain and characterise like no others the nature of Anabaptist spirituality.

It may come as no surprise that the nature and character of Jesus Christ that are highlighted in the beginning stages of Anabaptist spirituality mirror in fundamental ways those seen in the writings of the preceding ascetic and pious traditions. The late medieval period saw an ever-increasing emphasis on the humanity and suffering of Christ, which became the focal points for devotion and pious contemplation.[33] Thomas à Kempis' *Of the Imitation of Christ* represents only the best-known title of what was a large body of devotional material guided by a Christocentric emphasis. While there is no sign among the Anabaptists of the systematic affective devotions the Brothers of the Common Life practised, the parallels of understanding remain strikingly similar.

Jesus the Christ came into the fallen world to save sinners, but the salient point for the medieval devotional movements and for the Anabaptists was not the atonement as such – Christ's atoning work was assumed as a matter of course. What inspired the devout in the late Middle Ages was what had *enabled* the human Jesus to accomplish his work and, by extension, how human beings might likewise be enabled to do the same holy work. Late medieval piety answered the first question with emphatic clarity: Jesus Christ did God's work on earth only because he submitted his will to God's will, accepted pain and suffering, embraced the cross, and trusted absolutely in God. The answer to this first question provided the answer to the second: if we are to do Christ's holy work in this world, we must do as Christ did. Hans Hut explained the process by speaking of the 'essential' inward baptism:

> Christ had to be baptised first, as an example for us . . . Christ came to be baptized by John in order to humble himself beyond other men; to retake upon himself our proud nature which had deviated from God; and to make it obedient to God again through the baptism which he shows, and in which each must be baptized into a new creature through the killing of our evil, disobedient, insolent nature.[34]

To 'follow after' Christ thus means, in the first and most fundamental instance, to overcome our fallen human nature and be ruled by the 'mind of Christ' – that is, to take on the obedient 'mind' that led Jesus willingly to the cross.

Taking on the 'mind of Christ' was for the Anabaptists a biblical way of speaking about the process of self-denial, denial of the flesh, denial of the world, and an affirmation of the life of the spirit that comes in and with Christ. We return here to the attitude of *contemptus mundi*, to the centrality of a spirit of *Gelassenheit*, to the yielding of one's will to God, in the same manner as Jesus Christ did before us. To 'deny oneself' is thus fundamental to 'following after Christ'. Thomas à Kempis would write, 'Learn now to die to the world, that then you may begin to live with Christ. Learn now to despise all things, that then you may go freely to Christ.'[35] Less than a century later, an anonymous Anabaptist hymn-writer in the dungeon at Passau would write:

> Whoever wants to be my disciple
> Must forsake the world,
> Become pure in heart
> And hate his own life.[36]

Parallel testimonies from late medieval and Anabaptist texts alike could be multiplied many times over.

If the key to the nature and character of Christ was his willingness to suffer and to yield up his will to God, 'following after' Christ will be a painful experience (at least initially), and not a triumphant one. One need only look to Jesus' life for a demonstration of how one can expect things to go with his followers on this side of eternity. Balthasar Hubmaier, writing as an Anabaptist pastor, would say:

> For where Christ is and dwells, there he brings the cross with him on his back from which he gives every Christian his own small cross to carry and to follow after him. We are to expect this small cross and if it comes accept it with joy and patience, and not pick and choose our own chips and bits of wood in false spirituality, selecting and gathering them up without divine understanding.[37]

A critique of an external Catholic piety can be heard in Hubmaier's statement; the self-chosen 'chips and bits of wood' appear to be a derogatory reference to practices of self-denial that Hubmaier had known, practised and counselled others to practise during his tenure as a Roman Catholic priest.[38] But while the pious practices as such were criticised, the ideal path remained the same: the cross of Christ must be accepted as one's own. Before there can be the triumph of glory, there must be the pain of the cross. Our own particular cross will be revealed in due time, Hubmaier believed, in the course of human events. Hubmaier was writing in a context of state persecution, not from a cloister. His experience had taught him that there would be no need to impose suffering upon ourselves; we need only be sincere in the desire to follow after Christ, wait for the cross Christ will choose for us, and be ready to accept it when it arrives.

The early Anabaptists assumed that the process of being 'shaped' into a Christ-like person would be a painful one. Thus from the earliest point in Anabaptist beginnings, suffering was understood to be central to the spiritual life. This emphasis also fed on a long and deep spiritual tradition. Anabaptist expressions on this subject sound remarkably similar in content and form to earlier devotional exhortations. In his tract *On the Mystery of Baptism*, Hans Hut wrote:

> Yes, we would all gladly find Christ and boast about it. But no one wants to suffer with him.[39] Yes, if God's spirit were given to the world through pleasure and splendor, the world would be full of Christians. But Christ conceals himself beneath the flesh. And he only allows himself to be seen so that we notice him in the suffering of the greatest resignation (*Gelassenheit*), in which he shows himself to all his brothers . . . Then the person becomes conformed to Christ, the crucified son of God . . . Then the person lives no longer, but Christ.[40]

The path of yielding self-will, the flesh and the world to Christ in 'resignation' had been clearly marked long before the sixteenth-century biblical critique began, and long before adult baptism became an issue. The baptisers were walking a well-worn road in their understanding of the process of self-knowledge, repentance, contempt for the world, yieldedness and acceptance of suffering that must stand at the beginning of a genuine Christian life.

Finally, the Anabaptists were convinced that the call to would-be disciples would be an uncompromising one – the Christian life is all, or nothing.[41] Dirk Philips, along with many other Anabaptists, interpreted the call to 'follow after' in terms most stark:

> Christ also taught us in the gospel that one must for his sake, forsake all things, that is, father, mother, brothers, sisters, wife and children, in addition to his own life, take his cross upon him and follow after him, Matt. 10[:36]. And whoever loves anything more than him, that one is not worthy of him.[42]

Discipleship, or 'following after' Christ, calls for self-renunciation, self-sacrifice, a dying to self and the world, a 'yielded' state of being that is willing to accept God's will in all things, an embracing of the cross, even at the expense of all that one holds dear in this life. In the Anabaptist understanding, the fundamental struggle to embrace the cross is a struggle that must first take place in the depths of the human heart. What is being called for is an ultimate commitment and seriousness of purpose, a resolute setting out on the narrow road to salvation, even unto death.

CONCLUSION

The beginning point of Anabaptist spirituality did not lie in popular Roman Catholic piety of the kind that concentrated on penitential practices such as pilgrimages and prayers to the saints. Neither can the Anabaptists be described as mystics in the sense that Tauler and Suso, for example, directed themselves to an ecstatic experience of direct union with God.

Neither can they be described as adherents of the 'Modern Devotion', practising affective spiritual exercises of the kind utilised by the Brethren of the Common Life. And certainly, the Anabaptist rejection of the power of sacraments, clergy and popular acts of penance emphatically removed them from the widest sphere of Roman Catholic spirituality. Nevertheless Anabaptist spirituality was grounded in a deeply personal acceptance of responsibility for sin. They held to the conviction that the process of attaining salvation would involve a painful process of renouncing self and following after Jesus Christ into suffering and the cross. These convictions, while they were interpreted and expressed within a self-consciously 'anti-popish' context of 'Scripture alone', still bear the marks of a strong and influential Christocentric and ascetic spiritual current that flowed within the broader Roman Catholic stream. And, while Anabaptists clearly took direction from that spiritual current, mainline Protestantism broke with it in very fundamental ways.

As we shall see in the chapter which follows, the Anabaptist understanding of the presence and power of God continued building upon the basic themes that informed the late medieval current of Christocentric devotional piety.

3 RENEWED BY THE POWER OF GOD: THE NEW BIRTH

A man named Valerius exercised the office of schoolmaster at Hoorn, Holland and Middelburgh in Zeeland in the middle decades of the sixteenth century. It is reported of him that because of his zealous Anabaptist faith, he would not cease from proclaiming judgement on the unrepentant and comfort to the penitent. He was soon in trouble with the authorities for this, and placed under arrest. He managed to be released from his first imprisonment, but was less fortunate following his second arrest in 1568, when he was apprehended in Brouwershaven in Zeeland. He languished in prison for over sixty weeks before his eventual execution, during which time he wrote two small books. In the second of these, called *The Proof of Faith*, he outlined his understanding of salvation, from which the following is a brief excerpt.

> Christ did not come to judge or to condemn that which was already judged, but to redeem from judgment and condemnation all those who rightly, by faith, accept His grace (Tit. 2:11), that is, those who die unto and forsake their sinful life, repent and amend; in a word, those who are born again live after the Spirit (John 3; Rom. 8), as the Scriptures abundantly testify in many places.[1]

Jesus Christ came to redeem those who accept his grace by faith – here is the phrase that resonated from Wittenberg with such dramatic results. But Valerius provides an Anabaptist interpretation of the Reformation dictum by clarifying its meaning: '*that is*: Jesus Christ came to redeem those "who are born again and who live according the Spirit of God".'

The Anabaptists were convinced that the living God is disposed to grant his Spirit to those who, in utter dependence, truly repent and call upon God. The result will be the granting of the gifts of God's presence and power, and the birth of a new person.[2] This experience is reflected upon in a variety of ways in Anabaptist testimonies. The experience of God's presence is sometimes described as the birth of faith in the heart; at other times, as the birth of Christ within; or again, the working of the Holy Spirit in believers. Yet another image, as we will see in the following chapter, is that of a spiritual baptism.

The varieties of descriptive language used by the Anabaptists point to the experience of a reality which, they were convinced, needed to define all Christians: personal transformation by the regenerating power of God. The presence of God's power will result in a spiritual birth, strengthening and consoling the sinner, bringing into existence a new person, empowered and enabled to live a new life. Those once dead in sin are now brought to new life by the power of God. In 1557, in a booklet he wrote on the baptism of Jesus, Dirk Philips described the new birth in brief and pointed terms:

> For what is the new birth other than the transforming and renewing of the person which God works in him through faith in Christ Jesus in the power of the Holy Spirit? Thus the person is created anew out of God, born of his seed, 1 Pet. 1:23, made in his image, Col. 3:10, renewed in his knowledge, becomes partaker of his divine nature, Eph. 4:24; new being of the Spirit, John 14[:17]; 16[:13], in holiness and righteousness all the days of his life, John 20[:22]; Luke [1:75]. Where this takes place and is in process as a pregnancy, there is the genuine new birth; there is the new creature in Christ Jesus, John 3:3; Gal. 6[:15].[3]

This process of being born again, from its beginnings in repentance to its outcome in a holy life that reflects the newly born

Christ-nature, was not newly minted by the Anabaptists, but rather reflects a well-established spiritual and pious tradition within late medieval Catholicism.[4]

All Anabaptists, without exception, were convinced that Scripture – when read simply and with no attempt to escape the cross – demanded repentance and a new birth, by the power of God. It is this new birth by God's power, and not faith alone, baptism, or even a new life of discipleship, that stands at the very heart of Anabaptist spirituality. The new birth depends upon a prior preparation: genuine repentance (acknowledgement of one's own disobedience) and yieldedness to God. And the new birth will likewise have a concrete result: a life of discipleship and 'following after' Christ. But the crucial point on which all turns is the 'transforming and renewing of the person', as Dirk said. Without such a transformation by the power of God, all else is in vain. In fact, without such a trans-formation, water baptism, as the Anabaptists understood it, loses its meaning entirely. Thus to describe Anabaptist baptism as a 'believers' baptism' is to use far too anaemic a phrase. Anabaptist baptism was a baptism of the 'spiritually reborn'.

SALVATION BY GRACE THROUGH FAITH

The centrality of the new birth becomes evident when we examine the Anabaptist interpretation of the well-known Reformation dictum: saved by grace through faith alone. What Martin Luther meant by the phrase became increasingly clear in the 1520s: sinners are saved by Christ's death on the cross, in which they participate by faith alone. There can be no use-ful human activity relative to salvation; no human works can count for righteousness in God's sight. Or, as Luther himself explained in his treatise on Good Works (1520), faith is the only 'work' which counts in God's eyes – and it is no human 'work' at all. Salvation is entirely a work of God's grace, who graciously implants faith in the human heart and considers the sinner righteous because of this faith in Christ's atoning work on the cross. The righteousness necessary for salvation is, start to finish, God's work in and through Christ; it is an 'imputed righteousness'. Sinful humanity is grateful because of God's gift in Christ and performs works of virtue out of this gratitude, but human beings remain essentially and unredeemably sinful, this side of eternity. There will be no individual 'saints', let alone a visible 'community of saints', this side of heaven. Luther's break with the ascetic and regenerative tradition that preceded him was radical and remarkable.[5]

The Anabaptists simply could not agree. The former Franciscan, then Anabaptist leader, Leonhard Schiemer, had left the cloister and the Catholic Church under the influence of the Reformation, but he spared no criticism of Luther on this point when writing from his prison cell: 'The reason for the errors is that Luther comes *to* Christ, *to* God, *to* the light. He will not have any of them *in* him, but only beside him, under him, near him.'[6] The Anabaptists, although they spoke the Reformation language of grace and faith, could not follow Luther's lead but rather restated – after their own fashion – the emphasis on spiritual rebirth and new life that had been present in an earlier tradition of piety. Leonhard Schiemer critiques Luther from the perspective of one who stands closer to the understanding of Johannes Tauler, who in a Christmas sermon described three births of Christ, the third of which takes place 'when God is born within a just soul every day and every hour truly and spiritually, by grace and out of love'.[7] Or again, the Anabaptists were striving for the result described by the anonymous author of the *Theologia Deutsch*, who in concluding his mystical tract wrote: 'If you can come to the point where you are to God what your hand is to you, be content.'[8] The Anabaptists believed, emphatically, that Christ must be born in the heart of every believer (by grace through faith), and that this birth was a transforming power that produced actual (not imputed) righteousness.

CHRIST'S ATONEMENT FOR SIN

The Anabaptists were overwhelmingly of the common people,

the vast majority self-taught, with little theological education. Their understanding of Christ's work on the cross was rudimentary, but not confused or silly for all that. Valerius, being a schoolteacher, articulated the basic understanding with more clarity than some. He used the simile of a doomed criminal, a harlot, to illustrate his understanding; we can still hear the schoolmaster behind the words.

> Now suppose that the doomed criminal . . . were condemned to the most shameful death that could be devised; and the King should send His only, beloved Son from His kingdom and glory into great poverty, imprisonment, suffering and an innocent death, in the stead of the unclean harlot, who by all manner of contempt and evil-doing had angered the King, and merited death a thousand times, but is now nevertheless, out of grace, through the death of the King's Son (on condition of her amending) reconciled to the King, made at peace with Him, liberated from prison, and delivered from death, and remains alive, a partaker and heir of all the riches of the King; ought she not to accept this great love and grace, love the King, amend her ways, and be greatly afraid of vexing the King any more all her life, who cleansed her, forgave all her evil deeds, paid all her debts, espoused her as his beloved queen, exalted her into his glory, and protected her as himself from all enemies? But if she should not amend (according to her promise), and should again anger the King, and do worse than before, were this not great ingratitude, worthy of sorer punishment than before? Hereby we we may prove ourselves, whether we that are redeemed through the grace of God, also keep the promise of amendment.[9]

The atonement parable of the harlot certainly hinges on the 'satisfaction' rendered by the king's son: he dies in the harlot's place. But this is not the full extent of the story, nor even its central point in the Anabaptist telling. The harlot, Valerius notes, has promised to live a new life as a condition for her commuted sentence; her liberation is *conditional*, not absolute. Her salvation is, of course, a great and unexpected gift of the king and a tremendous reversal, but the harlot must do as she promised: in return for her spared life, she will be a faithful spouse and queen, wedded to the king. Her salvation hinges on a covenant, with reciprocal promises and obligations.

Central to the Anabaptist understanding of Christ's satisfaction for sin, then, is not simply 'believing' that the saving act has happened historically and 'believing' that the historical atonement applies to the forgiveness of one's personal sin, but further, there must be a 'proving' of the already-accomplished redemption by means of concrete response and action. Redemption is not simply about sins being forgiven in heaven (although it is about that); it is also about the cessation of actual sin, here and now. Will the king *continue* to love and forgive a disobedient, recalcitrant, unfaithful spouse, who insists upon acting the harlot? The Anabaptist answer is an emphatic 'No'. True faith requires (must be 'proven by') faithful living. Or, as the early Anabaptist leader Hans Denck put it, 'Woe to the perverse, who know the will of their Lord and do it not, and yet want to be regarded as justified.'[10]

GOD'S GRACE

It is important to note the extent to which the grace and power of God is emphasised by the Anabaptists in their description of the process of rebirth and regeneration of the person. Because of the very visible Anabaptist emphasis on living a new life, a common reproach of Protestant Reformers against the Anabaptists was that they had fallen into the Pelagian error, namely that they relied on human goodness and human effort, denied God's grace and preached a 'salvation by works of righteousness'. It was an unfair accusation, but it is true that the Anabaptists understood God's grace in a different way than did the Reformers.

The Anabaptists understood God's saving grace not in a forensic manner – as conferring righteousness only in God's sight – but rather God's grace, they believed, is a living power that actually transforms sinners, here and now. In his book *The New Birth and the New Creature*, Dirk Philips would explain:

> John says, 'As many as have received Christ, he has given power to become children of God . . .' Out of all this, it is clear that the new birth is actually the work of God in the person through which he is born anew out of God through faith in Jesus Christ in the Holy Spirit.[11]

This basic understanding of God's grace as a *power* that enables the doing of the good is in direct line with a significant regenerative tradition within Western Christianity,[12] but stands in significant discontinuity with mainline Protestantism.

FAITH

To believe, or have faith in Christ for the forgiveness of sins, was for the Anabaptists a gift of God, but it was a gift that required something of human beings, both before and after the gift. The Anabaptists refused to remove the weight of responsibility for sin from human shoulders. They sometimes spoke of 'election' by God, but they did not mean by this a predestination to salvation, free from human consent or involvement. When God's call is heard, human beings must do their part. God calls, but the sinner must desire and long for grace and call upon God's help. And, it is possible, believed the Anabaptists, perversely to resist God's call. So Dirk Philips would write:

> This sweetness and power of the true heavenly bread no one can taste except he who hungers and thirsts after righteousness and says with David, 'As a hart longs for fresh water, so thirsts my soul for you, oh God. My soul thirsts for the living God,' Ps. 42:1[–2] . . . Whoever is now thirsty for the living God, hungry for the bread of heaven, and desirous for the water of life, they shall without doubt

> be well satisfied, as Christ said . . . 'I am the bread of life;
> whoever comes to me shall not hunger, and whoever
> believes in me shall never thirst,' John 6:35.[13]

There must be a genuine thirst for the living God, after which
the Gospel promises that whoever believes in this way will be
eternally satisfied. But likewise, true faith will lead to a life
that overcomes temptation and the world. A stanza in a hymn
preserved in the *Ausbund* explains:

> For what is born of God
> Overcomes the desires of the flesh,
> Sin, devil, world, also possessions and riches,
> The Faith that is within us gains the victory.[14]

The fiery preacher Hans Hut wrote a tract called *On the
Mystery of Baptism* in which he describes his understanding of
the process by which faith is born in the human heart. He is at
pains to distinguish the Anabaptist understanding from the
Protestant understanding (as he saw it). Hut heaped scorn on
the 'profit-seeking, pleasure-loving, ambitious, hypocritical
scribes who preach for money'. Their teaching, he said, 'is nothing but "believe!" and it goes no further. They do not explain
through what means one should come to faith.'[15] A true and
genuine faith, Hut explained, only results after a thorough
preparation and cleansing: 'If God wants to use or take pleasure in us, first we have to be justified by him and made clean,
inside and out (2 Tim. 2:21). Inwardly, from desires and lusts,
outwardly, from all unjust conduct and misuse of creatures.'[16]

   As Hut saw it, we are not 'justified by grace through faith'
before God in some heavenly process, but rather we must first
be 'justified' by God (*von im gerechfertiget*: 'made righteous' is
also a possible translation) in the here and now, before we can
be said to have come to a genuine faith. This justification (or
making righteous) must take place within every individual.
Hut and other Anabaptists sometimes called this process the
'true baptism'. Hut continues:

Whoever wants to be a disciple of the Lord must be baptized in this manner, and he will be cleansed in spirit through the bond of peace toward the one body [the community of Christians] (Eph. 4:4 and 5). God thus makes his own blessed and capable (1 Peter 2), and everything occurs by means of this covenant of the Holy Spirit's rebirth and renewal in faith. God works this according to his great mercy, so that we are justified [made righteous] alone through this same grace, and in hope we are heirs to eternal life (Titus 3:5). In this way one is washed, healed, purified, and born again (Romans 8).[17]

The biblical images tumble over each other in Hut's prose, but the message is clear enough: 'God makes his own blessed *and capable.*' The emphasis on God's grace and power is unequivocal, but so also is the message that God performs the work of justification in his own, here and now. Thanks to the grace and power of God, believers are purified, reborn and renewed. The harlot is transformed into a beloved spouse and a queen. Thus Hut can conclude that the Gospel is not a matter of words, or intellectual belief, but of power.

For the kingdom of God does not consist of talk or an exterior thing, but of power. Thus, the Gospel is not a speech but a power of God (1 Cor. 2:4), which is given only by God and which completely renews the person, from his mouth to his heart, and in all his conduct and behavior.[18]

Hut, naturally enough, tied together the process of rebirth with the need of human beings to 'submit' and 'yield' to God's grace. There must be a giving way before God, if a sinner is to be cleansed, justified and led to a genuine faith. This 'giving way' is the way of the cross.

God exercises his justice on us through the suffering of the holy cross, which he lays on each one . . . Here all the lusts to which we have been accustomed in this creaturely life will be rooted out and broken. Thus the world's yoke of total sin will be thrown off, so that the world no longer rules, but Christ. The law of the father will be fulfilled in us through Christ, as in his members. Then there is a desire and love to do the will of God in true obedience. His burden is light and his yoke sweet to such people (Matt. 11:30), and everything is possible that was not possible before. Then a person might indeed say, 'Christ has extinguished my sin.'[19]

In the final analysis, the evangelical statement of faith, that one's sins have been taken away by Jesus Christ, is for the Anabaptists not simply an historical statement about the atonement of Christ on the cross, and one's personal faith in the forgiveness of sins through the work of Christ. A true statement of faith, Hut and the Anabaptists would insist, is an existential statement that can be made only by those who have been willing to submit to the power of the cross, to be cleansed by the cross; by those who have been led to a love of God's will through a rooting out of their own will and their own sin. Faith is essentially a living manifestation of the truth and efficacy of the work of Christ on the cross, a result of the working of the power of the cross within each yielded sinner.

The cleansing that leads to faith thus requires human co-operation – albeit, the 'co-operation' of yielding or 'getting out of the way' – and likewise, the presence of a genuine faith also will be manifested in human behaviour, and also will not occur without human co-operation. Dirk Philips would write: 'For where the fear of the Lord is, there the commandments of God are kept, there persons live holy and right (yet in weakness), Wisd. of Sol. [6:10]. Yes, there the person does not live anymore, but Jesus Christ lives in him through faith, Gal. [2:20].'[20] What it means to have faith is that a rebirth has taken place and, in a real way, the reborn believer lives no more, but rather, Jesus Christ lives through the believer. Galatians 2:20 appears again and again, quoted in Anabaptist testimonies.

Yielding to the living power of God marks not only the experience of the cross and rebirth, but remains a mark of the entire Christian life. The illiterate needle peddler and evangelist, Hans Nadler, reponded to questioning in prison by quoting a favourite Anabaptist text from James: 'We all speak of faith, but we don't much do the works of faith. James says in his epistle that faith without works is dead. He says that the devil also believes and trembles, but will not be saved for the sake of his faith [James 2:17–19].'[21] True faith will be active in deed and proclamation, in which one's true citizenship and allegiance to God are manifested. True faith will *necessarily* (not incidentally) produce good fruit, or it denies itself in deed; faith will be true to God regardless of the human consequences. In short, because faith in Christ is evidence of a transformation by the power of God, it will be evident from one's speech and one's actions whether one has truly yielded (has faith) or not. The visibility of faith leads directly into the Anabaptist conception of the church as the visible Body of Christ.

WORD AND SPIRIT

Just as the Anabaptist language of atonement, grace and faith – at first hearing – suggests a strong link to the teaching of the Protestant Reformers, so also the Anabaptist emphasis on Scripture suggests the same. The early Anabaptists, however, drew a distinction between the letter that could be read and preached, and the living Word that led them to rebirth and regeneration. Hans Umlauft, in a letter written to his friend in 1539, wrote:

> [The righteous persons] glory in that they understand God their Saviour and know him, not through the dead letter which you call God's Word, since it is only a witness of His Word, but through the indwelling of Christ, Gal. 2[:20], cessation from sin, 1 Pet. 4[:1ff]; Rom. 6[:6], and lowliness before the world, 1 Cor. 1[:27], 2[:1ff] one is raised up, and becomes righteous before God in one's heart, Luke 2[:79].[22]

Umlauft's conception of the written letter of Scripture is that it functions as a 'witness' to the true and living Word. This 'living Word' is described as 'the indwelling of Christ' which, in turn, leads to visible and tangible results: a cessation from sin and a genuine (not an imputed) righteousness. Dirk Philips wrote in a similar vein, 'For the heavenly Father generates or bears the new creature, but the Word of the heavenly Father is the seed out of which the new creature is born.'[23]

An early Anabaptist sermon, preserved in the writings of the Hutterites, ties together the Anabaptist understanding of the living Word and the experience of rebirth.

> [The living Word of God] comes to us always, but we do not wish to have it in us, and for this reason we cannot enter into the kingdom of God, as Christ the true Son of God teaches us: unless we are born again we cannot see the kingdom of God (John 3). There is no other birth than hearing God's Word and receiving it into one's heart . . . But those who hear the Word and refuse to do what the Word teaches (which proceeds from God and was opened up by Christ), these can never be born again until they hear the Word in their hearts and obey it, as Christ taught us. This is the law of God which Christ teaches us, which is sealed and which may never be broken, as Christ says: Before one tittle or letter of my law passes away, heaven and earth must rather pass away (Matt. 5).[24]

An important connection is made in this passage between the living Word of God that must be born in the heart, and the obedience that must follow from the rebirth. The birth of the spiritual Word in the heart is primary; it is the power-without-which sinful humanity can do nothing good. But the living Word of God operates in concert with the revealed will of God. The Word is also a teaching that must be heeded, and that requires obedience. The teaching Word proceeds from God and is 'opened up by Christ'. So it is that the birth of Christ within will result in a life of obedience that will manifest the external marks of Christ, as Scripture testified of him, as the earlier pious tradition had taught.[25]

THE SPIRIT AND THE FLESH

In 1536 the parish priest of the village of Witmarsum in Friesland, the Netherlands, left his post, accepted baptism and went into hiding. Menno Simons, the man in question, had been a Roman Catholic priest for twelve years. He joined a baptising group that was in turmoil, since the apocalyptically minded Anabaptists who had taken and held the Westphalian city of Münster for a year and a half had been defeated only the year before. Menno emerged as the most significant leader of the reorganised Anabaptists of the post-Münsterite period in the Netherlands and northern Germany, giving such sound pastoral and spiritual direction that many subsequent baptisers accepted the name 'Mennonite' as descriptive of their group.

Menno Simons published many writings of edification, guidance and defence, and so it is significant that the very first booklet he published – in 1536, the same year as his baptism – carried the descriptive title *The Spiritual Resurrection. A Plain Instruction from the Word of God Concerning the Spiritual Resurrection and the New or Heavenly Birth.*[26] Here Menno expounded with great clarity the process of repentance and rebirth that, as we have seen, the baptising movement as a whole placed at the centre of its spirituality. Menno's main point can be summarised as 'Put off the old, fleshly person; put on the new, spiritual person.'[27] Within the polar world-view that saw spirit and flesh in enmity with one another, there was a choice to be made between which nature one would follow. Menno followed the Anabaptist way when he called for a 'mortification' of one's earthly nature. 'There can be no resurrection from sin and death unless this body of sin be first destroyed and buried and have sensibly endured pain and the burden of sin, that is, penitence and remorse on account of sin,' Menno emphasised.[28]

There must be death to the sinful person, which will involve suffering: 'None can rejoice with Christ unless he first suffer with Him.' But there is assurance on the other side of the death of Adamic nature: 'For this is a sure word, says Paul, If we be dead with him, we shall also live with him; if we suffer, we shall also reign with him. This resurrection includes the new creature, the spiritual birth and sanctification, without which no one shall see the Lord.'[29] In short, Menno says, 'all those who are born and regenerated from above out of God, through the living Word, are also of the mind and disposition, and have the same aptitude for good that He has of whom they are born and begotten.'[30] The spiritual birth results in a new, spiritual nature within a person.

More importantly, the nature, mind and disposition that has been born of the 'living Word' in the heart, will correspond to the nature of Christ, as witnessed to in the written Word.

> For Christ has expressly portrayed Himself in His Word, that is, as to the nature which He would have us understand, grasp and follow and emulate . . . according to His life and conversation here on earth, shown forth among men in works and deeds as an example set before us to follow so that we thereby might become partakers of His nature in the spirit, to become like unto Him.[31]

Furthermore, it is no secret just what Christ's nature, now born in believers, is.

> Christ is everywhere represented to us as humble, meek, merciful, just, holy, wise, spiritual, long-suffering, patient, peaceable, lovely, obedient, and good, as the perfection of all things; for in Him there is an upright nature. Behold, this is the image of God, of Christ as to the Spirit which we have as an example until we become like it in nature and reveal it by our walk.[32]

All regenerate children of God are thus minded as Christ was minded, and will look to Christ 'as an example' after whom they will faithfully walk. This is the meaning of Paul's word in Galatians 2:20:

We must spend the remainder of our days not after the lusts of men, but according to the will of God, so that we may say with Paul, I am crucified with Christ; nevertheless I live; yet not I, but Christ liveth in me; and the life which I now live in the flesh I live by the faith of the Son of God who loved me and gave himself for me. For he died for all, that they which live should not hence-forth live unto themselves, but unto him which died for them and rose again.[33]

The very essence of the spiritual walk, then, is to be prepared to follow after Christ in word and deed. This is done, not out of heroic acts of the will, but by the power of God, born of God's living Word in the heart. It is the nature of Christ in the heart that will be made manifest to the world; the Christ life, as witnessed to in Scripture, will be seen again in all those who have been reborn of his Spirit. 'For they have put on Christ and are purified through the Holy Spirit in their consciences from dead works to serve the living God; bringing forth through the Spirit the fruits of the Spirit, whose end is eternal life,' Menno concludes.

CONCLUSION

We might summarise the central point of this chapter with Menno's confident words: '[The believer] is clothed with the power from above, baptized with the Holy Spirit, and so united and mingled with God that he becomes a partaker of the divine nature and is made conformable to the image of His Son.'[34] This has the unmistakable sound of a mystical stream of piety. To what extent was Anabaptist spirituality mystical?

If by 'mysticism' one means the aspiration for, and practices leading to, an 'ecstatic union with God', there probably is not even one Anabaptist who would qualify as a practitioner of mystical piety.[35] Recent studies, however, have usefully broadened the understanding of Christian mysticism in a way that sheds helpful light on Anabaptist spirituality.

In his magisterial multi-volume history of mysticism in Western Christianity (still in process of completion), Bernard McGinn does not link mysticism to an 'ecstatic unitive experience', central though such experiences may have been, and may be, to individual mystics. He maintains that what is central to Christian mysticism is 'an immediate consciousness of the presence of God'.[36] Therefore, the mystical stream in Christianity is a way of life; the 'mystical element in Christianity' is 'that part of [Christianity's] beliefs and practices that concerns the preparation for, the consciousness of, and the reaction to the immediate or direct presence of God'.[37]

When the essence of mysticism is seen as preparing for, being aware of and responding to the immediate *presence of God*, we can see immediately that the Anabaptist tradition incorporated the mind-set and process of Christian mysticism to a significant degree. We shall return again to this question in Chapter 8 below; here we wish only to point to the importance of the mystical legacy for the beginnings of Anabaptist spirituality.

The experienced presence of God is absolutely central to the first two stages of Anabaptist spirituality. First, the presence of God is to be sought in repentance and submission to God. The Anabaptist tradition unanimously insists that the presence of God must be wholeheartedly desired, sought, cultivated and actively accepted. As we have noted, the diagnosis of the human problem as one of wilful disobedience, whose solution lies in the fear of God, repentance and obedience, was a path already well marked in the mystical tradition. The path leading to the presence of God is described by the Anabaptists in ways that closely parallel the language, concepts and images used in the mystical tradition of the West. The crucial objective was the same: the experienced presence of God.

In the second place, the presence of God defines the experience of rebirth without which, the Anabaptists maintained, there could be no new life. The experienced reality of God's living presence was described by the Anabaptists in ways that closely mirror aspects of the preceding mystical tradition in the West. Even the Reformation dictum of salvation by faith through grace was interpreted in the Anabaptist stream in light of the regenerating presence of God with believers.

As a consequence, some of the central themes and attitudes of the broad mystical tradition were appropriated (and modified) by the Anabaptists. Central among these is the theme, or attitude, of *Gelassenheit*. In the earliest Anabaptist writings there is an emphasis on how one must 'yield' one's will and creaturely impulses in trust to God, if there is to be a true experience of the presence of God. In a later stage of Anabaptist development, *Gelassenheit* would be described as something akin to 'accepting God's will in all things', both at the hands of the will of the community and in the face of the persecution of the world.

The medieval mystical tradition insisted that 'Christ must be born in us' if there is to be a Christ-like life. This is a Christocentric understanding of the experience of 'the presence of God', and it was heartily embraced by the Anabaptists. Here mystical and Anabaptist spirituality contrast dramatically with Reformation spirituality: The accent falls on the experienced presence of the living Christ within, transforming believers with power, rather than on the historic work of Christ's atonement on the cross.

The mystical tradition asserted that God was in Christ perfectly, and to the extent that the presence of God dwells in the hearts of believers, to that extent will believers be conformed to Christ.[38] The expectation that the birth of Christ within will be efficacious in regenerating those who have 'yielded themselves' to that power is most evident in the late medieval mystical tradition, and increasingly so as we approach the sixteenth century in movements such as the Brethren of the Common Life. The presence of God was expected to express itself in individual believers by 'Christ-formed' action in the world. In the mystical and the Anabaptist traditions the same virtues of Christ's nature are to be reflected in the reborn: humility, patience, complete yieldedness to the will of God, perfect love, obedience.

Were the Anabaptists mystics? Because the focus of so many

Christian mystics fell on the 'ineffable' or ecstatic experience – which formed no visible part of the Anabaptist experience – one would be inclined to say 'No'. Anabaptists were not mystics in this narrow sense. But the question has been poorly posed. Anabaptist spirituality manifestly expresses the 'mystical element in Christianity', since it cannot be understood apart from the 'beliefs and practices that concern the preparation for, the consciousness of, and the reaction to the immediate or direct presence of God'.

Anabaptist spiritual life was based on the decisive presence and power of God; God's living presence would change everything. This they believed and, according to their testimonies, this they experienced. If, for Eckhart and other medieval spiritual practitioners, the experience of God's presence was one of ineffable rapture, for the Anabaptists God's presence was an experienced power that led them to repentance, to a new life in community and to a Christ-like life in the world. It was God's immediate presence and power that strengthened them in the midst of their suffering. The 'mystical element' of the immediate presence of the God in and with believers stands at the heart of Anabaptist spirituality, a foundation built upon and made plainly visible in the unique ecclesial practices and structures they would develop, as we shall see in the chapters that follow.

4 THE BAPTISM OF WATER: THE COVENANT OF A GOOD CONSCIENCE

Hans Schlaffer held the office of Roman Catholic priest for fifteen years. He had a brief one-year career as an Anabaptist before he was arrested, tried and executed in Austria in 1528. The *Martyrs Mirror* reports his answer to the question of adult baptism:

> They also asked him, in what the foundation of these anabaptistic sects did properly consist. To this he replied: 'Our faith, practice, and baptizing is founded on nothing else than the command of Christ: "Go ye into all the world, and preach the Gospel to every creature. He that believeth and is baptized shall be saved."' (Mark 16:16; Matt. 28:19); and many other Scriptures.[1]

Hans Schlaffer's answer to the question of adult baptism was to point to Jesus' Great Commission, as given expression in both Mark and Matthew. In this he was utilising a scriptural proof that was repeated innumerable times by Anabaptists in the sixteenth century. 'First teach, then baptise,' Jesus himself commanded. Here was a plain and simple biblical order of things that seemingly could not be disputed without doing violence to the text itself. True, the practice of infant baptism was brought into question, but this seemed a small price to pay for bringing church practice in line with Jesus' intentions. Paul Glock summarised a few of the scriptural arguments in a letter he wrote in 1573 from prison to his home church in Moravia.

We are happily satisfied with the words of Christ, since he does not bid [infants] be baptized. For if they had to be baptized, he surely would have commanded it. [Further], Jesus says: 'Every plant which my Father has not planted, shall be rooted up' [Matt. 5:13]. Infant baptism is no plant of God, otherwise Christ would have mentioned it. [Finally], Christ says: 'Teach all nations and baptize them' [Matt. 28:19]. Observe: the nations are first to be taught, otherwise you baptize the untaught.[2]

The rejection of infant baptism and the baptism of adults were two of the central points of contention between Anabaptists and the mainline churches. Anabaptists were questioned about their doctrine and practice of baptism virtually every time they were arrested. The result was a ubiquitous repetition of the arguments summarised by Hans Schlaffer above, as any reader of Anabaptist testimonies knows well.[3] The Anabaptists held to the Reformation premise that church practice should be shaped by Scripture, and so they clung to these texts with a tenacity that frustrated their interlocutors.[4]

If one were to summarise the Anabaptist understanding of baptism on the basis of the Scriptures most often cited in prison testimonies, the impression would be that Anabaptist baptismal theology was naive, narrowly literal and legalistic: Jesus said, first this, then that, and so we must do it in that order. But there was more: there is no command to baptise infants in the New Testament, nor any direct evidence that the apostles baptised infants – the texts concerning the baptism of 'households' were not considered convincing proof of infant baptism by the Anabaptists.[5] The literal New Testament evidence thus combined a direct command of Jesus to first teach and then baptise (which could not apply to infants), with the absence of a command to baptise infants, as well as a lack of evidence that the early church baptised infants. These simple biblical arguments were repeated often, but of them all, Anabaptist prisoners utilised Jesus' command in the Great Commission especially, with repetitive frequency.

But reviewing the common biblical arguments does not go far enough. The obvious New Testament texts were cited in the contentious settings of courts and disputations, and often do not make clear the pivotal importance of water baptism in the spirituality of the Anabaptists. In many of their own writings the Anabaptists spoke of baptism as a *threefold baptism* of spirit, water and blood, making reference to 1 John 5:6–12.[6] 'Baptism', understood in its full-orbed meaning as a threefold baptism, was in fact a shorthand description of a spiritual process that could apply only to fully conscious adult persons. The Anabaptists believed that Scripture, when read with no attempt to avoid the cross, called for this spiritual path to be followed by all members of Christ's body.

Water baptism is, first of all, intimately tied to, and dependent upon, the baptism of the Spirit, providing a visible witness and testimony to the inner changes wrought by God. In the second place, water baptism is a public witness that testifies to one's confession of sin, repentance and the commitment to live a new life, by the power of the resurrection. Third, water baptism is a visible sign of a conscious commitment to the body of believers. Whereas the spiritual struggles up to this point have been largely individual and private, after water baptism one's spiritual life takes on an irreversible public dimension because of one's personal pledge to the community of Christ. The baptismal sign in water is thus a crucial step in the spiritual life that signifies a covenant made not only with God in the heart, but also a covenant made with the living members of Christ's body. The covenant of water baptism witnesses to one's sincerity and good intention. It is a binding affirmation that one is prepared to receive and give counsel and admonition as a member of a community of believers, in the spiritual struggles of life's pilgrimage. Finally, water baptism signifies the willingness to accept a baptism in blood. The baptism of blood points not only to possible martyrdom, but also to the 'denial of self' and inevitable suffering entailed in living as a child of God. In none of these forms of 'baptism' can the path be undertaken by infants or children.

Technically speaking, water baptism was understood to be a 'sign' only, but the Anabaptists considered it a necessary sign, since it had been commanded by Christ himself.[7] Furthermore, although it was a 'mere sign' and no sacrament, a genuine water baptism was to reflect, accompany and be conjoined to spiritual realities, and thus carried a very rich cargo of significance for the Anabaptists. In what follows we will examine in more detail some of the themes indicated by the threefold baptism, and the place of water baptism within that wider understanding.

BAPTISM OF THE SPIRIT

Hans Schlaffer was convinced that the water baptism of adults had scriptural warrant based in the Great Commission instituted by Jesus himself. Nevertheless, as he explained in more detail in a writing from prison to his Anabaptist brothers and sisters, baptism in water was to be preceded by a prior and more important baptism which comes about by faith.

> This faith is . . . a work of God in a person. Through . . . faith God makes a covenant with a person and that person with God . . . This is not the old covenant which he made with the Jews who were his people then (Deut. 26) . . . Christ himself calls it the new testament in his blood which is shed for the forgiveness of sins (Heb. 8[:8–13]). It is impossible to say too much in words about this new testament. For it only is the work of the Spirit in the human heart and is at the same time the baptism of Spirit and fire with which Christ baptizes.[8]

It is through faith, which is God's free gift, that the new testament in Christ's blood is planted in the human heart. This new and true covenant is, says Schlaffer, a baptism of Spirit and fire. By means of the baptism of the Spirit, God provides the good conscience necessary for the step of water baptism.

Spirit is the assurance in the conscience of the grace and mercy of God for the forgiveness of all committed sins no matter how great or how many, for Christ has taken them all away and annulled them. The Spirit of God witnesses to our spirits that we are the children of God.[9]

The baptism of fire that accompanies the Spirit, according to Schlaffer, is the purifying love of God.

The fire is the ardour of the love of God and the neighbour in the heart. It enables him to suffer whatever befalls him because of the witness to God's truth, including death. Nothing can turn such a believer from the witness of the truth in the heart. This fiery love of God overflows towards the neighbour, that is, the brothers and sisters, not only with words but with deed and truth. Such goodwill is given also to enemies and evildoers (Matt. 5[:44]), for Christ himself teaches us and says: 'By this everyone will know that you are my disciples, if you have love for one another' (John 13[:35]).[10]

For Hans Schlaffer and the early Anabaptists, the spiritual baptism – that powerful rebirth and redirection of the sinner in the heart, by the power of God – was the 'true' baptism, without which water baptism could mean nothing. In the words of Hans Denck, 'Who indeed would venture to wash the red off the brick and the black off the coal . . .? It would be useless work, because (the) nature is not basically changed and overcome. Likewise it is also futile to wash externally the man whose body and soul are by nature unclean if he is not initially penitent and won over from within.'[11]

When contemporaries focused on the act of water baptism – the visible ecclesial sign – they were missing an important point. For the Anabaptists, the waters of baptism by themselves had no inherent spiritual or sacramental power, even when they were administered within a community of believers. Insofar as the water exercised power, it did so only in conjunction with a genuine spiritual transformation of the individual receiving water baptism.[12] Seen from one perspective, the water was 'just' water – it had no magical power – and so to focus on the act of water baptism was to be misled.

On the other hand, however, the waters of baptism were not inconsequential for all that. Throughout the sixteenth century Anabaptists battled spiritualists inside and outside their congregations who maintained that 'outward ceremonies' such as baptism were harmful and even useless, since Christ intended to found a purely 'spiritual' church. The 'baptisers' persisted, arguing that the 'ceremonies' of water baptism and the Lord's Supper could not simply be cast aside. Baptism, the Supper and other 'external witnesses' are indissolubly linked to inner realities, thanks to the power of Jesus' institution and command. Furthermore, although water was 'just water', the genuine administration of the 'sign' of baptism conjoined that sign and the 'visible life' that was to follow the sign, to the inner, experienced reality that both preceded and followed the outward sign. What Jesus intended, the Anabaptists maintained, was a seamless integration of outer witness with inner truth, of faith and practice, word and deed, aptly summarised in the act of water baptism but expressed throughout the Christian life.

The integration of inner, spiritual reality with outward witness characterises Anabaptist spirituality generally. Just as the inner reality was to be governed by the Spirit of Christ, so the outward witness was expected to reflect and mirror the life of Christ by a visible obedience to his explicit commands and a life in conformity to the witness of his life and that of the apostles. Anabaptist spirituality emphasised integrity, a coincidence between the hidden and the manifest, the measure always being Jesus Christ and the witness of Scripture. It is therefore fitting that Anabaptist spirituality is first marked visibly by the water baptism commanded by Jesus, which brings together the inner and the outer lives in a tangible way. The integration of inner and outer will shape both individual and church practice, as we shall see below.

The Anabaptists were asked frequently whether salvation is possible in the presence of a spiritual baptism, but in the absence of water baptism. Their answer was 'Of course!' Accepting water baptism is a step of obedience in fulfilling Jesus' intentions for his followers; it testifies to a deeper truth, and leads directly into a new life within the community of believers. But salvation is by faith and obedience, not by water. If for some reason a believer finds it impossible to witness to genuine faith by water baptism, the true baptism has already been received. And so Hans Denck wrote, putting an interesting twist on the Mark 16:16 proof text: 'External baptism is not required for salvation . . . But internal baptism . . . is necessary. Thus it is written, he who believes and is baptised will be saved (Mark 16:16).'[13] Denck read 'baptism' in the Mark passage as referring to the baptism of the Spirit, not the baptism of water. Although the outer 'ceremonies' and 'ordinances' commanded in Scripture need to be practised as commanded where possible, the power of the 'outward signs' is conditional on the more fundamental spiritual realities to which the signs point and to which they give witness.

We have reviewed some of the images of rebirth and regeneration in the previous chapter. Here we wish to underline how the language of spiritual birth was intimately connected to water baptism, thus linking inner change, rebirth and regeneration with the ecclesial sign of Christian initiation. Dirk Philips summarised the relationship between inner and outer baptism succinctly:

> We believe and confess that there is a Christian baptism which must take place internally and externally, internally with the Holy Spirit and with fire . . . but externally with water in the name of the Father and the Son and the Holy Spirit, Matt. 28:19. The baptism of the Spirit is administered by Jesus Christ himself to the penitent and believing, just as John the Baptist said: 'I baptize with water for repentance, but he who is coming after me is mightier than I, whose sandals I am not worthy to carry; he shall baptize you with the Holy Spirit and with fire,' Matt. 3:11.[14]

In the Anabaptist reading of the New Testament, the baptism of the Spirit and the baptism in water were intended to accompany each other; the Spirit leads to the water.[15] In Balthasar Hubmaier's catechism, for example, the question is asked, 'After faith what do you desire? Answer: Water baptism.'[16] Although the water does not of itself *convey* spiritual power, it is a sign that is necessarily conjoined to the experienced regenerative power of God in the heart and witnesses to one's embracing of the cross.[17] Anabaptist baptism carried a profound regenerationist and ascetic significance.

REPENTANCE AND WATER BAPTISM

As we have seen above, the Anabaptists believed that a heartfelt, profound repentance is a necessary step for those who have become aware of their sinfulness, their complicity in sin and their resistance to God. This repentance must take place deep in the human heart, but the Anabaptists believed it had to be recognised publicly as well. From the earliest days of the baptising movement, baptism in water was understood as a visible sign of a genuine, heartfelt repentance for sin, as well as a sign of the forgiveness of sins.

Just a few days after the first nocturnal baptisms in Zurich, a series of baptisms took place in the nearby village of Zollikon. These baptisms were characterised by highly emotional scenes of repentance. On 25 January 1525, a group of nine people shared an evening meal and a time of reading from the New Testament. All of a sudden Hans Bruggbach stood up and began to weep, telling the others 'what a great sinner he was'. He asked for prayer and the sign of baptism, both of which requests were met. After prayer, he was baptised in a simple ceremony: a metal kitchen dipper was used to hold the water, and Hans was baptised in the name of the Father, the Son and the Holy Spirit.[18] The day after this event George Blaurock, who performed most of these early Zollikon baptisms, told Marx Bosshart: 'Up to now you have been a carefree young man; but now you must become another person, putting off the old Adam, putting on a new man, and become a better person.' Blaurock then asked Marx if he 'desired the grace of God', and when Marx said yes, Blaurock baptised him.[19]

The Reformed historian Fritz Blanke has described the Zollikon events with detailed clarity and commented on the 'revival movement' character of these earliest baptisms. The process of repentance among the Zollikon baptisers begins, Blanke noted,

> when the consciences of individual persons begin to assault them and they become disquieted because of their sinfulness. The next step is that they implore God for full conviction of sin. Then follows the break-through of this conviction; their own guilt and sin are uncovered before them . . . Forgiveness is experienced in baptism . . . for it is regarded as the visible sign that God has pardoned the sinner . . . Baptism is a sign of grace.[20]

A full conviction of sin, followed by a heartfelt repentance are preludes to the sign of water baptism, which signifies (among other things) a genuine acceptance of the forgiveness of sins offered, in Christ, to the repentant sinner.[21]

BAPTISM AND THE NEW LIFE

In late February 1527, a clandestine gathering of Anabaptists was held in the Swiss village of Schleitheim. The group, under the guidance of Michael Sattler, a former prior of the Benedictine monastery of St Peter's of the Black Forest, came to agreement concerning seven articles.[22] The first of these concerned baptism.

> Baptism shall be given to all those who have been taught repentance and the amendment of life and [who] believe truly that their sins are taken away through Christ, and to all those who desire to walk in the resurrection of Jesus Christ and be buried with Him in death, so that they might rise with Him; to all those who with such an under-

standing themselves desire and request it from us; hereby
is excluded all infant baptism, the greatest and first abomination of the pope. For this you have the reasons and the
testimony of the writings and the practice of the apostles
(Mt. 28:19; Mk. 16:6; Acts 2:38; Acts 8:36; Acts 16:31–33;
19:4). We wish simply yet resolutely and with assurance to
hold to the same.[23]

Schleitheim's summary of early baptismal theology covers
well-known ground: first teaching, then baptism; first repentance and faith in the forgiveness of sins, then baptism. What
is striking about Schleitheim's formulation, however, is the use
of the Pauline image of dying to sin, dying to the world, dying
to the old Adam, and rising in Christ, in baptism, to a new life
(cf. Romans 6:3–4; Colossians 2:11–13). Pauline baptismal
images were particularly relevant to the Anabaptists, linking
baptism to the denial of self, 'dying to the world of sin' and the
regenerative process of rebirth by the Spirit of God, all of
which was to result in 'walking in newness of life'.

Added to these images of death to sin and birth into a new
life was the apostle Paul's equating of baptism with the new
circumcision, the mark of the new covenant, the sign of a good
conscience. Pilgram Marpeck, commenting on Colossians 2,
wrote:

Here, it is clearly understood how Paul interprets circumcision. He says that the Colossians have been circumcised
by the circumcision of Christ; they have taken off the body
of sin, which happens through faith in the knowledge of
Jesus Christ. When, therefore, we confess and also believe
that we have desire only toward Him, flee from all sin and
totally lay aside the sinful body, which we have taken off,
then we, too, are buried with Christ in baptism. If we
henceforth walk in a new life, commit ourselves to do so
with Christ, and seek no longer to walk in the old sins, we
are raised up with Christ.[24]

For Marpeck and the Anabaptists generally, having faith in

Christ meant not simply to believe, but actually to 'lay aside the body of sin'. This is being buried with Christ in baptism. Likewise, rising with Christ to a new life is 'no longer to walk in the old sins'. Baptism is the sign that indicates the joining together of the inner change with the intention to live a visibly new life.

In January of 1540, a group of 90 Anabaptist prisoners began their march from Passau on the Danube to Trieste, where they were condemned to be handed over to Admiral Andrea Dorea as galley slaves. Their confession of faith neatly summarises the manner in which Anabaptists wove together the biblical themes of denying oneself, following after Christ in life (Matt. 16:34; Mk 8:34; Lk 9:23), dying to sin, and being raised again in Christ in baptism.

> Christ says: whoever does not deny all that he has and takes up the cross and follows me cannot be my disciple. Thus we have completely died to sin, so that as Christ was raised from the dead through the glory of the Father, so we too should walk in newness of life. Scripture says further that we have been circumcised without hands with the circumcision of Christ through putting off the sinful body, the flesh. You have been buried with him in baptism and raised up through the faith which God gives. He has made you alive with him when you were still dead in sin (Col. 2[:11–13]).[25]

Along with Jesus' Great Commission and the New Testament evidence of apostolic practice, the apostle Paul's language and imagery concerning baptism was central to the Anabaptist understanding of baptism. The Anabaptists found in Paul's writings explicit links between baptism and a life of self-denial, devoted to living in a Christ-like manner – something no child could be expected to do.[26]

GELASSENHEIT, BAPTISM AND COMMUNITY

In 1527, Leonhard Schiemer wrote a tract in prison entitled 'On True Christian Baptism'. In it he connected the baptism of the

Spirit with *Gelassenheit* – complete surrender, or yieldedness.

> The first baptism is that of the Spirit to which one submits in obedience as Christ was obedient to his Father, even unto death on the cross, Phil. 1[:29–30] . . . In this baptism one surrenders to God with life and limb, but flesh and blood cannot surrender in that way without the Holy Spirit. Therefore a certain witness that one has the Holy Spirit is this complete surrender to God.[27]

The Anabaptists were convinced that a deep, personal yielding before God must precede water baptism and, in fact, constitutes the 'true baptism' before God. Had the Anabaptists not insisted that water baptism must accompany the spiritual baptism, they might well have formed a spiritualist group, perhaps such as the Society of Friends did later in England. But for the Anabaptists, *Gelassenheit* could never remain essentially private or individual. A profoundly personal yielding to God was simply the prelude to an equally profound yielding of the individual to the collective members of the Body of Christ on earth.

Along with Jesus' command to 'teach, then baptise', the Anabaptists encountered another scriptural command of Christ that they considered critical to the reformation of the church, and it was a command they always linked to the act of water baptism. In Matthew 18:15–18, Jesus described a process to be followed 'if a brother (or sister) sins against you'. First, confront the person privately and attempt a reconciliation. If that fails, return with 'one or two others' and do the same. If that fails, bring the matter before the congregation. At any stage in the process, the aim and the hope is a reconciliation and the 'winning back' of the erring brother or sister. But if the process fails entirely, a recalcitrant sinner is to be 'treated as a pagan or a tax collector', that is, expelled from the congregation. The passage in Matthew concludes with the declaration that what the church thus binds and looses on earth, will be likewise bound and loosed in heaven – a weighty responsibility which the Anabaptists took seriously.

The Schleitheim Articles of 1527, one of the earliest Anabaptist church orders to survive, make clear that baptism in water before the congregation not only witnesses to one's repentance, faith, rebirth and intention to live a new life, but also binds the one being baptised to 'the ban', 'brotherly admonition', or community discipline. The ban is to be administered by the *Gemeinde* (congregation) according to the 'command of Christ' as described in Matthew 18:15–18. The act of water baptism, therefore, marks the 'yielding' of one's individual will to the collective will of the body of believers.

We see here again the distance the Anabaptists maintained from the potential individualism of the spiritualists or a private spirituality of some later Pietists: the Christian life is not simply a matter of an inner baptism (being right with God personally), of a subjective 'sweetness of spirit' or an inner conviction of conscience of individuals. Rather, the faithful Christian life must be manifested in, and tested publicly, by the community of believers. Water baptism is the biblical 'sign' by which the shift from inner conviction to public commitment is made. Henceforth, the equally committed brothers and sisters will assist in testing and discerning God's will and the life of faithfulness for the individual.

The Schleitheim Articles make clear that the ban is to be exercised before the celebration of the Lord's Supper so that the unity of the body be maintained. The Lord's Supper, the third of the articles listed at Schleitheim, plays a central role in the maintenance of the Body of Christ. It is intended only for those who have been united beforehand 'in the one body of Christ, that is the congregation of God, whose head is Christ, and that by baptism',[28] and who have placed themselves under the discipline of the ban which is exercised by the community. This is a Supper open only to those 'who have been called out of the world unto God', an ascetic understanding that is cemented further by Scheitheim's fourth article, concerning separation from the evil and wickedness of the world.

The first three articles of Schleitheim (baptism, the ban, the Lord's Supper) thus make it clear that water baptism has transmuted *Gelassenheit* from a personal, subjective yielding before God in the heart, into a process of yielding to the public and corporate authority of the community. After baptism, believers will be called upon to 'yield' to one another, as fellow members of the Body of Christ. Balthasar Hubmaier had made the same point in his baptism book: 'the one who is baptised testifies publicly that he has pledged himself henceforth to live according to the Rule of Christ. By virtue of this pledge he has *submitted himself* to sisters, brothers, and to the church.'[29] The pledge of baptism, Hubmaier and Schleitheim emphasise equally, gives sisters and brothers 'authority over each other', to use Hubmaier's phrase. In the chapter that follows we will examine the specific shape assumed by Anabaptist community practice, as the baptising community struggled to make *Gelassenheit* visible in the community and before the world.

THE BAPTISM OF BLOOD

We have cited Hans Schlaffer before. He wrote eloquently about the threefold baptism, and especially about the baptism of blood – a subject on which he was well versed, since he wrote from prison, awaiting execution by beheading. His eloquent reflection bears repeating at length, for it weaves together many of the themes central to Anabaptist spirituality.

> The baptism of blood is the baptism about which Christ spoke: I have to be baptized with a baptism, and how afraid I am until it is accomplished (Luke 12f[:50]). Similarly he said to the two sons of Zebedee: Are you able to be baptized with the baptism with which I am baptized? By this he means the baptism of blood, that is suffering. That is why Scripture everywhere establishes that the true believers in Christ suffer only tribulation and every kind of opposition. Christians must be like Christ the head, whose members they are through suffering. For the disciple is not greater than the master nor the servant than his lord. Peter says: Christ suffered for us and left us

an example that we should follow his footsteps. He says further that whoever suffers in the flesh has ceased from sin. If we desire to be God's heirs and joint-heirs with Christ, as Paul says, we must also suffer with Christ. Thus the three baptisms are one even as the three witnesses, Father, Son, and Holy Spirit are one God. There is only one faith, one baptism, one God and Father of us all, and our Lord Jesus Christ.[30]

Just as there is no way to speak about water baptism without first understanding the baptism of the Spirit, Hans Schlaffer and the early Anabaptists were certain that one could not speak about either baptism in the Spirit or in water without speaking also about the baptism of blood.[31] The three baptisms were simply different aspects of the one true baptism. We will examine more dimensions of the baptism of blood in a later chapter on martyrdom. Suffice it to indicate here only that baptism in water points to and anticipates the readiness of those baptised to embrace suffering.

Baptism in water, then, testifies to the baptism in the Spirit, but also points beyond itself to a yielding to the community of believers and an acceptance of the baptism in blood. This threefold baptism, it is clear, is a baptism no infant can be prepared to accept, nor is it a baptism anyone may accept in someone else's place. This baptism is a covenant, a seal, a testimony, and a testament whose seriousness of intention is brought into sharp relief by the reality of the cross, accepted by those who accept the sign of baptism.

CONCLUSION

There are no direct parallels to the Anabaptist understanding of baptism in the preceding Catholic spiritual tradition. Infant baptism had been the common church practice since the late imperial period. The sacerdotal understanding of baptism and its sacramental function within the church of Rome was cemented by Pope Innocent III at the Fourth Lateran Council in 1215. Within Christendom, the only people to challenge this understanding had been groups labelled heretical, such as Albigensians and Waldensians who, for their different and respective reasons, suspended the baptism of infants. Those who challenged Christendom's ecclesial practice of infant baptism prior to the sixteenth century thus lie outside the Catholic tradition. Nevertheless, when we analyse the role played by baptism in Anabaptist spirituality, we see an interesting and important analogue in the mainstream monastic tradition in the West.

Anabaptist baptism was a sign that carried profound ascetic and communal signification, as we have seen. To accept baptism was to undertake a path of 'following after Christ'. This meant undergoing a process of spiritual harrowing that led to life in community, and which ended only at death, after one had traversed the narrow way of the cross. Marking an adult commitment to such a spiritual life was not new in Western Christendom. In fact, the rite and practice of water baptism functioned for the Anabaptists much as had the monastic vow for individual monastics. Although monastic profession was never described as 'anabaptism', it very well could have been. Already in the late patristic period the monastic profession of vows had come to be described as a 'second baptism, and came to parallel the baptismal rite in its own unique ways'.[32]

Granting the differences in ecclesial meaning given to the rite of baptism, the parallels of spiritual function between monastic profession and Anabaptist baptism are clear to those who compare, for example, chapter 58 in the *Rule of St Benedict*, which describes monastic profession, with Anabaptist writings describing the role of baptism. Common to both are the elements of a voluntary commitment to the path of following Christ unto death, submission of the individual to the community, with a 'dying to sin and rising in Christ' symbolised by the respective rites.[33]

Anabaptist baptism, like the monastic vow, witnessed to a profound intention, and was to be undertaken only by those who were prepared to commit themselves to a life of self-denial, a life devoted entirely to following in Christ's footsteps in the community of faith. It was a sign that indicated a fundamental process of repentance and faith, and signalled a conscious intention to 'walk in newness of life'. Because baptism signified these things – as did the fully conscious, pledged vow of the religious in the Catholic tradition – neither could properly be undertaken by children, but only by those who could responsibly meet the rigours and demands of the ascetic, committed life of following in the footsteps of Christ. It was perhaps for these reasons that Martin Luther, and the Lutheran tradition after him, described Anabaptism as 'a new monkery'.[34]

For the Anabaptists, water baptism was the biblically mandated 'sign' that crystallised like no other the entire inner process of coming to a fear of God, recognition of sin, repentance for sin, faith in the forgiveness of sins through Christ (believing the Gospel), rebirth, and the good intention of setting out in the living of a new and virtuous life within the community of believers, regardless of physical suffering, unto death. Here was a biblical 'covenant' or 'testament' that was established, commanded and exemplified by Christ himself, on which the visible church community was intended to be built. Far from being a 'mere' sign, the public pledge of water baptism by fully conscious adults testified to and symbolically made visible a wealth of spiritual experience, maturation, conviction, decision and intention – regardless of the cost – as a public document seals a contract. It was a covenant act that bound believers to the true way. Furthermore, understood in its threefold dimensions of Spirit, water and blood, the covenant sign of water baptism marked the phases of baptism received and lived out by Christ himself, to which he invited disciples when he said 'follow me'.

The very physicality of water baptism reveals a profound incarnational dimension to their spirituality that the Anabaptists refused to sidestep. Although they could never accept the sacramental premise that water, bread, wine or any other 'created thing' could 'convey grace' in the hands of ordained clergy, *ex opere operato*, neither could they accept that the Christian life would remain essentially invisible, a spiritual matter known to the believer and God alone. The Anabaptists were certain that the collective membership of the church of Jesus Christ would be marked by the 'visible signs of invisible grace'. They believed that the visible signs of grace had been revealed to humankind by God in Scripture and, most importantly, by the words and the life of Jesus himself. Baptism was the first of these visible signs; in the chapter that follows we will examine several more visible signs of grace that marked Anabaptist spirituality.

5 THE BODY OF CHRIST

The civil engineer and Anabaptist leader, Pilgram Marpeck, was deeply committed to building up the church. Although he was a self-taught theologian, he had a keen mind and a passion for shaping the church in a biblical manner. Marpeck was deeply committed to the spiritual foundations of the Anabaptist faith, but at the same time he came to oppose spiritualists of his acquaintance who wished to make the focus of the Christian life and church the 'inward' experience.[1] In response to the spiritualists, Marpeck emphasised a Christocentric and incarnational church, and so highlighted with particular clarity the common Anabaptist insistence on the unity of inner life, outer sign and outer witness. The following passage, from Marpeck's response to the spiritualist Caspar Schwenckfeld, is especially lucid.

> Under the Holy Spirit, inward and outward obedience flow together. First we need a birth into purity (Matt. 23). Then the inward obedience of our spirit belongs to the Spirit of Christ, who assures our spirit (Rom. 8) that outward obedience is possible for the outward person. The appropriate body now belongs to His Spirit. Through the divine Spirit the human spirit bridles the body for servanthood and cross bearing (Rom. 6, 8, 12; 1 Cor. 9; Gal. 5; Jas. 4). The external obedience of a wholly believing person makes such a person – spirit, soul, and body – a partaker of the obedience of the whole body of Christ, that is, His holy congregation. One becomes a member of the body of which Christ is the head, the lord, the ruler. Each one serves the other to the better-

ment of the body of Christ. For in every member there are gifts of the Spirit for the common good (Rom. 12; 1 Cor. 12, 14; Eph. 4; 1 Pet. 4). What is given to the spouse of Christ is applied through apostles, prophets, teachers, bishops, admonishers, and the like. This is the service of the whole congregation, carried out in and through the Holy Spirit, as members grow as branches on the Vine, who gives them guidance; without Him they can do nothing, externally or internally (John 15; Eph. 4; Col. 2) – neither baptism, communion, laying on of hands, footwashing, brotherly love, discipline, the ban, and the like. All of these issue from one Spirit to the praise of the one essence, that is, the God who is in all things, who wins us to and sustains us in eternal life unto salvation – one essence and one glory.[2]

Not all Anabaptists would have expressed themselves on this subject with Marpeck's focused clarity, but after their own fashion all the baptisers insisted that the inward and the outward lives of the reborn were two aspects of one, integrated reality. The one Body of Christ would be formed by members who had given themselves over to the one Spirit, and would be identifiable by the marks of a Christ-like life and obedience to Christ's explicit commands.

In the category of explicit commands were four biblical 'commands' that gave visible shape to the Anabaptist community of faith: the command to 'believe and be baptised', the command to observe 'fraternal admonition', the command to celebrate the Supper of remembrance, and the command (and example) to wash one another's feet. From one perspective, we can say that these four 'church ordinances' gave visible shape to the Anabaptist church; from another perspective, we can see that the practice of these ordinances was closely integrated with fundamental Anabaptist spiritual convictions.

THE BAN

Water baptism into the community of believers, the Body of Christ, was a covenant sign that signified the beginning of mutual obligations within that community. The illiterate needle-peddler and Anabaptist evangelist, Hans Nadler, gave the following account to the officials who questioned him.

> All that I have, body, soul, honour and goods, I have committed to God my Lord and to my brothers and sisters, in order to help where they need it. Therefore I accepted the sign of the water, that by it my brothers and sisters would know that I wanted to be united with them, and to be ready to be rebuked by the Word of God. Where I do wrong, I want to accept such a rebuke. They also will accept a rebuke from me, as Scripture shows when Christ says, 'If you see your brother err, rebuke him between yourself and him alone . . .' That is the Christian order we have among ourselves. If he comes to himself, he is again accepted into the congregation. In the meantime [the congregation] prays to God for him until he comes to himself.[3]

The 'Christian order' of mutual admonition was universally accepted by all Anabaptists, although there were some variations in practice. The ideal governing the practice was commonly acknowledged: the ban was to be exercised in a spirit of love, among those who had submitted to Christ and to one another in baptism. The ban was to be carried out in all humility, kindness and concern for the salvation of the person in need of contrition and repentance.

The Anabaptist ban took the place of the earlier sacrament of penance. It was by means of fraternal admonition and public repentance that the process of confession, absolution and the forgiveness of sins was carried out in the baptising communities. Those who had been 'inadvertently overtaken' by sin needed to demonstrate contrition and repentance, in a humble spirit, before the brothers and sisters. They could then be readmitted by the wider community into full fellowship in the Body of Christ. This practice found its scriptural warrant in Matthew 18:18: whatever you bind on earth will be bound in heaven. The penitential 'binding and loosing' function regarding sins and their forgiveness thus fell to the church community as a whole – it was not a clerical function or privilege. The congregation of baptised, committed believers was also the forgiving, reconciling and absolving community, with the power to 'bind and loose'.

The scriptural warrant for the practice of mutual admonition was clear: a direct command of Christ in the Gospel of Matthew. The practice of fraternal discipline in cloistered communities also had a long and venerable history, well known to all in the sixteenth century; it had been based on the same scriptural warrant.[4] But at the spiritual heart of the practice of the ban was the Anabaptist understanding of rebirth and regeneration by the Holy Spirit. The spiritual ideals and loving practices that were to govern the exercise of the ban were clearly expressed in many Anabaptist writings, testimonies and songs. Surely, regenerated believers (both those admonishing and those being admonished) would be guided by the Spirit that had regenerated them, and would approach fraternal admonition in the same yielded, penitential and humble manner as had brought them into baptism and the narrow way in the first place. Time came to show, however, that the ban was potentially divisive and problematic in real-life situations.

Anabaptist writings on the ban present a clear view of the ideal approach and practice.[5] In one of his earliest writings devoted to the ban, Menno Simons linked the practice of admonition to the love of believers to one another, particularly as people who are concerned with the salvation of their brothers and sisters and deeply involved in one another's lives.

> If you see your brother sin, then do not pass him by as one that does not value his soul; but if his fall be curable, from that moment endeavor to raise him up by gentle admonition and brotherly instruction, before you eat, drink, sleep, or do anything else, as one who ardently desires his salvation, lest your poor erring brother harden and be ruined in his fall, and perish in his sin.[6]

Exhort the sinner, Menno insists, and seek by prayer, word and deed 'to convert him from the error of his way, to save his soul'.[7] But do all of this 'with godly wisdom, discretion, gentleness, and prudence . . . not with austerity nor with cruelty, but rather with gentleness.'[8] We hear a genuine pastoral passion in Menno's words.

Still, with all the exhortations to compassion and gentleness, Menno still insisted that 'It is also the nature of those who are in God not to sin, as John says: Whosoever abideth in God sinneth not.'[9] Menno made this claim because of his understanding of the nature of rebirth: 'the birth of earth makes earthly minded, and the birth of heaven makes heavenly minded.' The birth from heaven leads to conformity with Christ: 'Then Christ dwells in our hearts. Then we are led by the Holy Ghost; we are the chosen generation, the royal priesthood . . . Then we are the temple of the Lord, the spiritual Mount Zion, the new heavenly Jerusalem, the spiritual Israel of God.'[10] But none of this will happen without a spirit of yieldedness: 'humble yourselves under the mighty hand of God; and sincerely deny yourselves.'[11] Only where there is a sincere yieldedness to God and an unfeigned love for one another will fraternal admonition function as it was intended to function: as an instrument of love used for winning back those who have momentarily strayed from the narrow path to salvation.

The practice of the ban was central to Anabaptist spirituality, based as it was on Christ's explicit command in the Gospel of Matthew, on a spiritual rebirth, on a continued attitude of yieldedness, denial of self, and a public commitment of all to walk 'in newness of life'. The Anabaptists recognized that even reborn human beings will stumble and fall – although early writings always maintained that these would be exceptional cases – and with the ban they attempted to institute a biblical practice that would enable new beginnings within the community. The process was fraught with danger, and did lead to schism and division. Nevertheless, the positive side of the story must also be told: the Anabaptists and their descendants came to be known for their piety, sobriety, modesty and honesty, living in communities where fraternal admonition and discipline were the norm. Admonition and loving discipline were instruments, when they functioned as intended, that served to maintain the integrity between the Spirit of Christ, born within, and the life of Christ that was to be lived in the world.

THE LORD'S SUPPER

The Lord's Supper, like baptism, was a constant point on which Anabaptist prisoners were questioned, particularly when they were arrested in Catholic areas. As with baptism, the Anabaptists rejected a clerical, sacramental understanding of the ordinance of the Lord's Supper. They were particularly emphatic in rejecting the doctrine of transubstantiation.

When Maria van Beckum was arrested in 1544 for being an Anabaptist, her sister-in-law Ursula voluntarily accompanied Maria to prison, prepared to share her fate. They were questioned repeatedly in prison by both clergy and state officials, but they could not be moved, citing Scripture in defence of their views. A commissar from the court of Burgundy asked them if they believed that Christ was present in the sacrament. They replied, 'as regards the Supper, we find that Christ left it as a memorial of His death, with bread and wine; as often as we commemorate it, we are to show forth His death till He come.'[12] The passage Maria and Ursula paraphrased was 1 Corinthians 11:23–27, the verses most often cited by Anabaptists being questioned about the Lord's Supper. In the Anabaptist understanding, the body of Christ was not physically present in or with the elements during the celebration of the Supper. Rather, the elements remained natural bread and wine; the Lord's Supper was a 'memorial' to be celebrated by the faithful until Christ returns. This was considered a heresy worthy of the most painful death in the Catholic Netherlands of the day, and death by fire was the sentence passed against these Anabaptist women.

Maria was burned to death first, and she died valiantly,

praying for those who were executing her. After Ursula had watched Maria being burned to death (she refused to be turned away to be spared the sight), she was offered her life in return for recantation. She refused and walked to the wood and the stake, where she began to pray the Lord's Prayer: 'Our Father which art in heaven,' to which the attending priest answered 'Yea, there you will find Him.' Ursula answered, 'Because I seek Him there I must die this temporal death. If I should confess Him in the bread, I might live longer.' Soon after she too died in the flames, having linked her death to her conviction that the body of Christ was in heaven, not in consecrated elements of bread and wine.

There was a stream of anti-clerical and anti-sacramental conviction that ran particularly deep among the Anabaptists, deepened and reinforced by occasions of persecution and martyrdom such as those experienced by Maria and Ursula van Beckum. Not only did priests lack the power to perform miracles of transubstantiation, but even more fundamentally, Christ's body, being in heaven after the ascension, simply could not be 'in' the bread. Here the Anabaptists followed Zwingli's argument, and commonly cited the Creed as evidence: Christ Jesus ascended into heaven and sits at the right hand of God the Father. It is Christ's Spirit (or the Holy Spirit, or the Spirit of God) that is present with believers, and not Christ's body in bread and wine. When Jesus said 'this is my body' he meant, 'this represents my body'. That is why he said 'Do this in *remembrance* of me.' The faithful remember Christ's sacrifice on the cross with each celebration of the Supper.[13] The bread, they insisted, is just bread; the wine is just wine.[14]

But, for all the radical talk, there is good reason to doubt that the Anabaptists meant, literally, that the wine of the Supper was just wine, and the bread of the Supper was just bread. If this were literally true, the Lord's Supper would have been nothing more than a snack of bread with a sip of beverage, along with some incidental remembering. The entire sacramental action would be trivialised and brought into question. And this, emphatically, was not the case, as is evident from the intense solemnity with which the ordinance was celebrated. But exactly how the elements of bread and wine were related to God's grace was not easy to explain – especially against the background of a doggedly sacramental view, that continually asked about the instrumental power of consecrated elements to convey grace, and could look no further.

As was also the case with the ordinance of baptism, if we restrict our understanding to the numerous repetitions of the memorialist proof texts, we will be misled about the true meaning and significance of the Lord's Supper for Anabaptist spirituality. Taken to one logical conclusion, the Anabaptist position seems to lead to a spiritualist view and to an 'invisible' church of the spirit. The Anabaptists, however, refused to countenance the spiritualist option. They insisted that spiritual communion with Christ and Christ's Body on earth must be incarnated, celebrated visibly *with the elements* Christ ordained for that purpose.[15] The elements of bread and wine were considered important enough that no Supper would be celebrated without them; but they were not to be used in a celebration of the Supper, unless the Supper could be celebrated 'worthily'.

At their celebrations of the Supper, the Anabaptists not only examined personal and fraternal spiritual relationships, they also sang hymns that explained how they understood what they were doing. Significantly, the hymns they sang were not much concerned to negate sacramentalism, but rather set out to explain the Supper's place within the Anabaptist understanding of the spiritual process of new birth and faithful living.

The Swiss Brethren hymnal, the *Ausbund*, contains two substantial eucharistic hymns; the Hutterites have preserved three. All of these hymns were composed in the first half of the sixteenth century. Eucharistic hymn 92 of the *Ausbund* is still sung in Old Order Amish communities on communion Sundays.[16] The 'Danksagung' or 'Thanksgiving' hymn was composed by Hans Hut before 1528. It has been preserved by the Hutterites and is still sung at every Hutterite communion service.[17] In fact, there is an interesting melodic continuity with the Catholic eucharistic tradition, which one would never guess simply by looking at Anabaptist anti-sacramentalism. Four out of these five eucharistic hymns carry instructions that they are to be sung to the tune of the *Pange lingua*, a Latin eucharistic 'hymn of the most blessed sacrament' composed in the thirteenth century by none other than Thomas Aquinas, for use during the office of the feast of Corpus Christi. The Anabaptists borrowed this well-known Catholic euchristic hymn tune – whose eucharistic associations would have been unmistakable in the sixteenth century – but changed the text to fit their own understanding of the Lord's Supper.

When we explore how the Anabaptists described the significance of the Lord's Supper in their own writings of edification – and especially in their eucharistic hymns – we find multiple layers of significance that tie the eucharistic celebration integrally to the spiritual life of the community of believers. It turns out, in the end, that the bread broken at the Supper and the wine that was shared actually were more than 'just bread and wine', even if that 'more' was not quite what traditional sacramental theology had understood it to be.

Remembrance

'For as often as we break it together, distribute it, and eat, we should remember his body broken for us on the cross and distributed to all those who eat and enjoy in faith.'[18] So wrote Balthasar Hubmaier, articulating the initial significance of the 'Supper of remembrance': the bedrock 'memory' that is activated by the celebration of the Supper is Christ's sacrifice on the cross, through which forgiveness of sins is offered to humankind. The eucharistic hymns presuppose the remembering of Christ's sacrifice, even if they do not linger there.[19] Hans Hut's eucharistic hymn connects Christ's sacrifice on the cross directly to the Supper in somewhat poetic fashion:

There the little grain of wheat was ground
That paid for our sins.
There the true bread was broken,
Of whom the prophets spoke.
The bread of life was given to us
When Christ hung on the cross.[20]

Christ's atoning sacrifice on the cross lies behind all celebrations of the Supper, and remembering that sacrifice calls for thankfulness. So Hans Hut's 'Thanksgiving' hymn begins with these verses:

We give you thanks and honour, O Lord God
For you nourish us all.
You give us food from heaven,
For which we praise you eternally, Lord.[21]

The Lord's Supper in the Anabaptist tradition shared with Christendom the *commemorative* and *eucharistic* nature of the celebration, giving thanks to God while remembering and commemorating Christ's sacrifice.

While these traditional eucharistic emphases are present in the Anabaptist hymns, it is striking how faint are the traces of traditional eucharistic emphases. A more typical and distinctive Anabaptist emphasis emerges at a second level of 'remembering'. The celebration of the Supper is meant to recall the spiritual process of repentance, faith, rebirth and new life that define the Christian walk. After its treatment of Christ's atonement, *Ausbund* hymn 92, stanza 12 says immediately, 'Understand! Christ the Lord has become a mercy seat for all who, *if they believe, are born in him.*'[22] In these words we hear again the conditionality Anabaptists attached to the atoning sacrifice of Christ on the cross. The celebrants are reminded that *through faith and the new birth*, the blood of Christ cleanses sinners, not in a removed 'heavenly' process of vicarious atonement, but in an immediate, actual way: sinners are born again by the Spirit. The atonement must be extended to each believer individually. The Spirit must humble each

believer so that the believer 'becomes like Christ' and is ready
to bear the cross.

The role of God's living Spirit is striking in all of this.
Repentance, faith, rebirth and the new life are the work of the
Holy Spirit; remembering this spiritual work is part of what
must happen at the celebration of the Supper. *Ausbund* hymn
55 says clearly:

> The Spirit teaches us to understand the communion
> Of partaking His flesh and blood,
> The old man must completely perish
> with his works, this is certain,
> the Spirit of Christ must work in us.[23]

Ausbund hymn 92, stanza 16 sounds the same theme:

> The Holy Spirit feeds souls.
> This is the pledge sent for the inheritance.
> He is called a seal
> for your eternal release from pain.
> You should, therefore, praise God
> through Jesus Christ at all times
> for this heavenly food.[24]

It is the work of the Spirit to 'feed souls'. This spiritual feeding
predates and also accompanies the celebration of the Supper,
as will be noted later. In fact, it was this 'spiritual feeding' that
led those once in darkness into the light. Thanksgiving for
spiritual feeding at the celebration of the Supper is a 'remembrance' of an experience shared by all the true participants in
the Supper. The remembering and thanksgiving for the
sacrifice of Christ on the cross merges into remembering and
giving thanks for the presence of the living Spirit in the souls
of those who have been led to repentance and have experienced
a rebirth.

This spiritual 'heavenly food' is foundational for understanding the Lord's Supper in the Anabaptist tradition,
because the Supper recalls the earlier, renewing work of the
Spirit, and invokes the Spirit's continuing work in the believer

and among the members of the Body. Just as the Christ's atonement is at once historic and actual, in the releasing from sin of individual believers, so also the presence of the living Spirit in believers is both historic and actual, both past and present. Both aspects are celebrated in the Supper.

For the Anabaptists, the liberation from sin that is celebrated in the Supper focuses not only on the historical event on the cross, but also on the actual, incarnational event that has taken place in the hearts and lives of believers. If such an event of spiritual renewal has not taken place within a believer, he or she cannot partake in the true Supper of the Lord. This is a crucial insight that informs the Anabaptist sacramental theology of the Supper. The focus is on the renewing work of the Holy Spirit in individuals, and not on the renewing work of blessed elements.

A third level of remembering indicated by the eucharistic hymns is their hearkening back to the seal and covenant of the new birth in baptism. Hymn 92 in the *Ausbund* says it this way:

> God now holds what you have
> promised to him in baptism.
> According to his command, take the cup,
> complete the sacrifice to him.
> How it is, then, for us in Jesus Christ
> three witnesses decide:
> two are called water and Spirit,
> the third, blood, that is, suffering.[25]

As the Anabaptist celebrants at the Supper sang this hymn, they were reminded that not only had they accepted Christ's sacrifice in their hearts, by faith, they had also made a covenant with water baptism, sealed visibly before God and the community. The Supper is a reminder of the commitment that was made to die to oneself, in order to live a new life in Christ.[26] Finally, the commitment made at baptism was also a promise to accept suffering, or the baptism of blood, should it come. Partaking of the bread and wine of the Supper was thus

an occasion for remembering and renewing the deep commitments signified by baptism in spirit, water and blood.

It should be clear, in conclusion, that a simple statement
asserting that the Anabaptists held to a 'memorialist' Supper
simply does not go deep enough. The 'remembering' that takes
place at the Supper celebration functions on several complex
layers simultaneously, pointing to Christ's sacrifice, of course,
but looking emphatically beyond Christ's atonement to the
living Spirit of God as the cause and reason for the celebration
of the Supper by these particular members of the Body of
Christ.

Unity and Communion

Whereas the 'memorial' aspects of the Supper suggest casting
one's mind to the past, the examination and celebration of
unity brings present realities to the fore. The celebration of the
Supper points, first of all and most importantly, to the *mystical*
unity of believers with Christ. We may cite *Ausbund* hymn 55,
stanza 5:

> The Spirit teaches us to understand the communion
> Partaking of His flesh and blood,
> The old being must completely perish
> With the old works, this must be noted,
> The Spirit of Christ must work in us.

We return to the process of repentance, yielding in faith, and
rebirth, seen here not as an event in the past now remembered, but as an event being fulfilled in the present.
Communion depends on the death of the old being, and the
coming to life of a new being, filled with the Spirit of Christ.
Galatians 2:20 was often alluded to and cited by the
Anabaptists at this point: 'it is no longer I who live, but it is
Christ who lives in me.' This sentiment appears in *Ausbund*
hymn 55, stanza 9:

> We must lay aside the old garment
> And purge out the old leaven,
> That He may have His work in us.

And again, in stanza 13:

> Christ lets His word be poured out,
> The fountain of life flows within us,
> When we open our hearts to Him.[27]

Likewise the second stanza of Peter Riedemann's eucharistic hymn says:

> Therefore [God] gave from heaven
> The true bread that gives us life,
> So that for us who rightly eat it here,
> We are made pure in conscience.[28]

The all-important verses from 1 Corinthians 11:27–29, calling for a self-examination prior to participation in the Supper, were heard by the Anabaptists as a call to reflect seriously on their present spiritual condition. *Ausbund* hymn 92 says:

> Whoever, without the Spirit
> eats this bread,
> walks in hypocrisy, stands in sin,
> and will be possessed with the devil,
> as Judas ate unworthily
> and trod Christ under foot . . .
> You must be clean, then, and pure
> when you want to partake of it.
> You must be fed with God's Spirit.
> His body should include you.[29]

The fundamental union of individual members to the living Spirit of God was to be re-examined carefully at the time of celebrating the Lord's Supper. It was not simply a matter of remembering graces past; one needed to re-examine one's true spiritual condition in the present. The threat of eternal condemnation was certainly reason enough for honesty in this matter.

Here it is apparent that far from being a simple memorial with 'mere' bread and wine, celebration with the elements of communion, as instituted by Christ, was laden with spiritual and material significance. When one took the elements, it was a public pledge and testimony of a clear conscience, of a present, genuine yielding to God and rebirth in the Spirit – and woe to liars, hypocrites and deceivers.

At a second and equally profound level, the celebration of the Supper points to the creation of one body out of many members. Eucharistic hymn 92 in the *Ausbund* uses evocative language pointing to the union of the gathered community with Christ:

> This community (*G'mein*) is in Jesus Christ,
> of his flesh and bones.
> The Holy Spirit brought her together,
> a united (*gemeine*) body of Christ.
> As the vine has many branches,
> so the community of Christ
> is included in His power.
> In this way one partakes of Him.[30]

The Holy Spirit not only regenerates individuals – a mysterious process in itself – it also brings those individuals together, like flesh and bones, into one body – again a profound mystery. The Body of Christ, as a whole, 'is included in Christ's power', and the communion that is celebrated in that Body is a present manifestation of that intimate spiritual relationship.

As was the case with individuals before God, so also in the case of individuals before the community: the words of Paul calling for 'discerning the Body of Christ' demand an honest evaluation of communal relationships. False members are those who outwardly pretend to be united, but inwardly refuse to be 'ground' or 'crushed' in the process of becoming one Body. The image of grains of wheat being ground for bread, and of grapes being crushed for wine, points to the 'submission' (yieldedness), patience and humility which marked the process of conversion and which continued to mark the communion of believers.[31] The presence or absence of God's Spirit will be discerned by the presence or absence of Christ's love. Peter Riedemann's hymn said it this way:

> In the bread it is prescribed for us,
> That we must exercise ourselves in love,
> Serve one another for improvement,
> We who are members of one body,
> With true hearts, truly without deceit.[32]

And Hans Hut wrote:

> Therefore we eat the Body of the Lord,
> As we are taught by the Holy Spirit.
> If we would truly see God,
> Godly love must burn in us.
> It makes us into vines, the Spirit gives life,
> And in this way the Body of Christ is given to us.[33]

The bond of Christ's love creates a united Body out of individual believers. It is this union and communion, based on divine love in action, that is celebrated with bread and wine.

In the third place, the celebration of the Supper points to the unity of the gathered community with Christ the Head. Of course, this unity has been implicitly affirmed at both the individual and communal levels already. Eucharistic hymn 55 in the *Ausbund* uses a variety of scriptural images to make the explicit point.

> He is the Rock and Cornerstone
> laid for the house of his community (*Gemeine*)
> which is His bride, wife and body
> through which He performs His work here.
> All members of His body
> pursue His work here always,
> according to His will, unto death.
> They are one bread with Christ here.[34]

The celebration of the Supper with the elements of bread and wine, makes visible and testifies to a deeper reality: the Holy

Spirit has already done (and continues to do) the work of unity, both within individuals and among individuals in the community, uniting them all with the Head. The spiritual community has already been formed of reborn members, united with Christ, who is the centre, the Head, the Bridegroom. The occasion of the Lord's Supper simply gives visible testimony to the profound spiritual identification that exists between Jesus Christ and the individual and collective members of his Body on earth.[35]

The process of 'becoming bread and wine', the Body of Christ in the world, is one that will require sacrifice. The eucharistic hymns make it clear that belonging to the Body of Christ will be painful, as it was in Jesus' own life in this world. *Ausbund* hymn 55 in particular sounds this note repeatedly:

> . . . the flesh must suffer
> If we want to possess the kingdom with him.
> The Lamb is eaten with distress,
> Covered with bitter salt,
> For whoever does not want to suffer with Christ
> Shall separate himself from His flesh and blood,
> He who is anxious about cross and affliction,
> To him the body of Christ remains hidden.

This eucharistic hymn underlines that for the Body of Christ on earth, the bread of unity will be accompanied by the bitter cup of suffering. The communion of the body and blood of Christ, incarnated in earthly members, will be visibly marked by the character and the marks of Jesus himself. This communion cannot be simply 'spiritual' or invisible, but will be marked by the visible 'witness' of bread and wine and lives of love and obedience, even in the face of suffering.

In their effort to be the visible Body of Christ on earth, the Anabaptists celebrated a 'closed' Supper. The celebration of communion with the elements of bread and wine was open only to those who had undergone the process of dying to self and rising in Christ, sealed by baptism, tested by submission to fraternal admonition in the community – the bread and the wine of communion were not for just anybody.[36] Far from devaluing the elements of bread and wine, eating and drinking together with other members of Christ's Body indicates 'coming to the Lamb'. The central themes of an Anabaptist spirituality – yieldedness to God, faith, humility, spiritual rebirth, baptism, new life and conformity with Christ unto death if necessary – are thus concentrated, recalled, examined and enacted in this celebration. It is this integrated unity, including celebration with the visible elements, which marks the Lord's Supper in early Anabaptism. *Ausbund* hymn 55, stanza 23 says:

> Just as one bread [is made] from many kernels,
> and one drink from many berries,
> So all true Christians
> are one bread and one drink, without deceit or duplicity,
> in Christ the Lord. He nourishes us,
> multiplying true love and communion.[37]

The source of the Supper is the living Lord. Just as it is the power of the living God, working in the hearts of believers, that brings them to the Body of Christ, so it is the power of the living God that turns mere bread and wine into a spiritual meal that 'multiplies true love and communion'.

What did the Lord's Supper mean to the Anabaptists who practised it in their communities in the sixteenth century? Their hymns and writings leave us with strong impressions of what the Supper meant to them. The Anabaptists refused to honour the elements and the ceremony as such, convinced as they were that too much power had been given to lifeless elements and clerics in the preceding tradition. But on the other hand, they valued the visible ceremony enough that they carefully examined all participants and excluded from participation all those who gave evidence that they were not in spiritual communion. The Anabaptist Lord's Supper was thus a celebration of remembrance and communion in which the elements of inner renewal, eating and drinking of the bread and wine, were simultaneously conjoined among those who honestly witnessed to a new life with a good conscience.[38]

Was the bread just bread, and the wine just wine? When Jacob de Roore was pushed in prison to explain the meaning of the celebration with bread and wine, he answered: 'the body of the Lord, in the breaking of the bread which we break, becomes for us one communion or participation; and . . . the cup of blessing, which we bless, becomes for us one communion or participation in the blood of Christ.'[39] *Ausbund* hymn 55 adds that in the celebration of the Supper, Christ the Lord 'nourishes us, multiplying true love and communion'. Likewise an anonymous Swiss Brethren's writing circulating in the 1580s noted that '[partaking] of the Holy Supper with all true Christians and children of God . . . feeds, refreshes and quickens the soul to eternal life'.[40]

At the heart of the celebration of the Lord's Supper, with elements of bread and wine, is the mystery of communion with the present, living Lord. It is the power of the living God, working in the hearts of believers and in their midst that makes of them the Body of Christ. And it is the power of the living God that transforms the plain bread and wine of their celebration into a spiritual meal that 'multiplies true love and communion', that 'feeds, refreshes and quickens the soul to eternal life'.

There was no presence of Christ *in the elements* of the Anabaptist Lord's Supper. The bread and the wine were not seen as instruments to *convey* grace. This does not mean, however, that the Anabaptists denied the living presence of Christ in and with their celebration of the Supper, only that observers were looking for the presence of Christ in places where the Anabaptists did not expect to find that presence. The mystery of communion with the living Christ in his Supper comes into being by the power of the Spirit, dwelling in and working through the collected members of Christ's Body.

So it was that the celebration of the Lord's Supper, with real bread and real wine, became the time for a profound re-examination of the entire spiritual path and new life on which the members, following after Christ the Head, had embarked, as

well as a time of public re-commitment to that path.[41] Menno
Simons' words are fitting:

> For all who eat of this bread and drink of this cup worthily
> must be changed in the inner person, and converted and
> renewed in their minds through the power of the divine
> Word. By faith they must become new creatures, born of
> God, and transplanted from Adam into Christ; they must
> be of a Christian disposition, sympathetic, peaceable,
> merciful . . . They must be led by the Spirit of God to be
> sincere Christians, and endeavor with all their powers in
> their weakness to be like-minded with Christ.[42]

FOOTWASHING

Although the practice of footwashing was not widely practised
as a church ordinance by Anabaptists until later in the
sixteenth century, in retrospect the broad acceptance of the rite
of washing one another's feet seems a natural development,
given the biblical bases of spiritual practice the Anabaptists
sought to institute. Jesus himself had provided the example by
washing the disciples' feet at the celebration of Passover, which
he followed by saying 'I have set you an example: you are to do
as I have done for you' (John 13:15).[43] Footwashing thus could
be interpreted not only as a graphic demonstration of Jesus'
own humility, but also as a dominical ordinance to be practised
in connection with the celebration of the Lord's Supper.
Furthermore, Jesus' own interpretation of his washing the
disciples' feet spoke to the heart of Anabaptist spirituality,
since it was a graphic and visible instance of the spirit of
humility, service and love: 'If I, your Lord and Master, have
washed your feet, you also ought to wash one another's feet. I
have set you an example' (John 13:14–15). Here was a visible
sign of *Gelassenheit*, ordained by Christ, in which members
visibly submitted one to another, promising to serve one
another, thus *following in the footsteps of Christ* by conjoining
the outward rite to a genuinely changed nature.

The historical evidence leads to the conclusion that, in spite
of later developments, footwashing was not commonly practised in early Swiss Anabaptism, although there are hints of
its being observed in some South German Anabaptist communities already in the late 1520s.[44] In his 'Three Kinds of
Baptism' (1527), Leonhard Schiemer wrote against the spiri-
tualisation or pure internalisation of Christian faith, and
listed footwashing as one of the external evidences of faith.

> Now you great scholars, doctors, academics, monks and
> priests, who care nothing for 'external things,' just how
> would you demonstrate to others that you are true
> disciples and followers of Christ except by feeding the
> hungry, giving drink to the thirsty, clothing the naked,
> sheltering the poor, comforting the sick and imprisoned,
> washing feet and showing love for one another?[45]

Although Schiemer does not elaborate on the comment, he may
well have been commenting on a practice that had been
adopted in his community as a 'demonstration' of the spirit of
discipleship.

Four years later Pilgram Marpeck, who had been strongly
influenced by Schiemer and his martyrdom, wrote about footwashing as if it were a common church practice in the congregations he led.[46] In his 'Clear Refutation' written in 1531
against spiritualists in Strasbourg, Marpeck insisted that
Jesus Christ had instituted 'external observances' to be carried out until he returns on the last day. Among the 'external'
things Christ instituted, Pilgram Marpeck lists 'to wash one
another's feet', echoing Schiemer's point.[47] In his 'Judgment
and Decision', written to the Swiss Brethren in the same year,
Marpeck listed footwashing as one of the 'external witnesses
of faith in Christ' and – along with baptism and the Lord's
Supper – called it a 'new ceremony of Christ' that is 'to be a
testimony and a revealing of every heart to his neighbor'.
There is little doubt, from the way Marpeck refers to the
practice, that the washing of feet was routinely practised as a

'ceremony' or 'external witness' in Marpeck's small circle of followers.[48]

Both Schiemer and Marpeck had followers living in Moravia in the 1530s and 1540s, so it is reasonable to assume that some Anabaptists in that territory practised the washing of feet. We know of at least one hymn referring to the washing of feet that was composed by someone who had lived in the Moravian area. The hymn was composed by an anonymous Anabaptist writer in the Passau prison, sometime between 1535 and 1537, and was eventually preserved in the *Ausbund*. The Old Order Amish of today still sing hymn 119 from the *Ausbund* during their footwashing services.[49]

The *Ausbund* hymn begins by stressing the importance of unity here on earth as a preparation for the unity of the coming Kingdom. The door to that Kingdom stands open, but it is the door of self-denial and discipline: 'Whoever wants to inherit the kingdom must beforehand, here on earth, entirely mortify the flesh so that he may be renewed.' From this common Anabaptist beginning point the hymn-writer moves instantly to renewal into Christ-likeness: 'Take to heart, therefore, the virtue of Jesus Christ in that he did not seek to be served.' The hymn describes Jesus washing the disciples' feet, as described in the John 13 passage, and draws the conclusion, 'Let it go to your heart what I now have done for you. In this way you should fulfill it: by loving one another.'[50] The rest of the hymn is devoted to explaining in what love consists: always unfeigned, demonstrated not in words but in deeds, in the sharing of possessions, in humility and in servanthood.

It has been noted that the hymn does not actually speak of footwashing as a church ordinance, and so cannot serve as a demonstration of widespread practice of the rite in Moravia in the 1530s.[51] Be that as it may, all the elements needed to integrate footwashing as an important spiritual practice within the Anabaptist community are presented in the *Ausbund* hymn. No changes needed to be made in order for the hymn to be sung in later celebrations of footwashing, once the practice became widespread.

Footwashing began to gain wider currency as an Anabaptist church ordinance in the Netherlands in the second half of the sixteenth century, and then later spread south to other Anabaptist groups.[52] It was the Dutch Anabaptist bishop, Dirk Philips, who especially advocated footwashing as a church-wide practice, beginning around 1560.[53] In his writing on *The Congregation of God*, Dirk Philips listed footwashing as the 'third ordinance' of the church, and gave a twofold interpretation of its significance. Jesus commanded the ordinance first, Dirk says, 'to give us the knowledge that he himself must cleanse us in the internal person, and we must let the sin which clings to us so closely . . . be washed away by him.'[54] According to Dirk, the celebration of footwashing was intended to promote growth in sanctity, reminding believers not only of the forgiveness of their sins through Christ's sacrifice, but also of the continuing process of cleansing from sin that each believer must pursue: 'So whoever is clean may become cleaner day by day.' The second point of significance Dirk attached to footwashing was the one more clearly indicated by the passage, namely 'that we should humble ourselves to one another . . . and hold the companions of our faith in great esteem . . . [for] they are the saints of God and members of Jesus Christ . . . and the Holy Spirit lives in them.'[55]

Footwashing became a widespread practice among Anabaptists in the Netherlands, achieving a wide enough acceptance that the Dordrecht Confession of 1632 included a separate article devoted to 'The Washing of the Saints' Feet'.[56] With the wide acceptance of the Dordrecht Confession among the Swiss Anabaptists in the seventeenth century, the practice of footwashing became established as a Mennonite and Amish ordinance. With the spread of the Dutch practice to the Swiss, the old *Ausbund* hymn 119, with its extended reflection on the meaning of Jesus washing the disciples' feet, gained a significance among the Swiss in the seventeenth century that it had not had in the sixteenth.

As with baptism and the Lord's Supper, footwashing was considered an 'ordinance', not a sacrament. That is, it was a visible ceremony instituted by Christ, to be practised by those who have given themselves to following after Christ. The Anabaptist understanding was that the essence to which the outward rite pointed would be found in the Spirit of Christ, invisibly joined to the hearts of believers, but visibly active in their lives. The spirit of humble servanthood, which typified Christ's nature and the nature of reborn disciples, was thus symbolically remembered, re-enacted and commended in the visible act of footwashing. *Ausbund* hymn 119 summarises the teaching of 'putting on the virtue of Christ':

> Therefore be minded just as
> Jesus Christ was . . .
> For he took on himself
> the form of a poor servant . . .
> He always showed
> humility and love.
> Let us therefore also be diligent
> to put on his virtue,
> so that we might keep
> love in purity.[57]

CONCLUSION

In 1 Corinthians 12 the apostle Paul uses the image of the Body of Christ when speaking of the various spiritual gifts manifested by believers. Whereas we tend to hear Paul's language as an extended metaphor, the Anabaptists heard it as a description of an actual reality. Ambrosius Spittelmaier, the Anabaptist preacher from Linz who was beheaded in 1528, expressed in vivid language the reality Anabaptists expected to see incarnated in the church.

> [The Body of Christ] concerns all those who belong to Christ through his godly Word, who are his members,

that is hands, feet or eyes. Such members must be joined
to Christ spiritually and not physically. Christ, the true
man in the flesh, is the head of such members through
which the members are ruled. With such a head and
members it becomes like a visible body, for just as in one
body there are many members doing different (unequal)
things, nevertheless they serve one another, for what one
member has the other member has as well. The members
are also humble with each other, and obedient to each
other.[58]

The Body of Christ, the church, encompasses two fundamental
and inseparable realities within itself and all its members: the
indwelling power of the divine Spirit, and the tangible and
visible reality of the Christ-like fruits produced by the Holy
Spirit in individuals and in the collective Body.

The poles of spiritual power and outward witness were tied
together by the visible, biblical 'signs' or 'ceremonies' commanded by Christ and practised by the apostles. While these
signs had no instrumental power by which they could convey
grace, it should be clear from the foregoing that neither were
they dismissed as useless external trappings. Even though the
precise way in which the 'ceremonies' functioned was never
clearly defined, nevertheless Anabaptist writing about the
'ordinances' makes it clear that they played a vital role in linking, making visible and strengthening the inner and outer
realities that made up the church.

The Anabaptists had come to a stunning conclusion that
may well have sounded blasphemous to their contemporaries.
They were convinced that when the living Spirit of God in
believers worked to bring them together by the outward signs
and ceremonies of their unity (as ordained by Christ), the
result would be the establishment of the very Body of Christ in
the world, visibly working through his members.[59] It was thus the
collective Body of Christ, the church, that was the closest Anabaptist analogue to the medieval eucharistic sacrament, for it
was in the church – thus conformed, united and marked –

where one would find the 'real presence' of Christ in the world. The real presence of Christ depended not on proper priestly administration, nor on human power of any kind, but rather on the living power of God, who alone could accomplish the work through the faith, trust, *Gelassenheit* and obedience of believers.

6 ANABAPTIST SPIRITUAL DISCIPLINES

The historian Walter Klaassen has described Anabaptism as 'neither Catholic nor Protestant', an insight amended slightly by Sjouke Voolstra, who preferred to describe the movement as 'both Catholic and Protestant'.[1] These descriptions have the merit of relating Anabaptism historically to the two major expressions of Christianity in the sixteenth-century West. When we consider Anabaptist spirituality through the lens of the spiritual disciplines that enabled the movement to grow and continue, we will suggest a more neutral description of Anabaptist spirituality as 'both biblical and ascetic'. This points to the same basic distinction noted by Klaassen and Voolstra, but avoids thorny issues of how to define 'Catholic' and 'Protestant', and to what degree and in what manner Anabaptists might fit within the varied definitions of each.

The Anabaptists exemplified spiritual ideals that were unorthodox primarily because the two major rival camps had decided not to embrace them in quite the same manner. To many contemporary observers, the impression was left of a pious people who were willing to give a public, biblical witness to the depth of their convictions, harrassed, hounded, incarcerated in the thousands, tortured, tried, and executed in savage public displays.[2] If we go beyond the explanations of their frustrated enemies, namely that this witness was possible only because the Anabaptists were fanatics, or possessed of Satan, we are faced with the question: What made such a steadfast witness possible? What were the spiritual disciplines that informed and strengthened this movement? What was the process that led people to become 'baptising brothers and sisters', that guided them through the wrenching decision to 'leave the world behind', committing themselves to membership in a persecuted and hunted group? What were the disciplines that strengthened these people as they faced the pressure to save their lives through recantation?

Song 67 of the *Ausbund*, whose author is unknown, summarises a vision of the 'new life in Christ' the Anabaptists hoped to incarnate, and in the process provides some clues about the way in which the new life could be lived.

> When the [reborn] child is sanctified,
> As Saint Paul teaches us,
> In the name and nature of Christ
> And in the Spirit of our Lord,
> He also subdues and teaches his Body
> And turns all things unto Christ
> With prayer and watchfulness.
> Lamenting his sin and becoming its enemy,
> He unites himself wholeheartedly to God,
> Which makes the angels rejoice.
> Then a person lives in obedience
> In the fear and will of God.
> His heart constantly strives toward heaven
> And he fulfills the law.
> He believes and loves, grieving no one,
> Exercising himself from the heart in God's Word
> Which is his nourishment and life.
> He richly gives forth
> Christian discipline and the fruit of faith
> Which Christ seeks among His own.[3]

These hymn stanzas richly describe the Anabaptist ascetic ideal: the aim is sanctification and holiness, which must be accomplished by the training and submission of the body, turning to Christ in prayer and watchfulness, lamenting sin in true penitence, living in obedience, in fear of God, keeping the divine law in faith and love. There is nothing here that could not have been written for a medieval monastic novice.[4] Given these strong parallels to late medieval ascetic movements of renewal we might expect to find analogous disciplines at work in the Anabaptist communities.

ASCETIC DISCIPLINES AND ANABAPTIST SPIRITUALITY

If we begin with 'training and submission of the body', we find that Anabaptist writings abound in ascetic exhortations to 'curb' the body so that the spiritual life might grow – phrases which sound odd indeed to Protestant ears, but not strange at all to vowed Religious. Balthasar Hubmaier wrote the memorable phrase 'The flesh must daily be killed since it wants only to live and reign according to its own lusts.'[5] The flesh must be crucified, in Christ.[6]

Anabaptists quite commonly framed their asceticism in terms of spirit and flesh, language that they found in the New Testament, especially in the Gospel of John and the writings of the apostle Paul. The schoolmaster Valerius painted a vivid picture of the 'lusts of the flesh' he had observed round about him:

> Many [unbelievers] are not willing to be reproved for the lusts of their flesh, in dicing, gambling, singing, jumping, dancing, strutting, boasting, in order to be nowhere the least, but everywhere the first, if possible; in vain, false, and renowned arts of earthly worldly and carnal wisdom; in litigating, suing, swearing; in subtle, fraudulent, wicked inventions and traffics; in lying, cheating deed, then with the heart; in hatred and envy, defaming, backbiting, foolish talking, jesting, joking, unprofitableness, impropriety, in all manner of lustfulness and wantonness. This is nearly everywhere as common as daily bread.[7]

Valerius concluded this passage with a call to repentance, an appeal to turn away from the world and the flesh, and turn back to God. The entire Anabaptist spiritual process, from repentance, rebirth, baptism and ban, through faithfulness, through persecution to the end, functioned within the stark and opposed polarities of flesh and spirit, of once-born children of this world and reborn children of God. To walk on the narrow way of salvation called for a conscious turning from the world, which could only be done by training, disciplining and controlling 'the flesh'.

Of course, in the final analysis the lusts of the flesh are overcome by the grace of God and the Spirit of God. Without the gift of the living Spirit, sinful flesh can do nothing – on this there is no equivocation in Anabaptist testimonies. Nevertheless, the Anabaptists were sure that the Spirit does not act alone, apart from human volition and effort, and here they sound the ascetic note as surely as did the cloistered Religious. Human beings must do their part in avoiding evil and pursuing good, in rooting out vices and cultivating virtues. Furthermore, this is not a solitary venture, between God and the believer alone: those who repent and begin the process of growing into holiness, mark their commitment by baptism into communities of like-minded believers. The church ordinances all serve to visibly mark, remind and encourage the living of this new life of the spirit. It is thus in community, in the Body of Christ alone, that one can learn the path of holiness and exercise oneself in the way of the saints.

Except for the novel institution and interpretation of church ordinances and the claims to be the only true church (and hence, the only true path to salvation), the Anabaptists might appear to be instituting a monastic foundation for lay, married members.[8] But there were significant differences in the spiritual disciplines practised in monastic and Anabaptist communities. Monastic communities were marked by a round of liturgical worship, prayer and work that was determined by the rule that governed life in that community. This regulated way of life was not incidental, but in fact was a central part of the path by which individuals worked to root out human vices, by which they practised the Christian virtues and grew in holiness within their communities.[9] When we look to Anabaptist communities, we find the same sentiment of 'overcoming the flesh' and 'growing in the spirit', of rooting out vices and growing in virtue – but we look in vain for a similarly regulated way of life.

The Anabaptists prayed frequently, fervently and often, but with very few exceptions they prayed informally or in their worship services, unlike the monastic tradition with its regulated programme of daily prayer according to set hours. Anabaptist records contain no breviary of prescribed or recommended prayers. Neither did they follow lectionaries of prescribed readings or prayers. Furthermore, we know of no Anabaptist writings describing an ideal or desired life of prayer, or setting out programmes for regulated prayer. In short, the liturgical underpinning of regular prayer, reading and worship that sustained medieval religious life from its earliest days is absent from Anabaptist testimonies. We can assume from this general silence in the sources that *regulated* prayer was not one of the Anabaptist spiritual disciplines.

Late medieval movements of renewal, such as the *Devotio Moderna* that began in the Netherlands, in many ways appear to be possible forerunners of Anabaptism. There are significant parallels.[10] Nevertheless, one of the things that made the 'new devotion' new was the structured and repeated pattern of exercises members undertook, meditatively focusing their minds on accompanying Jesus in different situations described in the gospels, thus experiencing an 'imitation of Christ' affectively and imaginatively.[11] Although 'following after' Jesus Christ was central to both the *Devotio Moderna* and the Anabaptists, the structured devotional exercises of the former are nowhere to be seen among the Anabaptists. Affective devotional exercises were, as far as we know, not one of the Anabaptist spiritual disciplines.

It would seem at first glance that there was no rule or orderly discipline by which Anabaptist community life was regulated, guided and directed. On more careful examination, however, it is apparent that the Anabaptists did not do away with the notion of a 'rule' altogether, nor were their spiritual lives devoid of discipline. To the contrary, the rule the

Anabaptists were striving to follow in life was no less than the unvarnished 'rule of Scripture'. This emphasis they owed to the Reformation, even though their approach to Scripture did not parallel the Protestant understanding. The central discipline of Anabaptist spiritual life – the discipline on which all others depended – was becoming thoroughly immersed in the words of Scripture, remembering them, internalising them, pondering them, all with a view to *living in obedience* to God's will as expressed in Scripture. Of course, the Bible was not read willy-nilly, but was parsed into its most significant components, at the heart of which was 'the Rule of Christ', a phrase that pointed to the core of Anabaptist reading and remembering. At the centre of Anabaptist spiritual grounding and life of witness lay a discipline that may described as a kind of *lectio divina*, that internalised a biblical and ascetic path to holiness and salvation.

LECTIO DIVINA

The Anabaptists agreed with the Christians of the Middle Ages that the words of God in Scripture were meant to be read 'slowly and deliberatively, meditatively and reflectively',[12] but they did not follow the methodical and structured manner of reading for a 'contemplative' end that had developed by the twelfth century.[13] It is not in the sense of a systematic 'divine reading' as a means to contemplation (as was practised in the monasteries) that we may speak of an Anabaptist practice of *lectio divina*. As a lay movement experiencing persecution, the Anabaptists did not follow the measured round of monastic life, nor did they have a contemplative aim. For the Anabaptists, learning, remembering and repeating the words of Scripture was a means to a practical end: it was *living the Bible continually* that really counted. It was in this sense of learning the Bible in order to live it – and not in the medieval (or modern) sense of a devotional 'exercise in divine reading' – that one may speak of an Anabaptist practice of something like *lectio divina*.[14]

LIVING THE BIBLE

Ausbund hymn 67, cited above, maintains that a reborn person needs to be engaged in 'Exercising himself from the heart in God's Word, which is his nourishment and life'. *Ausbund* hymn 19, translated from the Dutch hymnal *Het Offer des Heeren*, tells of the martyrdom of Peter of Werwijck, burnt at Ghent in 1552. It contains the same advice:

> One should exercise oneself
> daily in the teaching of Christ
> Loving one another heartily,
> Walking in discipline and respect . . .
> Let us secure the pure
> Word of God in our hearts,
> which we can feed upon in later times
> when we, in the future,
> are tempted by Satan's devices
> and his followers' power,
> so that we can prevail before them,
> and God Himself keep us.[15]

Anabaptist testimonies continually repeat this advice to young and old alike: exercise yourself in Christ's teachings; *keep the Word of God in your heart*. The *Martyrs Mirror* contains very many instances of this exhortation to biblical knowledge. It is said of Hans Bret that he was 'very diligently concerned and engaged with the study of the word of the Lord, in which he constantly exercised himself in the morning and evening'.[16] This served him well when he was tortured and questioned about his faith in prison. Joost de Tollenaer wrote in 1589, 'Friends, diligently search the Scriptures, which will sufficiently instruct you.'[17] Pieter van Olman wrote to his brothers and sisters in 1552, 'Take the Word of the Lord well to heart, and understand well what the Lord says, that you may stand fast valiantly.'[18] Examples could be multiplied with very little effort.

Of course, all these exhortations might be no more than

pious advice, more commonly ignored than practised. But in fact, we have good evidence that rank-and-file Anabaptists did undertake to 'exercise themselves' regularly in studying and learning Scripture. The convincing evidence comes from the many thousands of pages of interrogation records, recorded by court scribes and preserved in state archives to the present day.

The common mark of surviving Anabaptist court testimonies is the thoroughly biblical nature of the defences provided by Anabaptist prisoners, regardless of whether they were women or men, educated or uneducated, literate or illiterate. Anabaptist prison testimonies are often little more than patchwork quilts of biblical references, stitched together.[19] Ask an Anabaptist prisoner about baptism, and the result will be a recitation of a collection of New Testament texts they believed to be the indisputable evidence that the baptism of adults was the proper manner and divine order by which the Lord intended to establish the church on earth (Mark 16; Matt. 28, etc.). Ask an Anabaptist prisoner why she refuses to attend mass (or Protestant preaching) and the answer will be a string of Bible verses (often drawn from the Old Testament and the New) supporting separation from the ungodly and the impious (Jer. 51:6; Matt. 6:24; 1 Cor. 5, 6), as well as (not uncommonly) a sprinkling of verses condemning false prophets and those who follow them (Jer. 14:14–15; Matt. 7:15–20; 1 Tim. 4:1–5), and perhaps some verses condemning idolatry for good measure (Exod. 20:3–6; 1 Cor. 8:1–8).

The typical Anabaptist prison refrain was 'Prove to me from Scripture that I am wrong and I will agree.' This request (more of a challenge, really) was always backed up by text after text of scriptural proof, buttressing the Anabaptist position. Learned interrogators were frustrated. In May of 1569 the Anabaptist Jacob de Roore was questioned by a Franciscan monk, Father Cornelis, known for his temper and foul language. When Jacob made reference to the book of Revelation it provoked the following exchange:

Fr. Cornelis: 'Ah bah! what do you understand about St. John's Apocalypse? At what university did you study? At the loom, I suppose; for I understand that you were nothing but a poor weaver and chandler, before you went around preaching and rebaptizing out here in the Gruthuysbosch. I have attended the university at Louvain, and studied divinity so long, and yet I do not understand anything at all about St. John's Apocalypse; this is a fact.

Jacob: Therefore Christ thanked His heavenly Father, that He had revealed and made it known to babes, and hid it from the wise of this world, as is written, Matt. 11:25.

Fr. Cornelis: Exactly; God has revealed it to the weavers at the loom, to the cobblers on their bench, and to bellows-menders, lantern-tinkers, scissors-grinders, broom makers, thatchers, and all sorts of riff-raff, and poor, filthy, and lousy beggars. And to us ecclesiastics who have studied from our youth, night and day, He has concealed it. Just see how we are tormented. You Anabaptists are certainly fine fellows to understand the holy Scriptures; for before you are rebaptized, you can't tell A from B, but as soon as you are baptized, you can read and write. If the devil and his mother have not had a hand in this, I do not understand any thing about you people.

Jacob: I can well hear that you do not understand our way of doing; for you ascribe to Satan the grace which God grants our simple converts, when we with all diligence teach them to read.[20]

We have no hard evidence of how successful the Anabaptists were in teaching their converts to read, but we can document the fact that Anabaptist converts learned a great deal of Scripture. Furthermore, Anabaptist testimonies appeal almost exclusively to Scripture, with no reliance on 'church authorities' of the past.[21]

A marked characteristic of Anabaptist citation of Scripture was the 'topical' manner in which biblical citations were organised and presented. On reading the prison testimonies it soon becomes apparent that biblical information had been organised, taught and remembered under topic headings (such as 'repentance', 'faith', 'baptism', etc.), with selected Bible verses used to illustrate the proper understanding of a respective topic. A second striking feature evident from the prison testimonies is the way different prisoners, in different territories, use essentially the same Bible verses, again and again, to argue the same points. In other words, it becomes evident that there was a particularly *Anabaptist* way of reading and interpreting Scripture, and organising it into meaningful and coherent parts. These topically defined pieces of biblical proof formed the core of spiritual formation for the Anabaptists. The key words of Scripture on the central topics relating to the narrow way of salvation were learned, remembered and internalised as the words of salvation. They came flowing out in profusion when Anabaptists were called upon to present the biblical foundations of their faith and practice, as surviving court records testify.

Organising complex information by subject headings (or *topoi*) is an ancient mnemonic strategy, well understood in all cultures that rely on memory for oral communication. In spite of the recent invention of the printing press, sixteenth-century Europeans still relied heavily on the spoken and heard word for essential communication. For common people in the sixteenth century – and the Anabaptists were overwhelmingly from the artisan and peasant classes – the printed word was valued, as was the skill of knowing how to read, but the remembered word was of more practical worth than the mere printed word. The remembered word could be 'owned' by anyone who had a memory and the desire to remember. Even when relatively inexpensive printed Bibles became available, they cost more than a poor person could possibly pay. But anyone (literate or not) could 'own' a Bible simply by remembering the most important parts of it. Furthermore, this remembered word was completely portable, not subject to seizure at the moment of arrest, and readily accessible under questioning. Even literate Anabaptists committed large portions of the Bible to memory.[22]

Not only do the court records provide evidence that the Anabaptists utilised a 'topical' approach to remembering Scripture, the Anabaptists also composed and printed topical concordances for their own use. The Swiss Brethren printed such a concordance around 1540. It found its way to the Dutch Anabaptists, where it was translated and published in Dutch, and to the Hutterites where it was copied by hand; it was reprinted in at least fourteen German-language editions.[23] No other Swiss Brethren work – with the exception of the *Ausbund* hymnal – appeared in so many published editions. The Swiss Brethren Concordance, the end result of the organisation, selection and verbatim copying of biblical texts, was a kind of anthology of the Bible organised under 66 topical headings. It was a condensed Swiss Brethren Bible, distilled to what was considered its essentials, a theological and spiritual compendium ready to be read on its own. Although it contained no commentary, a theological interpretation was already built in with the selection of topics and Bible passages. Furthermore, the Concordance could be read directly in the absence of a Bible, in the presence of literate or illiterate hearers, in a form lending itself to memorisation. The Concordance provided access to the biblical word for people who, for the most part, had not enjoyed the benefits of higher education, and who still lived and worked in a predominantly oral culture.

By the late sixteenth century, one's standing as an orthodox Protestant was measured by one's command of catechism and confession, rather than by the knowledge of literal Scripture as such. By contrast, 'owning one's faith' for the majority of Anabaptists meant owning the biblical foundations of their faith in the form of specific Bible verses, memorised, stored and ready for use when one's faith was called to account.[24] One would not wish to claim that the Swiss Brethren Concordance functioned as the only biblical training manual for the whole of Swiss and South German Anabaptism. What the evidence does suggest, however, is a far-flung process of topical biblical organisation, teaching, learning and memorising taking place at the Anabaptist grass roots, even among literate Anabaptists. This remembered biblical knowledge came to expression in a wide variety of ways, in hymns, court testimonies, letters of admonition, sermons and concordances. The cumulative documentary evidence leads to the conclusion that it was this biblical grounding – this thorough owning of the biblical text and story – that was the source and foundation of Anabaptist spirituality.

The pattern of organisation of topic headings in the Swiss Brethren Concordance of 1540 is illuminating. The narrative thread running throughout is progress in the Christian life, lived in response to God's call. If one reads the topics sequentially, the Concordance leads readers through a collection of Bible verses concerning fear of God, repentance, rebirth, and life on the narrow way: the beginnings of the Christian life, the challenges faced by those who desire to obey God in the company of the faithful, the virtues to be nourished in a God-centred life, the vices to be avoided and rooted out, and finally the rewards promised to both the pious and impious. This organisation and selection of Bible passages is anything but random. The evident concern of the anonymous compilers was to provide practical direction for a life lived in the presence of God, in obedience to the divine commands expressed in Scripture. It appears to be no exaggeration to say that in the Swiss Brethren Concordance we have one striking example of an Anabaptist rule of life. It is, furthermore, a 'rule' that is as thoroughly biblical as it is ascetic.[25]

COMMUNAL WORSHIP

Living the words of Scripture was central to Anabaptist spirituality, not only as a focus for individuals, but as a communal focus as well. Scripture formed the heart of communal worship as well as being the primary spiritual discipline of individuals, for it was in their worship together that the Anabaptists reminded one another of the biblical truths that defined their path; in their times of worship they taught one another, consoled one another, and encouraged each other to remain faithful. In areas where persecution was intense, worship times could be occasional, and Anabaptists met whenever and wherever they could feel safe: in isolated locations such as forests, caves or behind closed doors in city homes.[26]

Most of what we know about Anabaptist worship services comes either from hostile sources or from the answers given by imprisoned Anabaptists. Most of the time, the early Anabaptists gathered in small groups.[27] Jörg Tucher's testimony in 1526 describes a typical small meeting. When he and his fellow believers gathered, Tucher testified:

> they prayed a prayer together, that God might strengthen them to be able to carry the cross patiently. After that they interpreted the Scripture according to each one's spiritual understanding, that they do nothing against God and act in love toward their neighbours, give enemies food, drink, and love them, etc. . . . In short, that all things should be held in common and each one should do their work, and if someone were needy, then they should share some of the common good with the needy.[28]

Jörg's compatriot, Wilhelm Echsel, added that 'When they gathered together, they admonished one another to beware of sin and disgraceful behaviour.'[29] We hear in these confessions the desire to be faithful to God's will as revealed in the Bible, and the wish to live a life of discipleship. The interpretation and understanding of Scripture stood at the centre of these small meetings, as well as biblical consolation, comfort and prayer.[30] There are frequent notices of small meetings where the primary purpose for gathering was simply to hear Scripture read. For example Ursula, a literate Anabaptist woman from Strasbourg, said at her hearing that she had 'instructed' no one: 'she simply went to the Becker house and to the house of Paul the weaver and usually read a chapter there.'[31] The distinction between 'instruction' and 'reading' was a fine one, as the authorities knew well: times of Bible reading were precisely the times when Anabaptist 'instruction' took place, but Protestant governments had difficulty forbidding Bible reading, given their stated Reformation principles.

These small gatherings were not only times of biblical study and grounding. They were also occasions to proselytise and invite others to the faith.[32] Women often were identified as the most active evangelists, making contacts and inviting others to come to the meetings. In the Basel region in the 1590s, a woman named Verena was particularly persistent in attending meetings (every four to six weeks, she confessed), and also quite successful in drawing others to the meetings. Soon after being expelled from the territory for her Anabaptism she was back at it, inviting her brother-in-law and a woman from another village to come to an Anabaptist gathering. It was reported that she continued to invite other women to the assemblies, even after repeated warnings and punishments.[33]

Larger and more formal meetings for worship were often held outside, in 'flecken, feldern und welden' (clearings, fields and woods) as official records often say. Large meetings often were held in woods or forests, where detection was difficult and sentries could give the warning to disperse if the authorities came to arrest Anabaptists. One of the most interesting accounts of such a meeting comes from the year 1545, from two young eyewitnesses who were mistaken for Anabaptists. These two young men played along and were subsequently led into the Eckelsheim Forest, near Strasbourg, where they observed what took place.

By ten o'clock at night some three hundred people had assembled deep in the forest, and the worship service began. A tall man began to preach a sermon that lasted 'until approximately one in the morning' – a three-hour sermon! The sermon dealt with the children of Israel during their time in Egypt and after their escape, and how God wished to make of the Anabaptists the one people of God. He also preached about the temple of God (Revelation 11). The temple of God could be found anywhere under heaven, not in a cathedral or stone church. After this biblical exposition, another person arose and read the eleventh chapter of Hebrews, but did not preach on the text. They also heard the story of Zacchaeus, and how he was an example of true penitence, since he returned ill-gotten tax money to the poor from whom it had been stolen. Then a third Anabaptist arose to preach. He said that when the Lutheran preachers said that Christ's death for our sins was enough, it was not true: we also have to do penance for our sins. He concluded by admonishing the assembled that they were not to believe people when they denigrated good works.

At this meeting there were five or six sisters who wished to be baptised, but this was not carried out at the time. Also one man was replaced in the deaconate by another. Then a time of prayer commenced in which they all prayed for their brothers and sisters, both in that assembly and elsewhere, frequently by name. These eyewitnesses claimed that 'they prayed with great earnestness, with cries and tears'. During the service one man went about with a light. It was his task to awaken people who had fallen asleep. When morning came, someone spread a cloth and placed pears and bread on it. Many ate the food, but others did not, and the crowd dispersed.[34]

Even this cursory description of an all-night Anabaptist church service reveals for us the 'biblical topics' that formed the backbone of instruction on this one occasion: deliverance by God of the children of Israel (figure for the true church, the one people of God); the 'Temple of God,' building on the prophecies of Revelation 11; then the story of the faith of the ancestors, who persevered through all persecution (Hebrews 11); the true repentance of Zacchaeus and the reordering of his economic life, as an example to all believers; and finally, an exhortation on 'true faith and works of love' as opposed to 'salvation by faith alone'. We may assume that the sermons and exhortations were supported with appropriate topical Scripture references, in the same manner as we see prison testimonies developed and documented.

Claus-Peter Clasen has noted that in the 1570s, Anabaptist

meetings in the Strasbourg-area forests, as well as those in Hesse, still followed the same basic pattern of biblical lessons and sermons, admonitions, greetings from brothers and sisters in other places, prayer, and sometimes song as well. The celebration of the Supper seems to have taken place commonly in the more intimate meetings, and although some baptisms are reported to have taken place in such-and-such a wood, they are more commonly reported as having taken place in someone's home.

The larger Anabaptist worship services had the general look of Protestant worship services, with Scripture and scriptural exposition at the centre, accompanied by singing and prayer. Nevertheless, the differences from Protestant worship were striking as well. In these early years there were no Anabaptist church buildings at all; pastors were most commonly persons chosen from the congregation, often craftsmen with no formal education; there was freedom for all participants to speak – in some cases, this participation was explicitly invited; the meetings were attended by those who had committed themselves to a dangerous path, for which they could be executed, and this undoubtedly added intensity to the gatherings. Claus-Peter Clasen concludes that Anabaptist meetings for worship 'seem to have filled a need for an intimate, emotional expression of piety that the official churches of the sixteenth century failed to recognize'.[35] The Anabaptists went to great trouble to meet together, but their times of meeting were rewarded by a strengthening of the scriptural bases of their faith and practice through preaching, prayer and a reconnection with fellow believers.

PRAYER

The Anabaptist approach to prayer may have been unstructured, in comparison to the prayer life of the cloistered Religious, but Anabaptist records leave no doubt that the Anabaptists believed in the power and efficacy of frequent and fervent prayer. Most reports of prayer at Anabaptist gatherings note that the members knelt to pray,[36] although there are also reports of Anabaptists 'falling on their faces' during prayer, or looking heavenward. The Lord's Prayer was often recited, but extemporaneous prayers were the most common. Many observers reported emotional prayers, sometimes with great sighing and weeping. One unsympathetic observer claimed that there was breast-beating and unintelligible mumbling during a public prayer time.[37] Public prayer during worship times was usually led by a pastor, but there seem to have been times of communal prayer included as well.

The use of the Lord's Prayer – one place where public Anabaptist prayer seems to coincide with the custom of the day – deserves further comment. Along with the Ten Commandments and the Apostles' Creed, the Lord's Prayer had been part of catechetical instruction for all European Christians. The early Anabaptists in South Germany, however, made it a point to teach Anabaptism by means of a reinterpretation of this commonly known biblical prayer.[38] The illiterate needle salesman and Anabaptist evangelist, Hans Nadler, for example, reported exactly how he proceeded to explain the meaning of the Lord's Prayer to interested persons.

> After that I began teaching, starting with the Lord's prayer, and said: 'You say, "Our Father in heaven." So you must learn, my brother or sister, and consider that you will now be a child of God when you say, "Father." You must live according to his divine will and must do as the Word of God and the Holy Gospel teaches, and which you have often heard. That you must do. Secondly you say: "May your name be made holy." Look, my brother or sister, why have you slandered the name of God? You are to make it holy, and you slander it. Look at your prayer. How did you pray? You have chattered a great deal but have not considered in your heart where it goes.'

And so Nadler continued, building Anabaptist meaning onto the familiar words and phrases of the Lord's Prayer: '"May your will be done." If God's will is now to happen, we must become completely and wholly yielded and rely upon the Lord, that his will may be done in us on earth as in heaven.'[39] It is safe to conclude that when Anabaptists recited the Lord's Prayer in their meetings, they were quite consciously investing the familiar words with Anabaptist meaning.

Prayer certainly was not confined to times of public worship. Anabaptist writings of exhortation commend frequent and fervent prayer, and other evidence confirms that prayer accompanied 'divine reading' of the Bible as one of the fundamental spiritual disciplines. The Anabaptists were known as a people who prayed often. Sebastian Franck noted that a minority took it farther than he thought proper.

> Some do almost nothing but pray and want to meet all misfortunes with their regulated prayer, just as though we did God an especially great service in making our mouth and ourselves tired by praying constantly. These also say that one must meet evil only with prayer, and will not permit their people any weapons for any reason. They are to be yielded and surrendered in all things and that no vengefulness be seen.[40]

A carpenter arrested on suspicion of Anabaptism declared himself innocent, and added that the worst he could say about the two Anabaptists with whom he had been arrested was that 'they prayed',[41] and a mercenary soldier and convicted murderer locked up in the same miserable dungeon as the Anabaptist Hans Schmidt said to the authorities, 'Why do you torment the poor devil? I can see nothing wrong in him except that he prays day and night.'[42]

Letters from Anabaptists in prison speak often about the importance of constant and fervent prayer. In a particularly poignant letter, the condemned Joost de Tollenaer wrote a last testament to his young daughter Betgen and advised her, 'Going, standing, working, always have the Lord before your eyes, calling upon Him with prayer and supplication.' He asked her to pray in the following way:

O Lord, my Lord, direct me in Thy ways; give me wisdom that comes from the throne of Thy glory, and cleanse me from all my sins, that I may be worthy to become a holy temple. Give me grace that I may be meek and humble of heart, and little in my own eyes, so that Thy Holy Spirit may dwell in me, and that I may grow up in Thy holy divine fear; to the eternal salvation of my soul and to the praise, glory and honour of Thy holy, most worthy, adorable name. O Lord, strengthen me, miserable one, since I am but dust and ashes. O Lord, be merciful unto me, and help me forever. Amen.[43]

The petitions contained in this prayer reveal a profound desire to be transformed and sustained by God's grace and power.

The Anabaptist leader Paul Glock, who survived an imprisonment of 19 years, invariably included admonitions to prayer in his letters to his Moravian brothers and sisters. Writing to his wife Else in 1563 he drew on the biblical example of Hannah.

Continue in prayer for us and for all saints. Remember Hannah, the mother of Samuel, how she prayed to God in her heart. She made no noise with her voice. Eli said she was drunk. But she spoke with modest words as is fitting for holy women: 'No, my lord, I am a sorrowful woman. I have not drunk wine or strong drink, but have poured out my heart before the Lord. Do not count your maid as a daughter of Belial. For I spoke only out of the heaviness of my heart.' And she was heard . . . Again we say with Christ: 'Watch and pray so that you may not fall into temptation.' Be firm and immovable for our work is not in vain in the Lord.[44]

Four years later, in a letter to the community, he concluded, 'Continue in prayer, in community, and in the love of God and also in true obedience, to which we have been called in Christ. May the Lord infuse and grant this in you through his Holy Spirit. Amen.'[45] And again in 1571, after yet another four years of incarceration, he wrote:

Pray for me at all times that he keep me faithful and true. I shall do likewise for you, as long as I live, and not depart from the truth in which God has set and established us, in which also we are saved with the strength and help of God and of your intercession to God for me. For I know that God hears us together for each other. To him be the praise.[46]

The majority of Anabaptist prayers seem to have been extemporaneous prayers of intercession, petition and thanksgiving; they were 'prayers of the heart', in contrast to the regulated structure of prayer in the cloisters. The Anabaptists were concerned to pray 'in spirit and in truth', and expected their prayers to flow from the heart.[47] As Joost wrote with full confidence to his daughter Betgen, 'If you, my child, thus betake your heart with all humility to the Lord, and unceasingly cleave to Him with prayer and supplication, He will delight in you.'[48] Hans Symons wrote to his wife while imprisoned at Antwerp in September, 1567, 'O dear lamb . . . let us pray together with a broken heart, an humble spirit and a pure conscience, lifting up holy hands, without contention or strife, praying to God steadfastly in the faith, then will our prayer be a sweet savour and an acceptable offering to God.'[49]

The Anabaptists prayed prayers of petition and intercession concerning everything they faced in life. The records document prayers for children, that they grow into faith, prayers for understanding of Scripture and God's will, for the sick, for those in prison, for protection and safety, for justice, for the brothers and sisters.

Anabaptist testimonies express confidence that their prayers will be heard and received by God. They were convinced that the sincere and pure-hearted prayer of a righteous person would be efficacious, because such was God's nature and expressed will. Endres Keller expressed a common view when he wrote from prison, 'the prayer of the righteous is powerful before God (James 5:16), but the prayer of the hypocrite is an abomination before God. God does not hear it, but the prayer of the righteous God hears at all times.'[50] Mattheus Bernaerts wrote to his children from prison in Ghent in December of 1572, 'keep your tongue from evil, and your lips from speaking guile. Eschew evil, and do good: seek peace, and pursue it; for the eyes of the Lord are over the righteous, and His ears are open unto their prayers: but the face of the Lord is against them that do evil. Ps. 34:13; 1 Pet. 3:10–12.'[51] Under the heading of 'Prayer', the Swiss Brethren Concordance collected a series of texts from the Old Testament and the Apocrypha that pointed to the same conclusion, well summarised by Proverbs 28:9: 'Whoever turns his ear from hearing the law, his prayer is an abomination' and Sirach 34:29: 'If one prays, and another curses, whose voice does the Lord hear?' A life of holiness grows from and reveals a pure heart. Together, a pure and humble heart and a life of holiness make it possible to offer prayers to God 'in spirit and in truth', and such prayers God has promised to heed and honour.

As Jan Wouterss awaited his sentence in 1572 at Dordrecht, Holland, he wrote the following, telling sentence to his congregation: 'Call upon the Lord for strength, and be assured in your hearts, that He hears your prayer. Ps. 145:19. *Present to Him in your prayer His own promises*, and you shall not be confounded, for He hears the prayer of the poor, says David.'[52] Anabaptists continually 'prayed back' the promises God had made in Scripture, and in the midst of their suffering they found particular consolation in this. Their intimate knowledge of Scripture was fundamental to their prayer life. Abraham Picolet's letter to his sisters from prison, just prior to his being burned alive in 1569, is a seamless integration of biblical promises, consolation and prayer. It serves as a fitting summary of the 'biblical' manner of Anabaptist prayer.

> Thus, my sisters, pray the Lord, who says: 'Ask, and ye shall receive; knock, and it shall be opened unto you; seek, and ye shall find; seek the kingdom of God, and his righteousness, and all that you need shall be added unto you.' Matt. 7:7; 6:33. Seek ye the Lord while He may be found,

call ye upon Him while He is near; the Lord is so merciful toward them who seek to fear Him, my sisters, as He says Himself: 'Come unto me, all ye that labour and are heavy laden, and I will give you rest. Take my yoke upon you, and learn of me; for I am meek and lowly in heart; and ye shall find rest unto your souls. For my yoke is easy, and my burden is light' (Matt. 11:28–30); 'And his commandments are not grievous.'[53]

SONG

If Anabaptists were noted as people who prayed constantly, the same could be said about their propensity to sing.[54] The earliest printed Anabaptist song collections date after mid century, but the songs clearly were composed years earlier. Songs were composed and began to circulate very soon after the first baptisms in Zurich and Zollikon, they were first transmitted orally, then written down, and thus preserved and passed on until they found their way into the print collections. By the end of the century there were well in excess of one thousand Anabaptist songs and hymns that had been printed and published in several collections; the total number of songs composed is a matter of conjecture, but it is not unlikely that two thousand Anabaptist songs, or more, were composed and sung from 1525 to 1600.

The Anabaptists sang their 'spiritual songs' everywhere, sometimes with negative results. Anna Janz of Rotterdam and her travelling companion, Christina Michiel Barents, were discovered as Anabaptists, arrested and ultimately put to death because an Anabaptist hymn they were singing while travelling on a public coach gave them away.[55] The surviving records document Anabaptist singing especially in prison and even on the gallows themselves. A song preserved by the Hutterites about nine men and several women who were executed notes that 'they joyfully sang in prison', before the nine brethren were beheaded and the sisters were drowned.[56]

The Hutterite *Chronicle* notes that 'even the sisters were cheerful and sang, which terrified other people'. It was common for Anabaptist prisoners to sing their spiritual songs very loudly, for the encouragement of the other prisoners and also as a testimony to others.[57]

The melodic witnessing of the Anabaptists was considered a serious problem by the secular authorities. In the Tyrol a document was circulated that read:

> The Mayor should prevent the Anabaptist prisoners from being kept together as a group, for then they sing hymns as is the practice in their sect. This causes trouble among the common people who hear them, and gives strength to the prisoners to persist in their heretical belief.[58]

Officials did their best to stop the singing, even gagging prisoners so that they could not speak or sing on their way to being executed.[59]

Just as the memorisation of Scripture under topical headings was well suited to the communication patterns of everyday people in the sixteenth century, so also the composition of songs provided a perfect vehicle for communication in a predominantly oral/aural world. Rhyming couplets set to catchy tunes were particularly easy to commit to memory. A favourite pastime in the sixteenth century was composing *contrafacta*, that is, composing rhyming verse to be sung to well-known tunes of all sorts, from bawdy folk tunes to hymn melodies.[60] At the time of the Reformation, anti-clerical and anti-sacramental sentiments were sometimes expressed in such spontaneous songs. In one (non-Anabaptist) example from Germany, the hymn 'Aus tiefer Not' (From Deepest Need) was changed into a satirical anti-clerical ditty which was sung on the streets: 'Aus tiefer Not, schlag Pfaffen tot, und lass kein Mönch nicht leben', which loosely paraphrased might read 'From deepest need, slay priests indeed, and leave no monks a-breathing'.[61] In St Gall, some unruly folks in 1524 were reported marching around St Katharine's nunnery, singing 'mocking songs' (*Spottlieder*).[62] Ribald verses were composed spontaneously and sung in taverns and inns, and 'news songs' that reported on the latest events of the day were commonly performed in market squares.[63] It was thus a most natural thing for Anabaptists to use this way of communicating, adapting it to their own circumstances and convictions. Helen Martens reports that Hutterite songs were sometimes performed by the missionaries as evangelistic 'news songs' for their audiences.[64]

Almost all known Anabaptist songs are *contrafacta*, with only a very few Anabaptist songs written to original melodies. Musical notation was virtually unknown. The standard way of indicating the melody to be sung was to identify the common folk tune or hymn: 'To be sung to the tune of . . .'. This resulted in some incongruous pairings of text and melody, such as a 'spiritual song' sung to the tune of 'Here comes a maiden with a jug', or penitential songs 'set to sprightly dance tunes'.[65] Nevertheless, joining rhyming couplets to popular tunes meant that the content of the songs was easily learned, remembered and taught to others.

In their subject matter, Anabaptist songs chronicle the events they were experiencing – martyr songs are numerous – but song collections also contain much didactic material, teaching perseverance, the nature of faith, the proper understanding of baptism, the Lord's Supper and the shape of the new life in Christ. One feature runs through all the songs: they constantly cite, paraphrase and allude to biblical passages, in the same 'thematic' approach that is seen elsewhere. There are some versifications of psalms and other passages of the Bible, but regardless of the theme, the Bible texts form the essential prose material that is shaped and versified. So it was that Soetgen van den Houte wrote in her last testament, 'Hence, my dear children, let no impure thoughts remain in your hearts, but engage yourselves with psalms, hymns, and spiritual songs, and evil thoughts will have no room.'[66] Singing such scripturally based hymns was a central spiritual discipline for Anabaptists. That it was so is clear from the evidence from prison and place of execution, when the songs thus learned and sung so often were sung again, to sustain the martyrs.

It was said that Claudine Le Vettre was 'beautiful of person, and a good singer, so that she moved the bystanders by her singing'. On the day she was executed, people gathered especially to hear her sing, when her sentence was read to her. The witness who furnished the account reproduced in the *Martyrs Mirror* reports:

> One who related it to me had heard her sing with a clear, strong voice the 27th Psalm of David 'The Lord is my light and my salvation; whom shall I fear?' And the people firmly believed that if they had not gagged her when they brought her to the place of execution, she would have departed life singing and praising God.[67]

After being betrayed and arrested in Leyden, in 1552, Adrian Corneliss, a glazier, reported on his incarceration:

> Without much delay, they shut me up above alone, where-upon I immediately began to sing the hymn 'Justice is turned back, and righteousness stands at a distance; for truth stumbles in the public square, and uprightness can-not enter' (Isaiah 59.14). I did not, however, enjoy a very long respite; since much people came, and hence they immediately came and took from me my Testament, and the hymn about our four friends, which I had composed.[68]

In the case of both Claudine Le Vettre and Adrian Corneliss, their songs were versified Scripture; but as Adrian reports, he himself had composed a song about four friends (presumably martyred previously). Reading the martyr hymns reveals that they are composed of biblical texts, woven together, based on the biblical themes shared by Anabaptists everywhere.

The scriptural warrant for composing and singing such spiritual songs was found in Colossians 3:16: 'Let the word of Christ dwell in you richly; teach and admonish one another in all wisdom; and with gratitude in your hearts sing psalms, hymns, and spiritual songs to God.' So Dirk Philips would write that when Christ, the one foundation, is established, then 'one sings to the Lord in the heart out of great joy of the Spirit, Eph. [5]:19; Col. 3:16.'[69] Mattheus Bernaerts recommended the same to his children from prison in 1572, as did Jacob van der Wege in the following year.[70] The point was not to sing beautifully, or artfully, but to sing 'in the spirit'. So Balthasar Hubmaier wrote in his catechism:

> *Leonhart*: Do you sing in church?
> *Hans*: Yes, with my mouth I sing understandable words, and with my spirit I reflect on the words, so that I do not honor my God with my lips while my heart is far from it, as the Pharisees did.[71]

So it was that the 'word of Christ' dwelling in these believers was remembered and brought to expression in spiritual songs and hymns, one of the spiritual disciplines that helped form their character as reborn children of God. Singing these songs helped keep the words of salvation constantly in their minds, as they proceeded through the routines of their daily rounds, or when they found themselves in desperate situations, in prison or facing torture and execution.

CONCLUSION

Anabaptist spirituality was 'biblical' in a focused way that would have been inconceivable without the Reformation, but it was not biblical in a recognisably Protestant way. The Anabaptist focus did not fall on the doctrines of salvation by faith through grace, predestination or at once justified and a sinner. Rather, the Anabaptists read the Bible in an ascetic manner that recalls late medieval movements of pious renewal. The words of Scripture were God's words that provided guidance for daily life. And so the Anabaptists made those words their own, in every conceivable way: through memorisation of biblical passages, organised thematically; through praying back the promises of God; through singing the words of salvation. Throughout it all they were convinced that it was the Holy Spirit that was at work, through the words of God. There was no evident discontinuity between Spirit and letter in their appropriation of the Word; both Spirit and letter witnessed to the same God and Christ, and the same path of salvation.

Although Anabaptist spiritual disciplines were not Protestant in shape, neither were they ascetic within the traditional Roman Catholic liturgical, sacramental and clerical structure. The rejection of 'man-made' rules, writings and interpretations led to a radical reliance on the biblical word that cut away centuries of spiritual structure and practice. The silence in the sources leads to the conclusion that the Anabaptists did not regulate their prayer lives in a systematic way; their memorisation of Scripture and reflection upon it was also unregulated; and their singing of spiritual songs was recommended and practised with great frequency, but also was not 'regulated'. The 'rule of life' they were attempting to follow was the Bible itself, which beyond general exhortations (such as 'pray without ceasing') contained no blueprint for calendars or exercises. Nevertheless, the evidence is clear that the early Anabaptists exercised themselves zealously in the spiritual disciplines of *lectio divina* (immersion in Scripture), worship, prayer and spiritual song, with a very clear focus on the words of Scripture, which they believed were (quite literally) the words of life.

In their approach to the spiritual disciplines, the Anabaptists were both radically biblical and radically ascetic, and thus represent a unique bridge between late medieval ascetic piety and the biblical spirituality of the Reformation.

7 DISCIPLESHIP: FOLLOWING AFTER CHRIST

> Those who are born anew in Christ, according to the inner working of the Holy Spirit, are those who are baptized with fire, who are aglow with love. Moreover, these children, born of the Spirit, see what the Father, working through Christ, does for the inner person; they, too, by co-witnessing in the Holy Spirit, immediately do likewise for the external person. Thus, the body of Christ is also built inwardly through the Holy Spirit, and externally through the co-witness of works. His church of communion is His bride, internally in the Spirit and truth, externally with praise to God, and to be a light before the world.[1]

With these words, Pilgram Marpeck pointed to his conviction that being born in Christ, and renewed by the Holy Spirit, would result in a 'co-witness' of works inspired by Christ and the Spirit.[2] Following after Christ is carried out in community, and is deepened by mutual obligations of love in the community. But at the same time, individual disciples are expected to grow into Christ-likeness and to give evidence of the regenerative power of God working in their lives.

In the Anabaptist understanding, Jesus Christ perfectly revealed, lived out and marked the path back to God. Christians are disciples who have committed themselves to following Christ on that path, yielding to God's will in all things as Jesus did, not claiming possessions for themselves, speaking the truth in all circumstances, humbly giving way in the face of evil power, living non-coercively, willing to suffer rather than inflict suffering on others. The visible 'shape' of Anabaptist spirituality is discipleship, the 'following after Christ' (*Nachfolge Christi*) in life.

Following after Christ in life will occur in three areas in which humanity is, by its nature, most particularly tempted not to be Christ-like: in the desire to claim ownership of possessions, in the temptation to lie and dissimulate, and in the temptation to coerce by using violence.

WORLDLY POSSESSIONS

The Anabaptists were convinced that no areas of life fell outside the 'spiritual' realm, and this included material possessions. At a disputation in 1532 the Swiss Anabaptist, Hans Marquart, provided a common Anabaptist explanation for the sharing of material goods in the community: 'Believers have in common one God, one faith, one baptism and all heavenly things. Since they have such spiritual things in common, they should likewise share with a member [who is] in material need.'[3]

It was inconceivable to the early Anabaptists that there could be reborn and regenerated Christians, baptised into the one Body of Christ, committed to faithfulness unto death, who would at the same time cling to surplus goods or wealth when they saw a fellow member of the Body in need. Lack of faithfulness in lesser, material things indicated a lack of faithfulness in higher, spiritual things. Members of the persecuted Body of Christ had pledged their very lives to God and to one another, to be true and visible members of Christ's Body even through torture and death. Such total commitment, to remain true to the highest spiritual truth, certainly placed earthly goods in a subordinate position. *Ausbund* hymn 119 explains:

> If one had this world's goods,
> Whether little or much,

> And sees thereby his brother,
> That he suffers want,
> And does not readily give of
> The gift which he did receive,
> How then would he give his life for him unto death?
> He that here in the small things
> Is not found faithful,
> And still seeks his own,
> To which he is attached,
> Who will then entrust him
> With the eternal good?
> Therefore let us determine
> To keep love in care.[4]

Although differences in application would soon appear, this basic understanding was universally Anabaptist, and given expression in the Swiss, South German, North German and Dutch branches of the movement alike.

The converse of the spiritual ideal of community were communities that called themselves Christian, but gave no evidence of a common spirit of Christ when it came to material possessions. The Anabaptists reproached the poverty they saw in evidence all around them, in the churches of 'Christendom'. Menno Simons spoke for many others when he wrote:

> Is it not sad and intolerable hypocrisy that these poor people boast of having the Word of God, of being the true Christian church, never remembering that they have entirely lost their sign of true Christianity? For although many of them have plenty of everything . . . yet they suffer many of their own poor, afflicted members (notwithstanding their fellow believers have received one baptism and partaken of the same bread with them) to ask alms; and poor, hungry, suffering, old, lame, blind, and sick people to beg their bread at their doors.[5]

The sign of true Christianity, the Anabaptists believed,

involved the avoidance of riches, and had to include the care of those who had need, particularly within the baptised Body of Christ. The 'spiritual' includes the 'material' in its scope.

The early Anabaptists were suspicious of the emerging capitalist forms of economic activity, which encouraged individual striving and the hoarding of surplus goods and capital. Trade and commerce were regarded with particular suspicion, based as they were on adding arbitrary cost to articles that had been produced or bought more cheaply. In their Confession of 1578, the Swiss Brethren in Hesse maintained that Christians should be engaged in 'honest hand labour', avoiding merchandising and similar activities.[6] Menno thought that there perhaps could be 'God-fearing merchants and retailers', but he was certain that they were in grave danger of being overcome by avarice.[7] Peter Riedeman expressed the Hutterite view that the work of a trader or merchant 'is a sinful business', and explained that 'we allow no one to buy to sell again'. It is wrong 'when one buys a ware and sells the same again even as he bought it, taking to himself profit, making the ware dearer thereby for the poor, taking bread from their very mouths and thus making the poor man nothing but the bondman of the rich.' Riedeman echoed other Anabaptists when he argued that Christians 'should labour, working with their hands what is honest, that they may have to give to him that needs'.[8] Rather than extracting wealth from the poor (which is how the Anabaptists viewed retailing and mechandising), Christian economic activity should be of benefit to the poor.

Likewise, the Anabaptists uniformly rejected the charging of interest on money at loan. Money collected in this way was simply described as 'usury' or 'theft'. In St Gall, Switzerland, in 1532, Hans Marquart argued that Christians should lend without any hope of recovering the *principal*; much less, then, may a Christian be allowed to collect *usury* on money lent.[9] The sentiment was echoed by the Swiss Brethren in their Confession of 1578. They argued that the reborn children of God should not invest their money to get interest, but should use their surplus to help the poor, 'to lend and give to them, and expect the reward from God'.[10] Menno Simons also opposed the charging of interest and the making of money with money; and the charging of interest was so far from Hutterite economic life that Riedeman did not even mention the subject.[11]

From the vantage point of the twenty-first century, this attitude towards individual striving and the accumulation of capital may seem retrograde and unrealistic. In the context of Anabaptist spirituality, however, one's attitude towards the larger community, towards money and how one earned it and disposed of it were all *spiritual* matters that directly involved the love of both God and neighbour. One's relationship to material possessions, they believed, directly grew out of, and reflected upon, one's spiritual condition. Believers, Menno Simons said, care for the needs of others, not because they are ordered to, but because they have been regenerated by the living Spirit of God. Reflecting on the repentance and conversion of Zacchaeus, the publican, Menno concluded:

> Therefore Christ cannot admit any other members to His church but those who are of one heart, spirit, and soul with Him, partakers of His Spirit, who die to all unrighteousness, bury the old evil life of sin, walk by faith, are unblamable in love, receive the truth joyfully, and willingly serve their neighbors as did this believing, regenerated, and renewed Zacchaeus.[12]

For Menno and for the Anabaptists generally, becoming a Christian meant passing from being a person concerned with self-advancement – a condition of sinfulness that would have clear and concrete economic manifestations – to being a person ruled by the Spirit of Christ, which was manifestly a spirit of love of God and neighbour, and a condition of grace. In the Anabaptist understanding, accepting God's offer of salvation by grace, through faith and the power of the Holy Spirit, concretely transferred one's mind, life and kingdom citizenship from the former kingdom of self-will and death, to life in Christ's Kingdom of joyful self-sacrifice, service and love.

Dealing with material possessions is a necessary part of life in this world, but it is a particularly dangerous activity because of the innate human propensity to claim possession of created things. Andreas Ehrenpreis wrote:

> The apostle Paul knew about the dangers of wealth. Therefore he wrote that those who want to become rich fall into many temptations, and he adds that we brought nothing into this world and can take nothing out of it when we die. And further that there is great gain in godliness with contentment, saying finally that the love of money is a root of all kinds of evil, 1 Tim. 6:6–10.[13]

Keeping economic activity under control and in its proper place was thus a matter of spiritual concern and could impact spiritual practice, as Anabaptist testimonies note explicitly from time to time. Jan Wouterss, who was put to death in 1572 at Dordrecht, wrote to his wife from prison and advised her not to allow the business to grow too large, 'lest your heart become overburdened, so that you can ill perform your prayers'.[14] It is a matter of having one's treasure in the right place, in heaven rather than on earth.[15]

The Anabaptists retained many elements of the late medieval understanding of the 'holy life', and did not follow the Protestant lead towards the encouragement of capitalist activity. They did not agree that salvation simply had to do with 'faith', and had nothing intrinsic or essential to do with one's attitude towards material goods. To the contrary, it was axiomatic to them that economic questions would have a direct bearing on salvation. As we saw in the case of the church ordinances of baptism, the Lord's Supper and footwashing, the life of the Spirit and life in the world are integrated at every point. There is no separating them. Entering into and walking upon the narrow way demands a fundamental change in one's actual spiritual condition, and a change in the life of the sinner on this earth. Living a life of discipleship according to the counsels of perfection (the words and the example of Christ) thus became paramount, just as it had been in the ascetic holiness traditions.

These were the shared principles, but in their concrete application the Anabaptists came to disagreement and, eventually, schism. The sharing of temporal goods in community became for the Hutterites in Moravia the litmus test of yielded discipleship. The Hutterite *Chronicle* contains the following clear description of the principle on which the practice of community of goods was established:

> Community, both spiritual and temporal, is a cornerstone and foundation of the entire Christian life of the believers, whose hearts grow together in mutual trust, bound one to another through grace. The inner community, attained through true surrender to God and his only Son Jesus Christ, is mirrored in their outward actions, in wholehearted, genuine service to all God's children, seeking not one's own advantage but that of the many. The whole life of Christ is our best example for this.[16]

'Temporal community' for the Hutterites meant a community in which goods were shared and private property abolished. The basic issue, they were convinced, had to do with *Gelassenheit*. One's readiness to abandon private possessions was a test of one's obedience to Scripture and true yieldedness to God and to the Body of Christ.[17] Andreas Ehrenpreis was particularly adept at pointing this out. He wrote, 'There is no doubt that if only love of possessions and self-will did not exist, and if we loved the poor life of Christ and his obedience as much as our wealth, the cross of Christ would not seem foolishness to us, 1 Cor. 1:18, but rather a clear illustration and example of love and community.'[18] Ehrenpreis was convinced that a reluctance to turn one's possessions over to the community was a result of human willfulness, and a refusal to embrace the cross. Again, Ehrenpreis wrote:

> There is little difference before God between poor persons who hoard their meager possessions and the rich who

hoard theirs; both are rich enough for disobedience. Our Lord Jesus Christ said in several instances that those who love something more than himself, and do not renounce everything, note everything, cannot be his disciples, Matt. 10:37–39; Luke 14:7–14.[19]

For the Hutterites, a refusal to accept full community of goods was a 'holding back' from true yieldedness and renunciation of oneself, and so an impediment to becoming a true disciple of Christ.

Hutterite community of goods, required as it was of all members in their Anabaptist communities, was the extreme position among Anabaptist groups, but the difference was one of degree, not of kind. Both the Swiss Brethren and the followers of Menno Simons in the Netherlands insisted that yielded believers, reborn by the Holy Spirit, had given up ultimate claims to property, and that selfless sharing of material goods was a visible sign of the Body of Christ. The later Swiss Brethren expected a good share of their members' economic activity to fall under the direct supervision of the church, for example.[20] But the Swiss Brethren and the Mennonites argued that relinquishing all private ownership and living in a full community of goods were not requirements for followers of Christ. The troublesome examples in Acts, chapters 2 and 4, they said, described only a limited practice in the Jerusalem church, and were not a blueprint for all believers everywhere.

The Hutterian Brethren, by contrast, took the spiritual principle of *Gelassenheit* and applied it radically and consistently in the matter of material possessions in their communities. In this, their communities came to mirror most closely the cloistered communities of monastic brothers and sisters of the preceding centuries, who also had insisted on the surrender of private property upon full acceptance into their communities.

THE OATH

In the case of how Christians should relate material possessions to sharing in community, there were biblical texts that could be interpreted one way or another; in the case of the swearing of oaths, there was a direct command of the Lord. The confession of faith composed by the brethren sent to Trieste as galley slaves put forward what was to be the common Anabaptist position and explanation:

> Christ says in Matthew 5[:33–37]: You have heard that it was said to those of ancient times, You shall not swear falsely, but shall keep your oath made to God. Christ, however, who is the fulfilment of the law says: But I say to you, Do not swear at all. He gives specific instances of swearing, and then concludes: Let your word be yes, yes, and no, no. What is beyond that is from the evil one. Thus we say and confess by the power and command of Christ that it is not proper or incumbent upon any Christian to pledge an oath or to swear.[21]

This basic scriptural proof was put forward in one judicial hearing after another, with predictable frequency. Nevertheless, simply noting the 'proof text' citation of this text misses the most fundamental points of Anabaptist teaching on the question. The deeper issue for the Anabaptists had to do with truth-telling, not simply rote obedience to a law of behaviour. Telling the truth – indeed, living the truth – was the real issue. As we have seen previously, what appears to be a simple 'literal obedience' by Anabaptists to a biblical command can sometimes obscure layers of more profound spiritual significance. This is especially true of the 'non-swearing' issue which, on the surface, appears to be a rather uninteresting, literalistic response to a saying of Jesus.

Anabaptist concern for the truth ranged from the mundane to the profound. In his last testament to his children, Janneken, Joosken and Mijntken, Mattheus Bernaerts wrote:

O my dear children, keep your souls with the greatest diligence, so that you also speak no iniquity with your mouth; and beware of lying, for man, says Christ, shall have to give account of every idle word which he shall have idly spoken. Matt. 12:36. Hence Paul says: 'Put away lying, and speak truth with one another.' Eph. 4:25. For idle words shall not go free, and the mouth that lieth slayeth the soul; and liars have no part in the kingdom of God, but their part shall be in the lake which burneth with fire and brimstone. Wisd. 1:11; Rev. 21:8.[22]

Speaking 'iniquity' or telling lies will slay the soul, and leads to perdition. The moral admonition to be truthful is frequently encountered in letters from prison, especially in those written by parents for the future edification of their children. Even in these admonitions, however, the point was not simply following a rule; the central point was integrity, expressing the truth with no dissimulation.

Endres Keller wrote from his prison cell, 'I [will not] simulate to please anybody or to harm him. I will tell the truth from the heart as David teaches us in Ps. 16[:3] and 24[:2]: "For God takes no pleasure in the hypocrite." There must be no hypocrisy.'[23] The truth must be told 'from the heart', regardless of those who might be pressing for a pleasing answer that is a lie. A Christian tells the truth; a believer's 'yes' is truly a 'yes'. We are back again at a central point in Anabaptist spirituality: the necessary coincidence between inner reality and outer expression.

The central truth for a Christian is the truth of the Gospel and, in its widest sense, the truth of the Word of God. The recognition of the truth is planted in the human heart and confirmed by the Holy Spirit. It is this foundational truth that must never be abandoned. Menno Simons wrote:

let every soul seek pure, Christian truth in purity of heart, and strive after the same with all diligence, and it will be well with him. Jesus says, If ye continue in my word, then are ye my disciples indeed; and ye shall know the truth, and the truth shall make you free. Those who trust in Him shall understand the truth, and the believing shall serve Him in love.[24]

It was this truth, planted in the heart, that the Anabaptist martyrs struggled not to deny as they faced torture and death. When Jerome Segers wrote from prison to his wife Lijsken, who was also in prison – they were both awaiting sentences that would result in their deaths – he wrote her the following words:

> I remember you day and night in my prayers, beseeching the Lord to strengthen you with *His Spirit of truth*, since I well know that you will have much conflict yet, before you will be released; and I also know that you will be greatly tempted by the cunning foxes and ravening wolves, yea, which are much more lions and dragons; yea, a generation of vipers, who will not spare your soul, but destroy, devour and murder it. Hence Paul says: 'Beware lest any man spoil you through false philosophy and the sleight of men, whereby they lie in wait to deceive.' Col. 2:8.[25]

To lie and to deny the truth that one knows in one's heart and conscience to be true, is to deny Christ; those who deny Christ will be denied by Christ before God the Father, to their eternal damnation (Matthew 10:33).

The Anabaptists believed further that another central truth that could not be denied had been revealed in Scripture, and that was the true path of salvation. Menno Simons wrote:

> My dearly beloved reader, take heed to the Word of the Lord and learn to know the true God . . . He will not save you nor forgive your sins nor show you His mercy and grace except according to His Word; namely, if you repent and if you believe, if you are born of Him, if you do what He has commanded and walk as He walks. For if He could save an unrighteous carnal man without regeneration, faith, and repentance, then He did not teach us the truth. But He is the truth, and there is no falsehood in Him.[26]

To believe in Christ is to believe in the way of salvation he indicated. The way of salvation is to repent, believe, be born of God, obey God's commandments and walk as Jesus walked. To deny these truths is to deny Christ and to proclaim God a liar.

Pieter van Olman, who was put to death at Ghent in 1552, had a heated exchange with his inquisitors in which he explained why, in his view, 'speaking the truth' was a far deeper matter than simply uttering the right words – even if the words that were spoken were those of the Bible.

> John says (I John 2:4): He that saith that he knoweth God, and keepeth not his commandments, is a liar, and the truth is not in him. Now, if there is not truth in him, how can he speak the truth? Else John must lie. Christ says (Matt. 7:18): A corrupt tree cannot bring forth good fruit. Again (Matt. 12:34): How can ye, being evil, speak good things? Solve this question, and I will believe you. I tell you, though he should take a Testament, and read it from beginning to end in your church, as the apostles have written it, yet I will prove to them, that they lie. But let a man speak the same words, who walks in the ways of the Lord, and he will speak the truth . . . if you should preach: For thy sake we are led to death, as sheep for the slaughter; would this not also be a lie from you? But a God-fearing man would speak the truth.[27]

In van Olman's testimony we see the profound connection between truth-telling and the Anabaptist spiritual path: 'the truth' is not in its essence a verbal truth that can simply be 'spoken'. We may say, the true words of Scripture are not simply 'doctrines' that are true or false, as verbal propositions. Rather, the profound truth revealed in God's Word is a truth that must be both grasped in the heart, and also *lived* in the lives of believers – and then also is spoken without fear of the consequences. Talk can be cheap; the truth is not, because 'speaking the truth' is confirmed by the Spirit in the heart, it corresponds to Scripture, and finally is made as visibly manifest as fruit from a good tree.

The words of Jesus, said the Anabaptists, are true: a follower of Christ does not need to swear mighty oaths in order to 'confirm' the truth of any statement. A follower of Christ speaks from a spirit of truth, which conforms to the commands of God, and is confirmed by a life of love and obedience. It was this tightly woven fabric of spiritual, biblical and lived truth that stood behind the 'oath refusal' of the Anabaptists. It was also this same tight weave that insisted on honesty and integrity in all dealings, that led members to admonish one another, and that supported plain speaking and a refusal to recant in prison, even in the face of torture and death.

NON-VIOLENCE

When we turn to the Anabaptist teaching on non-violence we find an analogous case in which a direct biblical command – in this case to turn the other cheek and to love enemies – is cited explicitly in many Anabaptist testimonies. In 1589, Joost de Tollenaer wrote to his daughter Betgen from prison:

> We are to wish evil to no one, though in the law of Moses the contrary is written: 'Thou shalt love thy neighbour, and hate thine enemy.' But Christ takes this away; for that was in the law of revenge, but now we are under grace. Hence we must also show grace, and not punish, as Christ says: 'Ye have heard that it hath been said, Thou shalt love thy neighbour, and hate thine enemy. But I say unto you, Love your enemies, bless them that curse you, do good to them that hate you, and pray for them which despitefully use you, and persecute you; that ye may be the children of your Father which is in heaven: for he maketh his sun rise on the evil and on the good.' Matt. 5:43–45. Hence, dear child, one may not wish evil to his enemy, much less do him any evil. And do not hate him, neither avenge yourself, but give place to wrath; and be slow to wrath, for the wrath of man worketh not the righteousness of God; but as you would that men should do unto you, so do to them, and

you will fulfill the law of Christ. Rom. 12:19; James 1:19, 20; Matt. 7:12.[28]

The words of Jesus to his disciples, particularly Jesus' words in the Sermon on the Mount, and the example of his own life, seemed clear enough scriptural testimony for disciples concerning God's will in Christ. The Anabaptist brothers who were marched to Trieste, condemned to be galley slaves, wrote in their confession of faith:

> All defence and physical resistance, all warring, fighting, insurrection, and resisting evil, and all litigation in worldly courts and quarrelling over temporal goods are excluded. Christ clearly forbids killing or angry resentment (Matt. 5[:38–40]). To this we add Paul who says: Do not avenge yourselves, my beloved, but give place to God's wrath (Rom. 12[:19]).[29]

Christ's command to his disciples is clear; so also is the testimony of the apostle Paul, and, for that matter, all apostolic testimony contained in the New Testament agrees.

The words of the New Testament were strong enough to make the point, but it was the example of Jesus himself that so often was held up in Anabaptist reflections on loving enemies and dealing with evil in the world. *Ausbund* hymn 46 contains the following lines:

> Yield yourself to God with wife and child,
> fully from the heart, with soul and body;
> He will truly enrich you.
> Show everyone spiritual fruit,
> love, and a gentle spirit.
> Meekly feed
> the enemy that troubles you.
> O brother of mine, show mercy
> to everyone,
> as does your Father . . .
> Be compassionate.
> Mirror yourself in the Lord Christ.[30]

Yieldedness (*Gelassenheit*) to God will bear the spiritual fruit of gentle love, a mirror image of Christ himself.

Placing Christ at the centre of the Christian life as the example to be 'mirrored' and followed was not original to the Anabaptists, but rather had been one of the strongest and deepest spiritual emphases in the late medieval West. Thomas à Kempis' classic, the *Imitation of Christ*, begins in book one, chapter one by saying:

> 'He that follows Me shall not walk in darkness,' says the Lord. These are the words of Christ, by which we are urged to imitate His life and virtues, if we wish to be truly enlightened and freed from all blindness of heart. Therefore, let it be our chief business to meditate upon the life of Jesus Christ. The teaching of Christ excels all the teachings of the Saints, and if a man have His spirit, he shall find therein a hidden manna.[31]

Christ is not to be 'imitated' in the sense of mere acting or aping, but rather those who 'study Christ' seek Christ's spirit, so that they can truly be imitators of Christ. So also the Taulerian *Theologia Deutsch* said:

> Where the true Light is, there is a true righteous life, pleasing and precious to God. Although it is not the perfect life of Christ, it is nonetheless formed and righted according to it; the Christ life is loved and what flows from it: rectitude, order, and the rest of the virtues.[32]

The Holy Spirit, the true Light, brings forth a righteous life that is formed according to the life of Christ.

The Anabaptists were deeply nourished by this Christocentric spiritual tradition. 'Obeying the command of Christ' was central, of course, especially in the polemical argumentation of the sixteenth century, but the literal biblical command still did not get to the spiritual heart of the matter. Weapons are rejected, and enemies shown love, insofar as Christ's Spirit has been born within. Pilgram Marpeck wrote:

Revenge is no longer permitted in the New Testament for, through patience, the Spirit can now more powerfully overcome enemies than it could in the Old Testament. Therefore, Christ forbade such vengeance and resistance (Luke 9, 21; Matt. 5), and commanded the children who possessed the Spirit of the New Testament to love, to bless their enemies, persecutors, and opponents, and to overcome them with patience (Matt. 5; Luke 6).[33]

It is the Holy Spirit that makes possible the blessing of enemies, the 'Spirit of the New Testament' granted by Jesus Christ to the reborn children of God.[34] Paul Glock wrote from prison:

> [Jesus] prayed life for those who killed him. In his last extremity he was still concerned about his enemies. Observe how the Father and the Son are one, friendly and forbearing . . . Oh, you dearly beloved brethren and sisters, how few people there are who have the mind and spirit of Christ. May the Lord have mercy on us that more and more we may be removed from the unrighteous and defiled Adam into the new and undefiled Adam who is from heaven, the innocent lamb without blemish and without spot.[35]

The Anabaptists knew that the mind and spirit of Christ are not granted in perfect measure to human beings, this side of eternity. Nevertheless they were convinced, as was the *Imitatio* tradition that preceded them, that a good measure of the Christ-like life was possible on this earth for the reborn children of God, and so also was forbearing enemies and not retaliating with violence. An Anabaptist witness in 1529 stated the case negatively: 'our neighbours, the sword users (*Schwärtler*), also think they are Christians, but their works and deeds prove something much different. Their life accords very little and not at all with the teaching and life of Christ.'[36] It is by the measure of Christ's life that one's true spiritual condition is made evident.

Because of the cruel persecution they experienced, the Anabaptists had ample opportunity to reflect upon unjust suffering and perseverance. Many Anabaptists in prison took comfort in the words of Scripture that promised God's justice on those who had perpetrated injustice.[37] But it was not unusual for them also to reflect on the positive actions to which they felt called, in imitation of Christ. Bartholomeus Panten, executed in 1592, wrote an instruction from prison 'to all lovers of the truth; together with a brief account of his examination', in which he admonished them:

> Dear friends, if we want to be of His servants, we must serve the Lord according to His divine will and demands. That is, we must suffer and bear here, and not resist; else we should live to ourselves, and not to the Lord, and so doing we should not <u>follow the footsteps of Christ</u>, for we must bless, and not curse, them that persecute us. As Paul teaches us: 'Provide things honest in the sight of all men. If it be possible, as much as lieth in you, live peaceably with all men. Dearly beloved, avenge not yourselves, but rather give place unto wrath: for it is written, Vengeance is mine; I will repay, saith the Lord. Therefore, if thine enemy hunger, feed him; if he thirst, give him drink: for in so doing thou shalt heap coals of fire on his head. Be not overcome of evil, but overcome evil with good.' Rom. 12:17–21.[38]

Not seeking vengeance is a necessary first step; overcoming evil with good is a further step beyond. Followers of Jesus are called to both. So Pilgram Marpeck wrote:

> Be glad for I have overcome the world (that is, in patience, hope, and faith). You will be in need of patience (that is, patience in time of evil tribulation). 1 Pet. 3[:9–11], Rom. 12[:21] And do not resist evil with evil, but overcome evil with good. Thus and in no other way had Christ overcome the world that we may be joyful in hope and so to over-

come and to await our Saviour, according to His promise, who will be our victory and our overcoming.[39]

Christ overcame the world by patient yielding, defeating evil with good; his disciples and children will overcome the world in the same way, through patience, hope and trust in Jesus' victory.

Of course, proponents of hard-headed political solutions in the sixteenth century posed the same questions as do their twenty-first-century counterparts: what do you non-violent Christians propose to do when enemies attack our territory? Hans Schmidt reported the following exchange in 1590:

> The overseer said, 'If a murderer came to you in the field and killed you while you could defend yourself and did not, you would be your own murderer. If the Turk were to come into the land, would you not defend yourselves either?' I said, 'No. We will defend ourselves with prayer and will refrain from fighting. God fights for us.'[40]

Reborn children of God do as Christ did: they do not take life, they give life. They do not kill or coerce others to make matters on earth turn out 'right', but rather they trust entirely in God and God's providential care for the world.

One of the earliest public expressions of this sentiment is found in the Schleitheim Articles of 1527, where Michael Sattler wrote concerning separation from the world: 'Thereby shall also fall away from us the diabolical weapons of violence – such as sword, armor, and the like, and all of their use to protect friends or against enemies – by virtue of the word of Christ: "you shall not resist evil."' As he explained at his trial a few months later: 'If the Turk comes, he should not be resisted, for it stands written: thou shalt not kill. We should not defend ourselves against the Turks or our other persecutors, but with fervent prayer should implore God that He might be our defense and our resistance.'[41] This was an answer that came perfectly from a spirituality of following after Christ in yielded submission to God's will, but it certainly was not a thought-out strategy for Christian participation in political affairs. The heirs of the Anabaptist tradition have had to struggle with the consequences of this spirituality down to the present day.

CONCLUSION

Anabaptist spirituality is visibly marked by a persistent insistence on discipleship – walking in the footsteps of Christ in the difficult matters of sharing material possessions, living absolutely truthfully and refusing to utilise violence. To live as a disciple was a visible expression of living 'scriptural' lives, in particular, living in accordance with Scripture that reflected the mind and nature of Jesus Christ. At the same time, they were convinced that the life of Christ that they sought to live would be a life of real spiritual yieldedness and renewal. Living 'biblically' was thus seamlessly joined to 'living a Christ-like life' which would be (as they read in Scripture) a life of yieldedness to God's will in all things.

We may conclude with the prison testimony of Jan Wouterss. Jan was martyred in 1572. His sixth letter from prison was addressed to his only daughter as a testament and letter of instruction. He particularly admonished her to read the Scriptures, when she was old enough, so that she would learn how to discern good from evil.

> When you see pomp, boasting, dancing, lying, cheating, cursing, swearing, quarreling, fighting, and other wickedness . . . think then: 'This is not the right way, these are not the words of Christians, as the holy Scriptures teach . . .' The Scriptures testify that they are Christ's who have the Spirit of Christ or are led by the same. Rom. 8:9, 14.

They who are Christ's, have the Spirit of Christ. This is the heart of the matter for Anabaptist spirituality. Joost continues:

> Thus, my dearest daughter . . . you will find, that we must follow Christ Jesus, and obey Him unto the end; and you

will also truly find the little flock who follow Christ. And this is the sign: they lead a penitent life; they avoid that which is evil, and delight in doing what is good; they hunger and thirst after righteousness: they are not conformed to the world; they crucify their sinful flesh more and more every day, to die unto sin, which wars in their members . . . they do evil to no one; they pray for their enemies; they do not resist their enemies; their words are yea that is yea, and nay that is nay . . . they are also these who bear the cross of Christ, for He says: 'If any one will come after me, let him deny himself, and take up his cross daily, and follow me.' Luke 9:23 . . . join these cross-bearers, that you may come to Christ, who bore the cross for us; for we must follow His footsteps, and be like our Lord, the disciple like his master; and as we suffer with Him, so shall we forever rejoice with Him.[42]

This testimony is a wonderfully rich summary of Anabaptist spiritual teaching. Those who have the Spirit of Christ *manifest* the mind of Christ with their lives. They quite naturally follow after Christ; they obey what Christ has commanded, in all things: in a penitent life, in avoiding evil, in delighting in the good, in hungering after righteousness, in non-conformity, in discipline and self-control, in dying to sin, and in loving enemies. Loving enemies, the ultimate test of the love of Christ, is not the exclusive Anabaptist mark of discipleship, but rather is part of a long list of 'cross-bearing' manifestations of the love of Christ within.

There really is only one simple point to be made from this: although there is a clear focus on the example and scriptural command of Jesus running throughout the Anabaptist calls to discipleship, when we take in the entire panorama of Anabaptist spirituality, we see that the sharing of possessions, truth-telling, the love of enemies and the forsaking of violent means are not simply requirements of a new law. These ways of living in the world are of the essence of Christ's Spirit, mind and example, and so will be of the essence of a regenerated believer's spirit, mind and life in this world.

Without regeneration, however, there can be only law and failure to keep the law. The Anabaptists were quite aware of the fact that a natural person who is informed of requirements that lie outside natural strength, is simply informed of inadequacy. The Anabaptists did not sidestep the question: how is unnatural sharing, truth-telling and loving to be accomplished? Their answer lay in the process of spiritual birth by God's grace, and growth through penitent and disciplined living, within the disciplined community. The 'obedience of faith' to which Christ calls us can only be fulfilled by the active work of the living Spirit of God. It is, then, the regenerated, yielded nature of the Christian life that forms the centre of the Anabaptist teaching on discipleship.

8 MARTYRDOM: THE BAPTISM IN BLOOD

They dance and jump in the fire, view the glistening sword with fearless hearts, speak and preach to the people with smiles on their faces; they sing psalms and other songs until their souls have departed, they die with joy, as if they were in happy company, they remain strong, assured, and steadfast to the point of death.

This description of the deaths of Anabaptist martyrs is notable because it was recounted not by an Anabaptist sympathiser, but by the Roman Catholic bishop Johannes Fabri, a staunch opponent of the Anabaptists who appears to have witnessed some executions personally. 'They remain so obstinate in their resolve that they also defy all pain and torment,' he concluded.[1] Even this stalwart defender of Rome did not deny the confidence and evident readiness for death of so many Anabaptist martyrs – even if he could and did question their 'obstinacy' and the cause for which they died.

Martyrs, Brad Gregory has observed, never represent the vast majority of average believers, but rather are the highest exemplars of religious observance: 'men and women self-consciously steeped in their faith, willing to make it their over-riding priority'.[2] The majority of Anabaptists did not have to face martyrdom. Nevertheless, martyrs made up a much larger percentage of the body of Anabaptist believers than was the case for other faith groups, and not surprisingly, martyrdom played a more significant role in defining Anabaptist spirituality than was the case for other contemporary Christian groups.

Martyrdom epitomised and exemplified the spiritual principles the Anabaptists espoused.

Anabaptists made up a small minority of dissent within the
larger body of European Christendom – the exact numbers are
impossible to verify, but even in the territories where they
were most numerous, they certainly never numbered even 10
per cent of the general population. Nevertheless, when we
consider the numbers of people martyred for their faith in the
sixteenth century, the Anabaptists take on a very large profile,
far beyond their absolute numbers. The best historical esti-
mates mark approximately 5,000 people killed for their faith
in sixteenth-century Western Europe, from the combined
Roman Catholic, Protestant and Anabaptist confessions. Of
this total number of martyrs, between 40 and 50 per cent –
between 2,000 and 2,500 – were Anabaptist martyrs.[3] This
extremely high proportion of martyrs stamped the rank-and-
file Anabaptist movement with a far deeper 'martyrological
sensibility' than was true for Roman Catholics or Protestants.

From its earliest days, 'even to ponder becoming an
Anabaptist was ipso facto to think about martyrdom', Brad
Gregory has noted.[4] The experience of persecution strengthened the Anabaptist conviction that the Body of Christ, the
church, would be separated from the world and would be
persecuted by the world, as Christ himself had been. This conviction, along with an astounding readiness to 'suffer God's
will, whatever comes', is evident in the many hundreds of
Anabaptist martyr testimonies that survive from the sixteenth
century. The testimony of the Bible, read through the lens of
brutal persecution, convinced the Anabaptists that the
'baptism of blood' was to be expected for those who had
accepted the baptisms of the Spirit and of water, and had set
out to follow Jesus in life. It was the way of all the 'friends of
God', from the prophets through Christ and his followers.[5]

It was not uncommon for rank-and-file Anabaptist members
to have known personally people who were killed for their
Anabaptist faith. Given the policy of authorities to seek out
and arrest Anabaptist leaders, many hundreds of people had

sometimes been baptised or instructed by a leader who was subsequently martyred. But there were some leaders who weakened and renounced their faith, just as there were many hundreds of 'ordinary' members, women and men, who persevered unto death. The faithful martyrs, leaders or not, immediately were memorialised, especially in song. This was an especially effective way for this grass-roots movement to remember their martyrs and to communicate the events surrounding their faithful deaths. The surviving collections of songs, some of which are still sung by the Amish and the Hutterites, are built around martyr accounts. They are didactic at every level: the martyrs exemplify the steadfastness required of disciples who 'have left all to follow Christ'; in recalling exchanges with inquisitors, the martyr songs also instruct and strengthen believers in the basic principles of the faith; and in providing examples of believers who 'died well', they paved the way for future martyrs to do likewise.

Because of the widespread persecution, Anabaptist martyrs were not incidental to their spiritual tradition – as if they were unfortunate random members who happened to be arrested and killed – but rather martyrdom came to define the very essence of the Anabaptist spiritual tradition. The spiritual roots for Christian martyrdom lay in the late medieval tradition of piety – for all martyrs of the sixteenth century, regardless of their denominational affiliation.[6] But the sixteenth century, with its appeal to Scripture and its persecution of dissenters, shaped the medieval spiritual roots in a unique way for the Anabaptists.

MEDIEVAL ROOTS

The highest example of the willing acceptance of death was, of course, Jesus Christ himself. His acceptance of the cross was emulated by the martyrs and saints of the early church up to the fourth century. With the arrival of Christendom, the possibility of martyrdom disappeared, except on the remotest missionary frontiers, and even these possibilities had disappeared by the high Middle Ages. Nevertheless, the medieval church continued to hold up the martyrs of the early church as saints and examples, and especially promoted the spiritual values of ascetic renunciation and faithfulness that had led the early martyrs to their deaths. Gregory the Great would write in the late sixth century: 'Even though we do not bend our bodily neck to the sword, nevertheless with the spiritual sword we slay in our soul carnal desires'; and further, 'If, with the help of the Lord, we strive to observe the virtue of patience, even though we live in the peace of the Church, nevertheless we bear the palm of martyrdom.'[7] The physical death of the martyrs was transmuted in Christendom into a spiritual martyrdom that sacrificed the 'carnal' side of life for the sake of a 'spiritual' life of patience, virtue and holy obedience. The spiritual virtue of yielding to God's will, regardless of cost, so graphically demonstrated by the martyr's death, could be exercised in the 'daily martyrdom' of the disciplines of cloistered spiritual life.

Thus although there were very few Christian martyrs in the centuries leading up to the sixteenth, the values that supported martyrdom had been upheld as the highest of Christian virtues for over a thousand years. It took only a change in historical circumstances for those values to apply to martyrdom again, and the sixteenth century provided those changed circumstances.

As we have seen above, the Anabaptist spiritual path was to begin in the fear of God, through deep repentance, in an attitude of contempt for this world, in full yieldedness (*Gelassenheit*) to God and God's will. The aim was to follow in the footsteps of Christ, as true disciples, yielding to the will of God as Jesus himself had done, in true abandonment and resignation. This spiritual path, as we have noted, had been marked out as the way of the Christian devout for many centuries – with the significant difference that the Anabaptists were not cloistered Religious, or even an accepted lay confraternity of pious people, but rather a persecuted group of religious dissenters. For them, the scriptural and spiritual admonitions of the preceding centuries suddenly took on a deeper and more fatal meaning.

Gelassenheit

The concept, or spiritual attitude, of *Gelassenheit* was mediated to sixteenth-century devout people through the late medieval mystical tradition: Meister Eckhart, Henry Suso, John Tauler and the anonymous Taulerian writing, popularised by Martin Luther, the *Theologia Deutsch*. The radical Reformers, Andreas Karlstadt and Thomas Müntzer, valued *Gelassenheit* and directly influenced some later Anabaptists.[8] But specific mediators of the virtue of *Gelassenheit* are not always identifiable, nor is it necessary to attempt to locate them. One did not have to be immersed in mystical writings to have understood the generally accepted late medieval truism that an attitude of *Gelassenheit* was indispensable to growth in the spiritual life.

The principle that the degree of one's attachment to God depends on the degree of one's disengagement from 'the creatures' was not simply a verbal or intellectual truism, but was a spiritual principle that could be measured by visible manifestations. To what extent had one turned away from the allurements of this world, and turned towards heaven? The answer would be visible in one's life. To what extent did one seek to impose one's own will on events in this world, as opposed to simply accepting what came 'from God's hand', in patient resignation? The answer would again be evident in one's life. To what extent did one share with the needy, relying on God to provide for tomorrow, as opposed to hoarding riches here today? One's entire way of living could be read as a book, revealing one's degree of *Gelassenheit*.

It was through the filter of *Gelassenheit* that the Anabaptists understood faith. Faith was less about 'belief' than it was about 'trust' evidenced in obedience and in life. To believe that Jesus Christ took away the sins of the world didn't amount to much, they said, if one did not trust in his promises and follow Christ in yielded obedience, wherever that might lead in this life. It was through the filter of *Gelassenheit* that they understood the willingness to be baptised, to accept the 'testing' of persecution, to accept the discipline of the community, and the willingness to walk the narrow way. It was, in the end, a question of yielded acceptance of God's will that led the martyrs to trust more in God's promises than in the promises of men who promised them temporal life in return for recantation.

The baptism of blood was the ultimate test of personal *Gelassenheit*: the readiness to yield one's life for Christ's sake was as convincing a piece of evidence as one could present, that one's own will had been set aside. But Anabaptist spirituality had been characterised by a search for true *Gelassenheit* from the very start of the spiritual path, as if in preparation for the final challenge. The numerous prison letters of Anabaptist men and women who were soon to be martyred reflect their struggles to trust entirely in God in their final moments on earth. The references to 'yielding to God's will' in surviving testimonies are so numerous that choosing just one example or two is almost arbitrary.

Walter of Stoelwijk suffered in prison for three years, before being burned at the stake in 1541. In a letter from prison he wrote:

> we must deny ourselves; that is, we must forsake our own will, and surrender ourselves wholly to Jesus Christ, so that according to the words of the apostle, we live no more unto ourselves, but unto Jesus Christ, who died for us, that He may be Lord both of the dead and living, and that no one shall live for himself, but unto Him who died for him, and rose again . . . We must follow and preserve only the teachings and commandments of Christ Jesus, and . . . we may in no wise live according to our own will, but are to consider that Christ Jesus Himself did not do His own will, but the will of His Father who sent Him.[9]

Raphel van den Velde's testimony is notable for its anguished human touch. He was imprisoned for his faith in 1576 at Ghent. From his cell he was able to write several letters to his wife and friends before he was burned at the stake. The following is from his first letter to his wife:

> no one knows what bonds are, except he that tries them, this I may well say, for which I thank and praise the Lord with a joyful heart. I hope that I am over the worst and my heart is much resigned in suffering or affliction, and in death, but when I begin to think of parting from my love, and my dear son, then I cannot compose my heart so easily. But this comforts me much, that my child can keep his mother. And be not over-careful, my love; the Most High cares for you and also for your child; and our dear Lord has shown us much grace, that He has permitted us to live together so long. Yea, be not too careful, this I pray you, my love; but cast your care entirely and gladly upon the Lord; He will provide for you, and give you another husband in my place, if it be for your good. Ps. 55:22; I Pet. 5:7; Phil. 4:6.[10]

Van den Velde was struggling to find holy 'resignation' in the face of the loss of his beloved wife and son, who were all that he held dear in this world. In the end, he accepted death as the price of following after Christ, trusting that this was God's will for him.

Hans Mändl, a Hutterite missionary who was imprisoned several times before he was finally martyred, wrote the following words to a song from the dungeon of a prison in 1548. The song is still sung by the Hutterites today.

> For to you only, o my Father,
> I have totally yielded myself . . .
> For God desires a pure heart,
> Which has totally submitted itself
> To Him and to the holy church
> With his whole life.
> For we must strive for the church

And yieldedness [*Gelassenheit*] here
If we wish to inherit the kingdom
With God and his saints . . .
How will he who does not put his complete
Trust in God and his church, With all that he has,
Prevail in the time of testing,
In tribulation and much suffering?
If he then has regrets, he will not be steadfast.
God desires only a devout people,
Who have submitted themselves,
Who have refrained from sinning,
And do His will. Have left house and possessions
And the world totally,
Have fellowship with God and His people,
And share their lives and counsel.[11]

Mändl's words give voice to the highest spiritual ideals of the Anabaptists: complete trust and yieldedness (*Gelassenheit*), first to God and God's will, and second, to the community of saints on earth. Mändl expressed a common view when he stated that only those who have practised an active trust in God, who have experience in yielding themselves daily to God and the community, only such people will be able to withstand persecution, unto death. Martyrdom, voluntarily giving up one's life, is the ultimate demonstration of one's complete trust in God.

Suffering with Christ

The theme of the righteous suffering on their way to God's Kingdom suffuses both the Old and the New Testaments, culminating in Christ's own suffering on the cross. This fact had been noted by the devout for centuries. The following collection of Scripture verses is a familiar one to anyone who has read Anabaptist testimonies.

What more? Does not the right and necessary way to the kingdom lead through distress? Does not Scripture say

'Many are the tribulations of the righteous' (Ps 33/34: 20/19) and we must 'go through many trials to enter the kingdom of God' (Acts 14:22)? And again: 'All who want to live piously in Christ Jesus will suffer persecution' (2 Tim 3:12). 'So if they persecuted Christ, will they not also persecute you' (Jn 15:20)? 'The disciple is not superior to his master' (Mt 10:24). Was it not 'necessary for Christ to suffer and thus to enter into his glory' (Lk 24:26)? Is it not necessary for us Christians, for whom Christ suffered, 'also to suffer and continuously to bear about in these our mortal bodies the mortification of Christ, so that the life of Jesus may be made manifest in our bodies'? For at all times, the Apostle says, 'we who live are given over to death, so that the life of Jesus Christ may be revealed in our bodies, in our mortal flesh' (2 Cor 4:10–11). For this reason, the Prince of the Apostles says, 'Christ suffered for us leaving us an example, that we might follow in his steps' (1 Pt 2:21), so that we might be made 'heirs of God and coheirs of Christ, for if we suffer with Him,' the Apostle told the Romans, 'we will be glorified with him' (Rom 8:17).[12]

This collection of Scripture verses was compiled not by an Anabaptist, but by the devout Roman Catholic brother Geert Grote, sometime around 1375. Grote was the founder of the *Devotio Moderna* movement in the Netherlands. He collected these verses not to strengthen the resolve of people facing martyrdom, but rather to strengthen the resolve of those who had dedicated themselves to a life of meditation and devotion.

Strikingly similar collections of biblical references were gathered also by Anabaptist prisoners but, a century and a half later, the suffering the Anabaptists had to face was no longer the 'temptations of the flesh' in a cloister, but the physical suffering of dungeon, torture and death. Walter of Stoelwijk wrote from prison in 1541:

Paul says: 'All that will live godly in Christ Jesus shall suffer persecution.' 2 Tim. 3:12. Yea Christ Himself says to

His apostles: 'Ye shall be hated of all men for my name's sake.' Mark 13:13. From all these words it must incontrovertibly follow, that all servants of God, all godly men, all disciples of Jesus Christ must suffer persecution for His name's sake; and be tried through manifold temptations.[13]

Or again, Lenaert Plovier wrote to his children from prison, in 1560:

Dear children, prepare while you have time . . . for we must enter into the kingdom of God through much tribulation. Acts 14:22. Therefore Peter says: 'Think it not strange concerning the fiery trial which is to try you . . . but rejoice, inasmuch as ye are partakers of Christ's sufferings . . . 1 Pet. 4:12, 13. Even Christ our Teacher and Master had to enter into the kingdom of God through tribulation and suffering; and the servant cannot be more than his master . . . Matt. 10:24, 25 . . . O dear children, lay to heart what Paul says: 'All that will live godly shall suffer persecution' (2 Tim. 3:12).[14]

And so on and on: examples could be multiplied many times over from Anabaptist testimonies, songs and writings. The message to be read in the biblical record was as clear to the Anabaptists as it had been to the medieval devout: suffering and the cross were to be expected for those who had yielded themselves entirely to God, and set out to follow after Christ. His yielded obedience had led him to the cross, and the disciple was to expect no better in this life, awaiting the reward of the fairhful in the next.

The biblical ideal of Christ's yielded, suffering discipleship had been well known, taught and emulated in the cloisters for centuries leading up to the sixteenth century, held up as the spiritual model for Christians from all walks of life. What changed in the sixteenth century were the historical circumstances; all of a sudden, there was a new meaning to be gleaned from the well-known biblical words, admonitions and examples.

THE BODY OF CHRIST

The dominical ordinances of baptism and the Lord's Supper occupied central places in Anabaptist spiritual life and practice, as has been noted above. Both ordinances took on more profound meaning for the Anabaptists in the crucible of persecution, suffering and martyrdom.

The Baptism of Blood

Baptism in the Spirit led believers to the visible commitment of baptism in water. Water baptism, in its turn, pointed beyond itself to suffering and the cross. 'Christians must be like Christ the head,' wrote Hans Schlaffer, giving voice to this fundamental Anabaptist conviction. This meant, as is written in 1 Peter 2:21, that the suffering undergone by Christ was no more and no less than an 'example' to those who really wished to follow after him. The 'cup of suffering' Jesus offered to the sons of Zebedee in Matthew 20:20–23 was identified with the baptism of blood Jesus himself spoke about in Luke 12:50.

This was a common Anabaptist understanding of baptism in the age of persecution. Shortly before she was drowned in Rotterdam in 1539, Anna Jansz wrote the following to her son Isaiah:

> Hear, my son, the instruction of your mother. Open your ears to hear the words of my mouth, Prov. 1:8. Look, I go the way of the prophets, apostles, and martyrs to drink the cup they all drank, Matt. 20:23. I go the way, I say, that Christ Jesus, the eternal Word of the Father, full of grace and truth, the Shepherd of the sheep, who himself is life and who went this way, and not another, and who had to drink this cup, as he said: I have a cup to drink, and a baptism to be baptised with; how anxious I am until this hour is fulfilled.[15]

There was no escaping the suffering indicated by Jesus, for it was the path he followed and the path on which he called his disciples to walk. Just as Jesus' baptism initiated his path to the cross, so it was also for his disciples. The 'dying to self and rising in Christ' indicated by water baptism was not an empty symbol or mere sign, but rather was a personal acceptance of the cross of Christ and, at the same time, an incorporation into the suffering Body of Christ.

The temptation of dissimulation or Nicodemism was a real one for sixteenth-century Anabaptists. Had they been willing to forego the visible marks of the Body of Christ on earth they could have lived in relative peace as a secret, purely 'spiritual' and invisible group. But the Anabaptist community was no invisible spiritual assembly, but a real gathering of physical 'members', marked by physical ordinances, actions and 'testimonies' as commanded and exemplified by Christ. As they read the biblical witness in the midst of persecution, it was as clear as it could be: Jesus Christ was still being persecuted in his members; Christ's Body on earth was still being led to the cross, member by willing member; Pilate still washed his hands, and the crowds still mocked. There was a terrible actuality to the passion of Christ that was intensely lived and re-enacted in the biblical ordinances of baptism and the Lord's Supper that the Anabaptists celebrated together. The act of water baptism, far from being a mere 'wetting' of believers (more than being 'just' water), was a public testimony to one's having become a living 'member' (appendage) of the incarnated Body of Christ. As such a member, the baptism of blood could only be expected.[16]

The Lord's Supper

The Lord's Supper was for the Anabaptists a celebration of remembrance and unity, as already noted, but it also pointed directly to persecution and suffering, along with Christ. Celebrating the Lord's Supper indicated uniting oneself to the sufferings of Christ as manifested in Christ's members, and a readiness to follow Christ to the cross. 'Remembering' Christ's sacrifice on the cross naturally led to reflection on the suffering of the members of Christ's Body on earth. A eucharistic hymn in the *Ausbund* says: 'Whoever eats and does not forget, but rather thinks about the Lord's death, how He gave himself up to hang on the cross, [such a one] is also minded in this time to suffer with the Lord.'[17]

The ancient eucharistic image of individual kernels being ground together to make one loaf, and individual grapes being crushed to make a cup of wine, was often repeated in Anabaptist testimonies. The images of 'grinding' and 'crushing' aptly suggested to them the pain of yielding to a larger process of transformation that the Anabaptists associated with faithfulness in following after Christ. Menno Simons wrote:

> Just as natural bread is made of many grains, pulverized by the mill, kneaded with water, and baked by the heat of the fire, so is the church of Christ made up of true believers, broken in their hearts with the mill of the divine Word, baptized with the water of the Holy Ghost, and with the fire of pure, unfeigned love made into one body.[18]

Jacob the Chandler wrote a confession of his faith for his children from prison in Bruges in 1569. He described the bread of the Lord's Supper as a 'mirror' in which each believer must examine oneself:

> For it is one bread baked of many grains, which must be alike among one another, because they are ground, made into a dough with water, and baked with fire into one bread ... Thus must we also be broken in heart, by the hammer of the divine Word (Jer. 23:29), being united together through the communion of the Holy Ghost.[19]

The bread which was being eaten in the Lord's Supper was symbolic of the ground hearts of the believers who were partaking in that Supper. The prism of persecution and martyrdom gave a powerful reality both to the assembly and to the deeper meaning contained in the emblems of celebration.

Even as the grinding of individual grains into one loaf suggested the suffering associated with becoming members of the one Body of Christ, partaking in the cup had even stronger associations with the suffering of Christ. *Ausbund* hymn 55 observes:

> The cup signifies to us Christ's suffering.
> All those whom the Holy Spirit circumcises,
> as his branches on the vine . . .
> these he gives to drink from His cup.[20]

Ausbund hymn 92 pursues the same thought further:

> Note! Suffering in this time is called the Lord's cup
> which the wine and bread signify . . .
> This cup is served
> by Jesus Christ to his community
> so that she, as did He, should drink the cup
> according to the Father's teaching . . .
> To be a member of Christ is also to suffer with Him,
> to shed one's blood for Him.[21]

The hymn then comes full circle, recalling the threefold baptism which led to the present celebration:

> God now holds what you
> promised to Him in baptism.
> According to his command, take the cup,
> complete the sacrifice to Him.
> Three witnesses decide
> how it is for us in Jesus Christ:
> two are called water and Spirit,
> the third, blood, which is suffering.[22]

The celebration of the ordinances of baptism and the Lord's Supper, carried out under the most trying conditions, were powerful symbolic actions, mandated by Christ himself, which testified to, strengthened and undergirded the commitment of participating members. More than 'mere signs', the celebration of baptism and the Lord's Supper in community were visible, tangible and real *actions* that sealed and ingrafted members to Christ's Body. Persecution and suffering made of these 'visible signs' much more than empty pointers, as the signs themselves became the reasons for which Anabaptists were persecuted and executed – and so the signs became visible markers of Christ's suffering Body on earth. With the celebration of the dominical ordinances, in contravention of the political mandates of the time, the Anabaptists were placing their hope in the power and promises of God.

THE PRESENCE OF GOD IN SUFFERING

The living presence of God, experienced in the heart, lay at the centre of Anabaptist spirituality. Anabaptists in prison, facing death, cultivated God's presence with earnest and fervent prayer, by continual singing of spiritual songs, and with reading and meditating upon the promises of Scripture.

Letters from prison often report divine comfort, but more than this, they also report that the Spirit's living presence had directed their replies to inquisitors' questions. From the frequency of these reports, it appears that Anabaptist prisoners fully expected divine aid in making their defences and replies. Claes de Praet reported that after six days of imprisonment, he was led into a room to be questioned at length about his faith. 'Then thought I: "O gracious God! now I find that Thou art faithful to Thy promise. Heb. 10:23. Lord, direct now my speech, as Thou has promised" (Luke 21:14–15).' Claes reported in detail the days of questioning and the answers he gave, noting at the end that he had 'told them a great deal, as the Lord gave me utterance'.[23] Matthias Servaes, an Anabaptist elder and teacher, wrote numerous letters from prison before his beheading in 1565. In his seventh letter he advised all prisoners to 'guard their lips, and bridle their tongues', and rather than speaking, to 'wait with patience until Christ speaks in you, or His Spirit, according to His promise, through you. Matt. 10:20'.[24] Matthias had already had ample occasion for testing this biblical promise, having been tortured and questioned at length. So too did Claesken Gaeledochter, who reported after rounds of questioning that 'I spoke without fear whatever the Lord gave into my mind.'[25]

The strengthening presence of God was often tested directly in the tortures routinely applied in sixteenth-century prisons. The objective of the authorities was less to obtain recantations (this was usually done by gentler means of persuasion and disputation with clerics), than to obtain names of fellow members and especially the names and dwelling places of leaders. It is reported that 53-year-old Anneken Heyndricks, who could neither read nor write, was suspended by her hands and tortured in order to 'extort from her the names of her fellow believers ... But they obtained nothing from Anneken, so faithfully did God keep her lips.'[26] She was burned at the stake in 1571.

One year later, Jan Wouterss managed to write to his brother-in-law and sister, after he had been tortured with the aim of obtaining the names of fellow believers and preachers. In this remarkable letter, he describes his struggle to remain true to his conscience in the face of repeated torture, and his reliance on God's presence during his struggle. Jan describes how, in the bitter cold of winter, he was taken to an unheated torture loft, stripped to the waist, with his hands tied behind his back and his feet tied to the floor. A rope was then attached to his wrists and he was hoisted aloft by that rope, arms behind his back, beaten with rods on his abdomen for good measure. He reported that 'the Lord be praised, they obtained nothing from me, though I had drank that bitter cup ... I prayed within myself, that the Lord should not suffer me to be tempted above that I was able.' Anabaptist prisoners had pledged life and limb to each other in the celebration of the Supper; under torture they struggled valiantly not to reveal the names of other members of Christ's Body.

Jan resisted the pain of torture through constant prayer. He wrote that he had not been able to sleep well on the night following the torture, 'But afterwards I received a great, peaceful joy and gladness of the Holy Ghost, so great that I cannot adequately describe it; because the Lord had so faithfully kept my lips, and not suffered me to be confounded in my confidence.' Jan knew that he would be tortured again in a few days. He wrote that although his 'flesh feared', he 'made supplication to my God, that He would not chasten me unworthy servant according to my sins, according to His justice, but according to His fatherly mercy, that He would keep my lips, and alleviate the pain, as He had done the first time'.[27] Again he prepared for his ordeal through fervent prayer, and again he withstood the second session of torture. He passed on this message to his co-believers:

> You beloved and saints of God, who have become partakers of the heavenly calling through Jesus Christ . . . I bear witness of Him, that He is a faithful helper in distress, as is written of Him; yea (He says by the prophet), though a mother forget the son of her womb, whom she brought forth, yet will I not forsake nor forget thee. Isa. 49:15; Heb. 13:5. Hence, all you that believe the Lord's promise, continue steadfastly.[28]

The message that came repeatedly from the prisons was: God's promises are true. In spite of external appearances to the contrary, God is present with us and does not forsake us in our tribulation, but strengthens and comforts us. He fights for us, and is faithful, and does not allow us to be tested beyond our means.[29] Sometimes human weakness prevailed, and prisoners named names or recanted, as in the case of Clement Hendrickss, for example, who admitted in a letter from prison to his parents that as he was being racked, scourged and having urine poured into his mouth, he did name four persons because of the severe pain but, he wrote, 'I hoped they were not in town.'[30] The overwhelming message in the martyrs' letters, however, was that the comforting presence and power of God was real, making possible heroic acts of resistance in the face of very real physical pain and suffering.[31] Those who had experienced the presence of God in the midst of their suffering anticipated finding the same strength and presence in their final trial, in their moments of death. Matthias Servaes wrote from prison, shortly before his beheading, 'Trust God; He will not forsake you even unto death.'[32]

THE PRESENCE OF GOD IN DEATH

One of the earliest Anabaptist martyr accounts to circulate was the report of Michael Sattler's execution in 1527. Wilhelm Reublin wrote a first-hand account of Sattler's death. He described how the hangman placed a sack of gunpowder around Sattler's neck prior to his being thrown into the fire, with the intent of hastening his death and lessening his suffering.

> When the powder went off and one despaired of his still being alive, he cried with a clear voice often and constantly to God in heaven. When he had been crying thus for a long time, he became unbound in the fire and raised his arms high with the first two fingers on each hand outstretched and cried with a powerful voice: 'Father, into thy hands I commend my soul!' And thus ended his life. The Lord be eternally praised. Amen![33]

Reublin here carefully recounts Michael Sattler's death agonies, the last, painful moments of his life; such descriptions appear very often in eyewitness accounts of Anabaptist martyrdoms.

What may seem to us to be unnecessary, gruesome detail was for sixteenth-century contemporaries the very heart of the matter and the question to be pondered, as did the Catholic bishop Johannes Fabri: how did they die? Were they firm in their beliefs to the end? Did physical pain overcome them in their final moments (an implicit confession of error), or did they pass through death triumphantly and at peace, as if they were moving through an open door into the rewards of life everlasting? Michael Sattler's pre-arranged signal of out-stretched fingers as his body burned was taken by the Anabaptists to be his final confirmation that God had strengthened him to the very end in the truth for which he was dying. Michael Sattler died a 'good death', remaining firm in the faith. Opponents of the Anabaptists, of course, placed a different interpretation on this 'obstinacy'.

In spite of the lack of medieval martyrs, the spiritual teachings of the late medieval devout had prepared the way for this concentration on the final moments of the martyrs' lives. Among the most popular spiritual texts in the century preceding the Reformation were two books collectively called the *Ars moriendi*, which contained instruction on the art of dying. The moment of death was considered to be a particularly telling and vulnerable time, when the unwary and unprepared could see their souls snatched away to hell by Satan. Renouncing this world, keeping the hopes of heavenly reward in view, and resisting the temptations of Satan all led to a blessed death, welcomed as one would a friend.[34] As Brad Gregory has noted:

> When crowds gathered to witness the execution of religious criminals, town squares displaced the domestic intimacy of the deathbed. Spectators scrutinized the condemned, looking for behaviour to which the *Ars moriendi* had sensitized them for more than a century.[35]

While the Anabaptists saw their sacrifices as the final test of their faith and the quintessential witness to the truth in the moment of death, the authorities carried out gruesome public executions in an effort to suppress the movement through fear of punishment. They wished to convince the public that the Anabaptists were being executed as criminals. The crowds that gathered to watch and who heard the songs and accounts of the executions were the audience being appealed to by both parties, as this lethal drama played itself out.

Of particular note were the high number of women martyrs among the Anabaptists. Approximately one third of all the martyrs commemorated in van Braght's massive *Martyrs Mirror* are women. Contemporaries were astonished. It was shocking enough to see so many women (many of whom were not literate) claim the Anabaptist faith for themselves. Not only had they decided to join this dissenting group of their own volition, they also knew exactly in what their faith consisted, as the prison records document. Anabaptist women ably debated learned clerics and court officials, defending their faith with numerous biblical texts, with ready wit and intelligence. It was even more astounding when these women, commonly considered the 'weaker sex', nevertheless withstood torture and faced death with 'manly courage', as contemporary accounts have it.[36] The martyr accounts describe the very same steadfastness from women facing death as from men. The case of Weynken Claes is typical. As she was being led to the fire, a monk persisted in asking her to renounce her faith. She rebuked him and 'After that she went joyfully, as if she were going to a Wedding Feast, and she did not flinch even when she saw the fire.'[37]

As in the case of male Anabaptist martyrs, the interpretation of unexpected displays of women's courage and perseverance depended on the perspective of the observer. Frustrated clergy proclaimed these women to be possessed of Satan;[38] to their Anabaptist compatriots, the power of God shone through their witness of extraordinary courage in the face of death. So the song commemorating the martyrdom by fire of Maria and Ursula van Beckum concludes:

> And so until the bitter end, these Lambs,
> Both of them, endured faithful
> And with their deaths recounted here
> Gave to God's word a seal.
> With great and patient suffering
> They fought to the end with courage brave,
> And have left for us
> An exemplum – understand this well.
> O Lord, do hear our crying,
> We beseech you, shorten these days,
> Pour into our hearts
> Your Spirit, without delay.
> Give us strength too, in our need,
> Like them, to battle to the death,

So that with greatest longing
We may receive the crown with them.[39]

Late medieval spiritual teaching had prepared sixteenth-century Europeans to focus on the time of death as 'the moment of truth'. On public scaffolds across Europe, many hundreds of Anabaptist men and women martyrs 'died well', in full view of the masses who had been congregated by the authorities to see just the opposite. It is not surprising that it soon became common practice to gag Anabaptist prisoners, to prevent them from singing and testifying in their last moments, and that some authorities took to executing Anabaptists in secret, rather than in public spectacles.[40]

CONCLUSION

Bernard McGinn has suggested that some of the Christian martyrs of the second century may well belong within the broader stream of mystical spirituality. Ignatius of Antioch (*c*. 110), for example, who interpreted the Christian life as an imitation of Christ, expected to 'attain' God by means of his impending martyrdom.[41] McGinn notes that insofar as mysticism is understood as a process of transformation driven by a desire for, and consciousness of, God's immediate presence, then a focus on the coming union with God after death may well fit within the Christian mystical tradition.[42] This observation certainly opens the door to a consideration of Anabaptist spirituality as in continuity with this broader, ancient Christian spiritual stream.

As the hundreds of prison testimonies give witness, Anabaptist prisoners contemplating their coming martyrdom expressed a confident hope in the better life with God that awaited them on the other side of death's door. George Steinmetz wrote in 1530: 'O God, sustain us to Thy praise and honor . . . give us strength . . . that we may never despond, but keep good courage and remain steadfast and proceed straight on in the narrow way, and at the risk of body-life, go on through

Christ to the Father. John 14:6.'[43] By suffering through Christ and entering the narrow way, the martyrs were confident that they would soon be in the presence of God. When nine brothers and three sisters were martyred in Austria in 1528, the youngest of the men offered to die first, and said 'God bless you, my beloved brethren; today we shall all be together in Paradise.'[44]

The prison witnesses often speak of the 'crown' they will receive when they meet the Lord in the hereafter, and sometimes about the new bodies they would receive. Jan van Hasebroeck wrote to his wife:

> My dear and much beloved wife, take good heed, that no robber deceive you by philosophy and vain deceit, after the rudiments of the world; and that you may not have labored in vain, but may receive your reward, so that no man may take your crown. Hence have your conversation always in heaven, from whence we look for our Saviour, Christ Jesus our Lord; who shall change our vile body, that it may be fashioned like unto His glorious body. Phil. 3:20–21.[45]

Cornelis the shoemaker likewise wrote to his 'dear wife' and 'most beloved lamb' reminding her of the promise that they would be clothed by God into eternity,[46] while Hans Symons wrote from prison, using the imagery of the labours of childbirth, and the joy of 'being delivered' in the end.[47]

Images of life after death, read as faithful promises, often were drawn from the book of Revelation. Lijsken Dircks wrote from her prison cell to her husband Jeronimus Segersz, who also was in prison:

> let us then be at peace in him, and take on our cross with joy and patience, and await with firm faith those promises which he has made us [Rev. 2:3], not doubting them, for he is faithful who has promised it. This is so we might be crowned on [2 Esd. 2:42; Rev. 7:9] Zion's mountain, and be adorned with palms, and might follow the [Rev. 14:4] Lamb.[48]

Maeyken Wens wrote to her son Adriaen in a manner often seen in letters from parents to children, and spouses to one another, expressing her hope and confidence in a reunion to come: 'Oh, my dear son! Although I have been taken from you here, if you will turn yourself to the fear of God from your youth, you will have your mother again in the new Jerusalem up above; there there will be no more parting.'[49]

There was little overt 'unitive' language to be found in the writings of the Anabaptist martyrs, as they contemplated life after death. Their expressions, drawn almost exclusively from scriptural sources, depend heavily on the images of life after death provided there: the faithful waiting under the altar, the crown of glory, the impending day of judgement, and the promises of eternal happiness in the New Jerusalem.

Whether or not we consider Anabaptist spirituality to have been 'mystical' – and there seem to be some good reasons for so understanding it – the striking fact remains that the living presence of God provides the axis around which all else revolves in Anabaptist spirituality. We have had occasion to note this fact at every descriptive stage of the Anabaptist spiritual path, culminating in the challenge of suffering and martyrdom. The pressing hour of death that was forced upon so many Anabaptists in the sixteenth century brought into view the immediate comfort of God's presence that they experienced in prison and under torture, as they prayed their way through horrific circumstances. They faced death with the hope and confidence that the power, presence and reality of the living God that they had already experienced awaited them in its full reality once they had put off their mortal bodies. How else to explain a statement of faith as that of Margret Hottinger, whose sentence of execution by drowning was underway when she was pulled from the water, still alive, and asked one more time to recant. She answered, 'Why did you pull me out? The flesh was almost defeated.'[50]

The very real possibility of suffering death for their faith distilled medieval ascetic themes for the Anabaptists, which in their turn were the themes of a sublimated martyrs' spirituality: suffering the loss of one's will by yielding to God's will and purposes; following after Christ in all things, including acceptance of suffering; accepting the enmity of the world as the price of obedience; struggling to overcome human weakness, and cultivating the Christ-like virtues; turning away from the temptations of 'the world' and 'the flesh'; living as a member of Christ's Body on earth; relying on God's power in the extremities of prison, torture and painful death.

In medieval mystical spirituality, the struggle between two competing spiritual realms formed the conceptual framework within which the experience of the presence of God took place. This framework remained for the Anabaptists, but with a different reality and intensity. The former Benedictine prior, then Anabaptist leader Michael Sattler, wrote to the reformers of Strasbourg that he could not agree with their broad, state-church approach because 'Believers are chosen out of the world, therefore the world hates them. The devil is prince over the whole world, in whom all the children of darkness rule. Christ is the Prince of the Spirit, in whom all who walk in the light live.'[51]

Not only must the 'flesh' make way for 'spirit' in order for the presence of God to be manifested, but once the path has been entered, the 'flesh' will attack the 'spirit' and the pilgrim will be assaulted on all sides.[52] Separation from the world for true believers, the Anabaptists were convinced – on rather good evidence in their time – is inevitable and necessary. Their life experiences confirmed their reading of Scripture, as they were attacked precisely for wanting to follow after Christ in all sincerity and conviction. In the contemplative tradition the attacks of the 'flesh' on the 'spirit' were suffered in cloistered contemplation; in the early Anabaptist tradition, the enmity between 'heaven' and 'earth', the spiritual struggle, became the stuff of everyday life.

Anabaptist spirituality was thus suffused with a 'martyrological sensibility' that directed and concentrated the reading and interpretation of Scripture and the understanding of the faithful Christian life. The path of following after Christ had been well marked by the devout of the church for many centuries, but the sixteenth-century reality led to the conclusion following a 'way of perfection' in a cloister, within the body of a broader Christendom, had been in error. The Anabaptists could not accept that a larger body of Christendom was pursuing salvation along a 'broader' way. Rather, they were convinced that the only true Body of Christ, the one and only Bride of Christ, was none other than the suffering remnant who had passed through the narrow gate and were walking on the narrow way that had been walked by Christ himself, as he carried his cross.

9 ANABAPTISM TODAY

The Anabaptist spiritual tradition took shape in response to the historical situation of its time. The relevance of the Anabaptist response, however, did not disappear with the passing of the sixteenth century. Anabaptist spirituality marked a challenging path that retains its prophetic relevance today, calling for surrender to the Spirit of the living God in all things, putting Christ's way into concrete practice in the 'real world' by following in his footsteps. No matter the historical circumstance, the Anabaptist example of living simply and with integrity in this world, according to the principles of the Kingdom announced by Jesus, speaks with as clear a voice in this postmodern era as it has in other times. Among those who continue to be challenged by Anabaptist spiritual principles are groups such as the Mennonites, the Amish, the Hutterites, the Brethren, the Bruderhof and the Baptists, all of whom claim Anabaptist origins.

One of the gifts of the Anabaptists to the wider Christian church is the insight that God calls every human being to a personal recognition of the truth, and to a personal commitment to a new life in Christ, recognising Jesus Christ as both Saviour and Lord. Jesus called us not simply to be believers, but to be disciples.

Putting Christian discipleship into practice is no easy matter, for the costs are high, and what appear to be less painful alternatives abound. The Anabaptist spiritual tradition, however, resisted the temptation to disconnect a private, interior 'spiritual life' from the less-than-spiritual actions that are supposedly necessary for life in a public and secular world.

Rather than privatising the spiritual life and divorcing it from life in the world, the Anabaptists insisted on applying the rules of the Kingdom of God to all of life. They insisted that we are called to lives of integrity, the integrity of faith and obedience, of belief and action, of hidden conviction and public behaviour. The final measure of all this is the life, the words and the person of Jesus, to whom one makes the highest commitment in baptism.

In a world in which one hears the insistent call to be spiritually 'born again', an experience which apparently changes one's heavenly status with no corresponding necessity for a life in conformity with the life of Christ, the challenge of Anabaptist spirituality remains clear. The spiritual rebirth of which the Anabaptists spoke was indivisibly linked to a radical discipleship.

In the second place, Anabaptist spirituality was premised on the loving presence and powerful action of the Spirit of God, regenerating and empowering believers. It is the power of God that makes disciples, and not simply good human intentions. This reminder is needed far more in the secularised and wealthy Christianity of the industrialised West than in the Christian communities of the two-thirds world, where the living presence of God is experienced as the primary motive force calling the church into being and sustaining the church day by day. Anabaptist spirituality, speaking from its own reading of Scripture in its own difficult situation, continues to provide inspiration to contemporary Christians who live under conditions of oppression and lack. As the Anabaptists learned, the presence of God gives birth to hope for those who sincerely seek God's Spirit.

Anabaptist spirituality understood the reality of human weakness and sin, and the need for the presence and power of God in all things. As such, it challenges the modern liberal temptation to assume that human beings, being good, can simply build on their goodness, work hard and achieve a better world. All good grows from the living power of God, working in those who sincerely open themselves to that power of good. On the other side of the ledger, Anabaptist spirituality rejected the view that saw human beings as so thoroughly depraved that no spiritual good could hope to be achieved by faithful action in this world. To the contrary, the Anabaptist spiritual tradition held that those who open themselves to the power of God will work to incarnate the Kingdom of God in this world, not by their own power, but by the power of the risen Christ.

The Anabaptist call to radical discipleship outlines an ethic of following after Jesus, but more fundamentally, the Anabaptist call to radical discipleship insists that disciples are those who allow the spiritual power of the risen Christ to manifest itself in their lives. The disciples of Jesus will live lives that remind the world of Jesus, not because they are superhuman rule-keepers, but because they have yielded to the power of the risen Christ in their lives. It is this spirit of *Gelassenheit*, of 'yieldedness', that corresponds to a non-violent life, a life that refuses to insist on the forceful imposition of one's will on the world.

The Anabaptist spiritual tradition refused to abandon or relativise the high demands that Jesus passed on as blessings to those who heard him speak on the mountain: blessed are those who truly need God and who are sorrowful, those of a gentle spirit who hunger and thirst for righteousness, those who show mercy, the pure of heart who are peacemakers, and blessed are those who are persecuted for the sake of the Kingdom. The Anabaptists were convinced that these blessings were to be lived and experienced by the power of God, in full view of the world. The gentle and peace-loving spirit of Christ creates disciples who refuse to violate others socially, economically or with violence of any kind. Not only did Jesus exemplify these blessings with his entire life, he called on his followers to do the same.

Christians are to be peacemakers, loving enemies, sharing and not hoarding God's good gifts, not arrogating power to themselves, but comforting, healing and loving. This timeless message is at the heart of the Gospel, the good news that followers of Jesus proclaim to the world. Experiencing forgiveness through Christ is good news for us personally; putting forgiveness into action gives living witness to the Gospel and extends the good news to others. The Anabaptist spiritual tradition continues to challenge those who would believe in Christ as spiritual Saviour, to fearlessly follow Jesus Christ also as Lord of all life, walking the way that he himself indicated in both word and deed.

In the third place, Anabaptist spirituality insisted upon the central importance of the united community of witnesses, the incarnated Body of Christ, as the natural place in which the earthly pilgrimage of individual members would unfold. It is in the communal setting of the Body of Christ that one can profess one's faith openly, and pledge to live according to that faith, with the help of other members. It is within the Body of Christ that the 'habits of heaven' are practised and acquired. It is the Body of Christ, driven by the Spirit of Christ, that will follow Christ the Head in uncompromising obedience, in face of any opposition presented to it by the powers of 'the world'.

The Anabaptists insisted that the community is the Body of Christ, and so opposed the spiritualistic individualism that was already emerging in the sixteenth century. The Anabaptist spiritual tradition continues to challenge spiritual expressions that focus exclusively on the private spiritual state of the individual. The spiritual life of Christians, the Anabaptists believed, is lived in relationship of members to the Body, under obedience to Christ the Head.

The Anabaptist spiritual legacy represents a significant witness to a postmodern world. To a predominantly non-Christian world, the Anabaptists promise the possibility of a personal encounter with the living God, and a vital owning of one's faith on the basis of that encounter. As spiritual and ethical standards are increasingly relativised in the indust-rialised West, the call to focus on the person of Jesus Christ measures our convictions and our lives by the one indubitable and certain measure of faith and life. In a world increasingly dominated by an exaggerated individualism, the Anabaptist recognition of the centrality of the faith community is a call away from the seduction of a 'God-and-me' spirituality. To be Christian is to be responsible and responsive to God's call in Christ, then to other members of Christ's Body, then to all members of the human race, and finally to the health of God's creation itself.

In an increasingly post-Christian world, Anabaptist spirituality reminds us in no uncertain terms of the lordship of Christ in all things. Historically, mainline churches have often joined forces with the powers that be, sometimes in the service of questionable causes. All too often, an acculturated 'Christian church' has become all too willing to bless the social, political or economic status quo of its era, to the detriment of what should be a genuine Christian witness. Speaking with integrity from an era still dominated by the idea of Christendom, the Anabaptist spiritual tradition counsels the churches of post-Christendom to maintain a judicious distance from political power, and also specifically notes the areas in which this distance needs to be maintained.

The Anabaptist experience does suggest that maintaining such a clear witness vis-à-vis the reigning culture or state may well result in social, political and economic difficulties for the church. The question it poses to believers in our time, and in any historical era, is whether we have counted the cost of following Christ with a total and unreserved commitment. The Anabaptist experience is a sobering and realistic reminder of the costs of discipleship, of the significance of the baptismal pledge and commitment to follow after the one who said, 'If any want to become my followers, let them deny themselves and take up their cross and follow me.'

NOTES

Abbreviations used in the Notes

Ausbund   *Ausbund, das ist Etliche schöne Christliche Lieder, wie sie in dem Gefängnis zu Passau in dem Schloss von den Schwiezer Brüdern und von andern rechtglaubigen Christen hin und her gedichtet worden.*

BH   *Balthasar Hubmaier*, ed. Wayne Pipkin and John H. Yoder (Scottdale, PA: Herald Press, 1989).

Chronicle   *The Chronicle of the Hutterian Brethren*, vol. 1 (Rifton, NY: Plough Publishing, 1987).

CWMS   *The Complete Writings of Menno Simons*, trans. L. Verduin, ed. J. C. Wenger (Scottdale, PA: Herald Press, 1956).

LhBr   *Die Lieder der Hutterischen Brüder*, 4th edn (Cayley, AB: Macmillan Colony, 1974).

MM   Thieleman J. van Braght, *Martyrs Mirror* (Scottdale, PA; Herald Press, 1972).

QGTS, I   *Quellen zur Geschichte der Täufer in der Schweiz, 1. Band*, ed. L. von Muralt and W. Schmid (Zürich: Theologischer Verlag, 1952).

SBC   *Biblical Concordance of the Swiss Brethren, 1540*, ed. C. Arnold Snyder, trans. Gilbert Fast and Galen Peters (Kitchener, ON: Pandora Press, 2001).

SSGAA   *Sources of South German/Austrian Anabaptism*, ed. C. A. Snyder, trans. W. Klaassen, F. Friesen and W. Packull (Kitchener, ON: Pandora Press, 2001).

TA, *Hesse*   Günther Franz (ed.), *Urkundliche Quellen zur hesseschen Reformationsgeschichte* (Marburg: N. G. Elwert'sche Verlagsbuchhandlung, 1951).

WDP   *The Writings of Dirk Philips*, ed. and trans. C. J. Dyck, W. Keeney and A. Beachey (Scottdale, PA: Herald Press, 1992).

WPM   *The Writings of Pilgram Marpeck*, ed. and trans. William Klaassen and Walter Klaassen (Scottdale, PA: Herald Press, 1978).

1. Anabaptist Spirituality in Historical Perspective

1. By far the most comprehensive description remains George H. Williams, *The Radical Reformation*, 3rd edn (Kirksville, Mo.: Sixteenth Century Journal Publishers, 1992). For a more limited treatment of the subject, see Arnold Snyder, *Anabaptist History and Theology: An Introduction* (Kitchener, ON: Pandora Press, 1995).

2. *Sources of South German/Austrian Anabaptism*, ed. C. A. Snyder, trans. W. Klaassen, F. Friesen and W. Packull (Kitchener: Pandora Press, 2001), p. 248. (Hereafter *SSGAA*.)

3. See, for example, Hans-Jürgen Goertz, *The Anabaptists*, trans. Trevor Johnson (London: Routledge, 1996), a translation and expansion of *Die Täufer. Geschichte und Deutung* (Munich: Beck, 1988).

4. *The Chronicle of the Hutterian Brethren* (Rifton, NY: Plough Publishing, 1987), vol. 1, p. 45. (Hereafter *Chronicle*.)

5. *ibid.*

6. The Donatist movement of North Africa, which began after the Diocletian persecutions of the third century, practised re-baptism, not because infant baptism was being resisted (which at that time still was a minority practice in the church) but because of a rejection of baptism that had been carried out at the hands of apostate bishops. The imperial church of the next century decided against the Donatists, and by Augustine's time re-baptism was an imperial crime, punishable by death. Augustine provided the essential theological and biblical arguments for 'compelling' Donatists into the church by force. Some eleven centuries later, the imperial mandate of Speyer (1529) explicitly identified sixteenth-century Anabaptism with Donatism ('condemned and forbidden many centuries ago') and decreed that 'every Anabaptist and rebaptized man and woman of the age of reason shall be condemned and brought from natural life into death by fire, sword, and the like, according to the person' (Williams, *Radical Reformation*, p. 359). St Augustine's arguments for compelling the Donatists into the church by force were also found useful by some in the sixteenth century. The Lutheran pastor Urbanus Rhegius borrowed liberally from Augustine's anti-Donatist writings in composing his influential *Justification for the Prosecution of Anabaptists* (1536). The latter writing is translated in *SSGAA*, pp. 213–27.

7. F. Bente (ed.), *Concordia Triglotta. Die symbolischen Bücher der evangelisch-lutherischen Kirche, deutsch-lateinisch-englisch . . . herausgegeben . . .* (St Louis: Concordia Publishing House, 1921), p. 839 (from the *Epitome* or summary; see the virtually identical statement on p. 1097). Likewise, even if one were to grant that salvation was by faith and not by the merit of works, if one went on to say that works subsequent to faith were necessary for salvation, as did the Anabaptists, this was also said to be a theological error. *Ibid.* p. 945.

8. Walter Klaassen, *Anabaptism: Neither Catholic nor Protestant*, 3rd edn (Kitchener, ON: Pandora Press, 2001).

9. Sjouke Voolstra, 'Hetzelfde, maar anders. Het verlangen naar volkomen vroomheid als drijfveer van de Moderne Devotie en van de doperse reformatie', *De doorwerking van de Moderne Devotie. Windesheim 1387–1987, Voordrachten gehouden tijdens het Windesheim Symposium Zwolle/Windesheim 15–17 oktober 1987* [Uitgegeven P. Barge], ed. C. Graafland, A. Y. Yelsma, A. G. Weiler (Holdersum, 1988), 119–133.

10. *Chronicle*, p. 41.

2. The Human Condition: Coming to a Knowledge of the Truth

1. Thieleman J. van Braght, *Martyrs Mirror* (Scottdale, PA: Herald Press, 1972), p. 646 (Hereafter *MM*.)

2. *MM*, p. 11076.

3. First, in the 'Prologue', *RB 1980: The Rule of St. Benedict in Latin and English with Notes*, ed. Timothy Fry (Collegeville, MN: Liturgical Press, 1981), p. 159. Later in Ch. 7: 'The first step of humility, then, is that a man keeps the fear of God always before his eyes (Ps. 36:2) and never forgets it. He must constantly remember everything God has commanded.' *Ibid*. p. 193.

4. See the *Biblical Concordance of the Swiss Brethren, 1540*, ed. C. Arnold Snyder, trans. Gilbert Fast and Galen Peters (Kitchener, ON: Pandora Press, 2001). (Hereafter *SBC*.)

5. *MM*, p. 1079.

6. *MM*, pp. 1076–77.

7. Song 50, by Christoph Bisel, in *Ausbund, das ist Etliche schöne Christliche Lieder, wie sie in dem Gefängnis zu Passua in dem Schloss von den Schweizer Brüdern und von andern rechtglaubigen Christen hin und her gedichtet worden* (hereafter *Ausbund*). First edition 1564; second expanded edition 1583. Subsequent editions to the present essentially reproduced the 1583 edition, with some minor additions. I have used, and slightly modified, a translation taken from *Songs of the Ausbund* (Millersburg, OH: Ohio Amish Library, 1999), vol. 1, p. 100.

8. *SBC*, p. 66. For a full collection of Scripture passages on this theme, see *ibid*. pp. 64–7.

9. For example, by Thomas à Kempis: 'The authority of the writer should not affect you, whether he be of little or great learning; but let love of the plain truth lead you to read. Ask not, Who said that? but consider what is said. Men pass away, but the truth of the Lord abides for ever. God speaks to us in many ways, without respect of persons.' *Of the Imitation of Christ*, Book I, Ch. 5, trans. Abbot Justin

McCann (New York: Mentor, 1962), p. 22. Or again: 'Fear God, and you shall not be afraid of the terrors of men.' *Ibid.* Book III, Ch. 36, p. 118. John Kessel, the cook in the Lord Florens House in Deventer, wrote: 'I must try, moreover, in all my works, words, and thoughts to fear God more than men, so that whatever I do be done purely to honor God and to please him alone. In whatever matters I might transgress, I should fear to offend God more than men.' John Van Engen (trans.), *Devotio Moderna: Basic Writings* (New York: Paulist Press, 1988), p. 208.

10. *SSGAA*, p. 209.
11. *MM*, p. 482. Elizabeth was subsequently tortured with thumb and shin screws. When she refused to reveal the names of her fellow members, she was condemned to death by drowning on 27 March, 1549.
12. *The Complete Writings of Menno Simons*, trans. L. Verduin, ed. J. C. Wenger (Scottdale, PA: Herald Press, 1956), p. 90. (Hereafter *CWMS.*)
13. *CWMS*, p. 92.
14. *CWMS*, p. 95.
15. *MM,* p. 1077.
16. *Ausbund*, hymn 51, stanza 4; translation from *Songs of the Ausbund*, p. 104, slightly modified.
17. Hans Denck, 'Whether God is the Cause of Evil' (Augsburg, 1526) in George H. Williams and Angel M. Mergal (eds.), *Spiritual and Anabaptist Writers* (Philadelphia: Westminster, 1957), p. 106.
18. Thomas à Kempis wrote in the first chapter of his spiritual classic, 'This is the highest wisdom: to despise the world and aim at the Kingdom of Heaven.' *Imitation of Christ*, Book I, Ch. 1, p. 17. The anonymous mystical author of the *Theologia Deutsch* advised, 'I should only wait for God and His work and leave aside all creatures with all their works, first of all my own self.' *The Theologia Germanica of Martin Luther*, trans. Bengt Hoffman (New York: Paulist Press, 1980), Ch. 9, p. 70.
19. *MM*, p. 905.
20. *CWMS*, pp. 56–7.
21. 'The labor of obedience will bring you back to him from whom you had drifted through the sloth of disobedience.' *Rule of St. Benedict*, Prologue, p. 157.
22. *The Writings of Pilgram Marpeck*, ed. and trans. William Klassen and Walter Klaassen, (Scottdale, PA: Herald Press, 1978), p. 510 (Hereafter WPM.)
23. One could cite many texts at length here. Johannes Tauler wrote: 'We encounter noble souls so steeped in truth that it shines forth in them. They permit God to prepare the ground, leaving themselves entirely to Him. By this act of self-surrender they refuse to cling to anything of their own, be it their works, their special devotions, what they undertake and what they leave aside. They accept all things

from God in humble awe and refer them back to Him in total detach-
ment, bowing lowly to the divine Will. Whatever God may send, they
are well pleased to accept it. Peace or strife are all one to them . . .
Their time is forever the same for they are unencumbered and
surrendered to God's will.' *Johannes Tauler: Sermons*, trans. Maria
Schrady (Toronto: Paulist Press, 1985), p. 47. Or Thomas à Kempis:
'Strive for this, pray for this, long for this: that you may be stripped
of all self-seeking, and thus naked follow Jesus naked; that you may
die to yourself and live eternally to Me.' *Imitation of Christ*, Book III,
Ch. 37, p. 119.

24. Hans Denck, 'Whether God is the Cause of Evil' in Williams and
Mergal (eds.), *Spiritual and Anabaptist Writers*, p. 109.

25. Translation from Michael G. Baylor, *The Radical Reformation*
(Cambridge: Cambridge University Press, 1991), p. 164.

26. As translated by Gordon Rupp, *Patterns of Reformation* (London:
Epworth Press, 1969), p. 392.

27. '. . . the more a man dies to himself, the more does he begin to live to
God.' *Imitation of Christ*, Book II, Ch. 12, p. 71. And again: 'My son,
in proportion as you can go out of yourself, so will you be able to enter
into Me.' *Ibid*. Book III, Ch. 56, p. 147. Or the anonymous *Theologia
Deutsch*, Ch. 5: 'The less he assumes on his own behalf the more
perfect and whole he becomes.' *Theologia Germanica*, trans.
Hoffman, p. 64. Johannes Tauler writes: 'If you go out of yourself, you
may be certain that God will enter and fill you wholly: the greater
the void, the greater the divine influx.' *Johannes Tauler: Sermons*,
trans. Schrady, p. 38.

28. Hermina Joldersma and Louis Grijp, *'Elisabeth's Manly Courage':
Testimonials and Songs of Martyred Anabaptist Women in the Low
Countries* (Milwaukee: Marquette University Press, 2001), p. 153.

29. Hymn 48, stanza 4, *Songs of the Ausbund*, p. 98.

30. John H. Yoder (trans. and ed.), *The Legacy of Michael Sattler*
(Scottdale, PA: Herald Press, 1973), p. 37 (italics mine). Menno
Simons wrote that if believers suffer a wound (i.e., sin), having been
'surprised by their enemies, their souls remain uninjured and the
wound is not unto death, for they have the anointing of God . . . They
are not so wholly overcome that they cast asided their weapons and
surrender, to become servants of sin again and to be ruled by it.'
CWMS, p. 57. Dirk Philips wrote: 'But if anyone through human
weakness makes a mistake and is overtaken with a fault, then this
sin is not reckoned to him but it is forgiven and covered through the
righteousness of our Lord Jesus Christ, Gal. 6:23; Ps. 32:1; Rom.
4:7[–8]; 8:1 . . .' *The Writings of Dirk Philips*, ed. and trans. C. J.
Dyck, W. Keeney and A. Beachey (Scottdale, PA: Herald Press, 1992),
p. 243. (Hereafter *WDP*.)

31. Tauler, describing people who 'allow God to prepare the ground' in
yieldedness, says 'when tempted, through pride of carnal desire,

through worldly attachments, anger, or whatever else, they immediately surrender it all to God and they allow themselves to fall into His loving arms.' And again, when those who 'have died to themselves and to the world' are assailed by sin, 'they flee unto God and there can be no more trace of sin, for they now dwell in God's freedom.' *Johannes Tauler: Sermons*, trans. Schrady, pp. 47, 48. Thomas à Kempis writes: 'Fight like a good soldier; and if sometimes you fall through frailty, take again greater courage than before, trusting in My more abundant grace.' *Imitation of Christ*, Book III, Ch. 7, p. 81.

32. *SSGAA*, p. 89.
33. 'No ideal was more central to the spirituality of the later Middle Ages than that of the *vita apostolica*, that is, to live as Christ and the apostles had lived.' Bernard McGinn, *The Flowering of Mysticism: Men and Women in the New Mysticism (1200–1350)*, vol. III of *The Presence of God: A History of Western Christian Mysticism* (New York: Crossroad, 1998), p. 5.
34. Baylor, *Radical Reformation*, p. 168.
35. *Imitation of Christ*, Book I, Ch. 23, p. 45.
36. *Ausbund*, hymn 98, stanza 12; translation from *Songs of the Ausbund*, p. 207, slightly modified.
37. 'Summa of the Entire Christian Life', *Balthasar Hubmaier*, ed. Wayne Pipkin and John H. Yoder (Scottdale, PA: Herald Press, 1989), p. 364. (Hereafter *BH*.) Hans Hut, who disagreed with Hubmaier on other things, agreed with him on this point. He wrote: 'God exercises his justice on us through the suffering of the holy cross, which he lays on each one.' Baylor, *Radical Reformation*, p. 166.
38. Criticism of a 'self-imposed' cross predates the Reformation. The founder of the Brethren of the Common Life, Geert Grote (d. 1384), writes: 'Alas, many of us freely take up a cross which we have made for ourselves, such as a hair-shirt or private prayers or extraordinary fasts, but that which God makes for us, also truly ours to be borne and embraced, we not only fail to take up voluntarily but cast from us in horror.' Van Engen (trans.), *Devotio Moderna*, p. 88. It could be that the Anabaptists simply were repeating a pre-Reformation spiritualistic criticism of mechanical acts of penance.
39. cf. à Kempis: 'Jesus has now many lovers of His heavenly kingdom, but few bearers of His cross . . . All desire to rejoice with Him, but few are willing to endure anything for His sake.' *Imitation of Christ*, Book II, Ch. 11, p. 66.
40. Baylor, *Radical Reformation*, p. 169.
41. The anonymous writer of the *Theologia Deutsch* noted: 'If you wish to follow Him you must take the cross upon you. The cross is the same as the Christ life and that is a bitter cross for natural man. Christ says about the cross: He who does not leave all and does not

take the cross upon himself is not worthy of Me and is not My disciple and follows Me not.' *Theologia Germanica*, Ch. 52, p. 143.

42. *WDP*, p. 192. *Ausbund* hymn 98, stanza 14, says: 'Whoever . . . casts my cross away is not worthy of Me, because he is partial in his love towards me on earth, and so cannot be my servant.' Translation from *Songs of the Ausbund*, p. 207, slightly modified.

3. Renewed by the Power of God: The New Birth

1. *MM*. pp. 727–8.
2. *Ausbund* hymn 88, stanza 10, reads: 'Now if the Holy Spirit leads you, so that you no longer yield to sin, God has borne you anew in Christ Jesus his Son. You have been accepted in Him, chosen as His child.' *Songs of the Ausbund* (Millersburg, OH: Ohio Amish Library, 1999), p. 181; translation slightly modified.
3. *WDP*, p. 79.
4. To cite one example from the *Devotio Moderna* movement, Geert Grote (d. 1384) had written: 'In all things the most pure birth, right-eous life, and holy death of Christ are the only true antidotes to our impure birth, perverse thoughts, words, and deeds, so that the spiritual rebirth may radiate through our lives and the life of Christ may be made manifest in our souls and bodies through the mortifi-cation of our flesh.' John Van Engen (trans.), *Devotio Moderna: Basic Writings* (New York: Paulist Press, 1988), pp. 98–9.
5. On the question of faith and works, Gerhard Ebeling sums up Luther's view as follows: 'faith is not the power to act which makes good works, but is the power of the good which makes works good.' *Luther: An Introduction to His Thought* (Philadelphia: Fortress Press, 1970), pp. 168–9. The Anabaptists, by contrast, saw faith pre-cisely as 'the power to act which makes good works'.
6. *SSGAA*, p. 69. Hans Denck wrote: 'Yea, it is impossible to retain the creaturely, as the false Christians do, and at the same time to receive salvation.' (Evil, 97.)
7. *Johannes Tauler: Sermons*, trans. Maria Schrady (New York: Paulist Press, 1985), p. 35.
8. *The Theologia Germanica of Martin Luther*, trans. Bengt Hoffman (New York: Paulist Press, 1980), p. 149.
9. *MM*, p. 727. *Ausbund* hymn 97 also works with the themes of rebirth and the Bride of Christ. Stanza 3 reads: 'Since now your sin is forgiven through Jesus Christ, God has borne you anew in baptism through the Holy Spirit, so that you now are called a chosen bride of Christ. Keep yourself for your spouse alone; be prepared for him at all times. Accept no one else but Him alone.' *Songs of the Ausbund*, p. 201; translation slightly modified.
10. Hans Denck, 'Whether God is the Cause of Evil' (Augsburg, 1526) in

George H. Williams and Angel M. Mergal (eds.), *Spiritual and Anabaptist Writers* (Philadelphia: Westminster Press, 1957), p. 106.

11. *WDP*, p. 296.
12. Thomas à Kempis writes: 'O Lord, how supremely necessary for me is Thy grace, so that I may begin what is good, go forward with it, and accomplish it! For without it I can do nothing; but I can do all things in Thee, when grace strengthens me.'
13. *WDP,* p. 168.
14. *Ausbund* hymn 125, stanza 17, translation from *Songs of the Ausbund*, vol. 1, p. 308; translation slightly modified.
15. Michael G. Baylor (trans.), *The Radical Reformation* (Cambridge: Cambridge University Press, 1991), p. 153.
16. *ibid.* p. 159.
17. *ibid.* p. 163.
18. *ibid.* pp. 163–4.
19. *ibid.* p. 166.
20. *WDP*, p. 530.
21. *SSGAA*, p. 142.
22. *ibid.* p. 280.
23. *WDP*, p. 296.
24. *SSGAA*, pp. 115–16.
25. The anonymous mystical author of the *Theologia Deutsch* wrote: 'For where the Christ life is, Christ is also present. Where this life is not, Christ is not. In the Christ life one speaks with Saint Paul, who writes: I live, yet not I, but Christ lives in me. This is life at its noblest and best. For where that life is, God Himself is and lives, with all goodness.' *Theologia Germanica,* p. 132.
26. *CWMS*, pp. 52–62.
27. *CWMS*, p. 53.
28. *ibid.* The *Ausbund* hymn 47 includes the lines: 'By this a Christian is plainly known, he who turns away is born again, through the Word. Nor more to the flesh, but in the spirit, he lives soberly, brings forth spiritual fruit in this time of grace.' *Songs of the Ausbund*, p. 96.
29. *CWMS*, p. 54.
30. *ibid.* p. 55.
31. *ibid.*
32. *ibid.* pp. 55–6.
33. *ibid.* p. 54.
34. *ibid.* p. 58.
35. Mysticism has often been described as a process directed to an experience of union with the divine. The process was said to include the stages of awakening or conversion; self-knowledge or purgation; illumination, with possible voices and visions; surrender, and possibly a dark night of the soul; and union or consummation (contemplation in its ultimate sense). See, for example, Ray C. Petry, *Late Medieval Mysticism* (Philadelphia: Westminster Press, 1958), p. 21.

36. Bernard McGinn, *The Foundations of Mysticism: Origins to the Fifth Century* (New York: Crossroad, 1994), pp. xi–xix.
37. Bernard McGinn, *The Growth of Mysticism: Gregory the Great through the Twelfth Century* (New York: Crossroad, 1994), p. xi.
38. The anonymous author of the *Theologia Deutsch* wrote: 'I grant you, them, that no one lives totally and purely in this obedience, the way Christ did. It is, however, possible for man to approach and come so close to it that he can be called – and can in fact be – godly and divinized.' *Theologia Germanica*, p. 80.

4.   The Baptism of Water: The Covenant of a Good Conscience

1. *MM*, p. 425.
2. *SSGAA*, p. 356.
3. There are more than one hundred explicit references to the Matthew and Mark passages in the *Martyrs Mirror* alone.
4. In July, 1525, Balthasar Hubmaier published *On the Christian Baptism of Believers*, a foundational Anabaptist text that collated New Testament passages related to baptism. These texts continued to be cited by Anabaptists everywhere. See *BH*, pp. 95–149.
5. See Hubmaier's arguments in *ibid.* pp. 118ff. Modern studies seem to confirm what the Anabaptists deduced from their reading of the New Testament, namely that infant baptism was not a general apostolic practice, and came into wide use rather late in the imperial period. For one small sample, see *The Origins of Christendom in the West*, ed. Alan Kreider (Edinburgh: T & T Clarke, 2001). Particularly helpful are the contributions by Alan Kreider, 'Changing patterns of conversion in the West', pp. 3–46, and David F. Wright, 'Augustine and the transformation of baptism', pp. 287–310.
6. This is one of the texts cited under the heading 'baptism' in the Swiss Brethren Concordance of 1540. *SBC*, p. 15. In his *Interpretation of the Apostles' Creed*, Leonhard Schiemer wrote: 'Paul says, all of us who are baptized in Jesus Christ are baptized into his death, we are buried with him, Rom. 6[:3–4]. This is the reason for baptism, namely a willingness to die with Christ. It is he who comes with water and blood, not water alone. Note: there are three witnesses on earth, the spirit, water, and blood, and these three are one, 1 John 4, 5[:8]. Whoever separates these has broken it, like a chain.' C. J. Dyck, *Spiritual Life in Anabaptism* (Scottdale, PA: Herald Press, 1995), p. 34. See Balthasar Hubmaier's description of the threefold baptism in his 'Catechism', *BH*, pp. 349–50.
7. A scriptural command was held to be binding. Hubmaier wrote in his baptism book: 'Christ wants that one neither add nor take away from his Testament, Gal. 3:15.' *BH*, p. 136. Menno Simons likewise wrote:

'Thus has the Lord commanded and ordained; therefore, no other baptism may be taught or practiced forever. The Word of God abideth forever.' *CWMS*, p. 120.

8. *SSGAA*, p. 91.
9. *ibid.* p. 92.
10. *ibid.*
11. Clarence Bauman (trans. and ed.), *The Spiritual Legacy of Hans Denck* (Leiden: E. J. Brill, 1991), p. 61.
12. Balthasar Hubmaier's seminal booklet *On the Christian Baptism of Believers* states at the outset: 'Baptism in the Spirit and fire is to make alive and whole again the confessing sinner with the fire of the divine Word by the Spirit of God. The Spirit of God makes and effects this enlivening internally in the human being. Outside of the same all teaching of the Word is a killing letter.' *BH*, p. 100.
13. Bauman (trans. and ed.), *Hans Denck*, p. 63. Dirk Philips also wrote: 'In Christ Jesus no external sign alone is of any value without true faith, without the new birth, and without a sincere Christlike being, Gal. 5:6; 6:[15]; John 3:3.' *WDP*, p. 76.
14. *ibid.* p. 72.
15. Pilgram Marpeck wrote: 'before the transfiguration of Christ, no one received the Holy Spirit in the same measure as His apostles and all true believers now received Him. Thus, the true baptism of Christ in water and Spirit is instituted, grounded, and started by Christ. As the Lord said to Nicodemus: "Unless a man be born anew of water and the Spirit, he will never enter the kingdom of God" (John 3:3)'. *WPM*, p. 225.
16. *BH*, p. 349.
17. Leonhard Schiemer wrote in 1527 that keeping one's faith secret was simply a way of avoiding the cross: 'But our scribes (and other falsely famous ones) do not want anything external; the reason: they see how we are burned, killed, suffer, are beheaded, so they keep it in their heart and deny it orally, Matt. 10[:38–39].' Dyck, *Spiritual Life*, p. 220.
18. See Fritz Blanke, *Brothers in Christ*, trans. J. Nordenhaug (Scottdale: Herald Press, 1966), pp. 25–6. Original document in *Quellen zur Geschichte der Täufer in der Schweiz, 1. Band*, ed. L. von Muralt and W. Schmid (Zürich: Theologischer Verlag, 1952), #31, pp. 40–2; also #32, pp. 42–3. (Hereafter *QGTS, I.*) Document #31 contains several testimonies, all of which report similar experiences. Rudolff Breitiner reported that he began to weep and 'bewail his sins' prior to requesting baptism. *Ibid.* p. 41. Conrad Hottinger likewise confessed that he was a 'great sinner' and declared his resolve to stop sinning and live a new life. He sealed his confession with water baptism.
19. *QGTS, I*, p. 43.
20. Blanke, *Brothers*, pp. 32, 33. I have changed only one word of

Nordenhaug's translation, using 'assault' for 'beat' in rendering *schlagen* into English.

21. Hubmaier wrote: 'the outward baptism of Christ is nothing else than a public testimony of the inner commitments with which the person confesses and accuses himself before everybody that he is a sinner and confesses himself to be guilty of the same.' *BH*, p. 86. See also hymn 48 in the *Ausbund*, with its themes of repentance, forgiveness of sins through Christ's sacrifice, and salvation.

22. C. Arnold Snyder, *The Life and Thought of Michael Sattler* (Scottdale, PA: Herald Press, 1984).

23. John H. Yoder, *The Legacy of Michael Sattler* (Scottdale, PA: Herald Press, 1973), p. 37.

24. *WPM*, p. 192.

25. *SSGAA*, p. 264.

26. Menno Simons wrote: 'the Christian baptism which is commanded by God pertains only to believers . . . and not to . . . infants. For it is a washing of regeneration, as the holy Paul has taught and testified.' *CWMS*, p. 264.

27. Dyck, *Spiritual Life*, p. 219.

28. Yoder, *Legacy*, p. 37.

29. *BH*, p. 127 (italics mine).

30. *SSGAA*, pp. 98, 99.

31. For example, the *Martyrs Mirror* reports concerning Hans Huber, who was burned at the stake in 1542, that after the fire had reached his face and singed off his hair and beard, he was asked if he would recant. He refused and 'was immediately burnt alive, and thus *faithfully paid his baptismal vow unto the Lord Christ*'. MM, p. 466 (italics mine).

32. On profession as a 'second baptism', see *RB 1980. The Rule of St. Benedict in Latin and English with Notes*, ed. Timothy Fry (Collegeville, MN: Liturgical Press, 1981), pp. 15 n44, 441, 454ff, esp. 455 n32. One of the earliest patristic references is a letter from St Jerome to Paula: 'Only four months ago Blesilla, by the grace of Christ, was washed by a kind of second baptism, that of profession.' Cited in *ibid*. p. 15.

33. On profession in the Rule of St Benedict, see *ibid*. ch. 58, pp. 267–71. A common monastic practice in the sixteenth century was for professing monks to be covered with a funeral pall and surrounded by lighted candles, symbolising death to sin. *Ibid*. p. 455. The Anabaptists did not mirror the monastic rites. They intended to 'restore' the church to its early purity by following only biblically mandated 'ceremonies'. They considered baptism in water to be the biblically mandated rite and symbol for 'dying to sin', commitment to the community, etc. For further reflections on parallels and differences, see Snyder, *Life and Thought*, pp. 185–7; the parallel is also noted in the case of Leonhard Schiemer, the former Franciscan, in

Stephen Boyd, *Pilgram Marpeck* (Durham: Duke University Press, 1992), p. 35.

34. The definitive Lutheran Formula of Concord of 1580 used this phrase to describe Anabaptism. F. Bente (ed.), *Concordia Triglotta. Die symbolischen Bücher der evangelisch-lutherischen Kirche, deutsch-lateinisch-englisch . . . herausgegeben . . .* (St Concordia Publishing House, 1921), pp. 839, 1097.

5.   The Body of Christ

1. By 'spiritualists' we mean those in the sixteenth century such as Sebastian Franck, Caspar Schwenckfeld and Hans Bünderlin who maintained that only spiritual baptism and a spiritual Supper are 'true' ordinances. The physical elements of water, bread and wine they believed to be completely secondary, incidental and even positively harmful, since they caused much disunity and strife. The spiritualists advocated a 'spiritual church' that was not marked by outward signs and was thus essentially invisible.
2. *Later Writings by Pilgram Marpeck and His Circle*, trans. Walter Klaassen, Werner Packull and John Rempel (Kitchener: Pandora Press, 1999), p. 81.
3. *SSGAA*, p. 143.
4. See C. Arnold Snyder, *The Life and Thought of Michael Sattler* (Scottdale, PA: Herald Press, 1984), pp. 187–91, for a discussion of the parallels between monastic and Anabaptist discipline. See chapters 23, 24 and 28 of the Rule of St Benedict for an outline of monastic practice.
5. See, for example, hymn 56 composed by Hans Straub, in the *Ausbund*, devoted to the ban.
6. Menno Simons, 'A Kind Admonition on Church Discipline' (1541), *CWMS*, pp. 411–12.
7. *ibid*. p. 412.
8. *ibid*. pp. 413–14.
9. *ibid*. p. 415.
10. *ibid*. pp. 416, *passim*.
11. *ibid*. pp. 416–17.
12. *MM*, p. 467. See also C. A. Snyder and L. A. Huebert Hecht (eds.), *Profiles of Anabaptist Women: Sixteenth Century Radical Reformers* (Waterloo, ON: Wilfrid Laurier University Press, 1996), pp. 352–8 for more historical details.
13. See, for example, Balthasar Hubmaier's brief explanation in *On the Christian Baptism of Believers, BH*, p. 147, elaborated in more detail in 1526 in *A Simple Instruction, ibid*. pp. 314–38.
14. A phrase often repeated; an early example (1525) is found in Hubmaier's *On the Christian Baptism of Believers*: 'everyone can see

that bread is bread and wine is wine, like other bread and wine.' *BH*, p. 147.

15. For a fine study of three Anabaptist understandings of the Supper, see John Rempel, *The Lord's Supper in Anabaptism* (Scottdale, PA: Herald Press, 1993), in which the theological positions of Balthasar Hubmaier, Pilgram Marpeck and Dirk Philips are examined in detail.

16. The eucharistic *Ausbund* hymns are numbers 55 and 92. The text to *Ausbund* hymn 92 was written by Hans Betz from a prison cell in the castle at Passau on the Danube, around 1535. The tune was designated as 'O Son of David'. Dr Helen Martens suggests that 'O Son of David' may be the same tune as the medieval hymn *Veni redemptor gentium*. On the *Pange lingua* and *Veni redemptor gentium*, see Helen Martens, *Hutterite Songs* (Kitchener: Pandora Press, 2002), pp. 120–30, esp. p. 129 nn2 and 10.

17. Hutterite hymns have been preserved and printed in *Die Lieder der Hutterischen Brüder*, 4th edn (Cayley, AB: Macmillan Colony, 1974); hereafter *LhBr*. The three eucharistic hymns are by Hans Hut, pp. 38–9; a short anonymous hymn, p. 40; and a hymn by Peter Riedemann, pp. 453–4.

18. *BH*, p. 147.

19. *Ausbund* hymn 92 is the most complete, and devotes the first eleven stanzas to explaining how Jesus Christ, the food from heaven, the spotless lamb, fulfilled the Law and established the new covenant. *Ausbund* hymn 55, on the other hand, makes only passing reference to Christ's historic atonement on the cross, and makes only one oblique reference to remembrance during the Supper. The reference to the atonement comes in *Ausbund* hymn 55, stanza 3, which reads, in part: 'As Head You have given us Your beloved Son, the pure life, He has prepared the way before us.' Reference to 'remembrance' comes towards the end of the hymn, stanza 21: 'Therewith did Christ at the last institute a communion supper of His body, when he broke the bread with thanksgiving. He gave them to drink out of the cup, therewith to reflect (*denken*) on what he has given us, if we cling to His body.' Translation, with some modifications, taken from *Songs of the Ausbund*, vol. 1 (Millersburg, OH: Ohio Amish Library, 1999), pp. 112, 115.

20. *LhBr*, p. 38.

21. *ibid*.

22. *Ausbund*, hymn 92, stanza 12. Translation from Robert A. Riall, *The Earliest Hymns of the Ausbund*, ed. Galen A. Peters (Kitchener, ON: Pandora Press, 2003), p. 118.

23. Translation, with some modifications, taken from *Songs of the Ausbund*, vol. 1, p. 112, stanza 5.

24. *Ausbund*, hymn 92, stanza 16. Riall, *Earliest Hymns*, p. 119.

25. *Ausbund*, hymn 92, stanza 25. *Ibid*., p. 122.

26. As Hans Denck noted, speaking on the theme of righteousness, 'one

breaks bread many times but is baptized only once'. The reason for this, Denck said, was that 'the realization of the Covenant, which is righteousness, must be constantly practiced and pursued'. Clarence Bauman (trans. and ed.), *The Spiritual Legacy of Hans Denck* (Leiden: E. J. Brill, 1991), p. 195.

27. Translation, with some modifications, taken from *Songs of the Ausbund*, vol. 1, p. 113, stanza 9; p. 114, stanza 13.

28. *LhBr*, p. 453, stanza 2.

29. Also *Ausbund* hymn 55, stanza 24: 'For whoever eats this bread unworthily, Eats to himself judgment and death, He who carries guile and mockery in his heart, for him this bread will do harm.' Translation, with some modifications, taken from *Songs of the Ausbund*, vol. 1, p. 116, stanza 24.

30. *Ausbund*, hymn 92, stanza 14. Translation, with slight changes, taken from Riall, *Earliest Hymns*, p. 119.

31. The Anabaptists loved this ancient eucharistic image. It is cited in all branches of the movement. Menno Simons wrote: 'Just as natural bread is made of many grains, pulverized by the mill, kneaded with water, and baked by the heat of the fire, so is the church of Christ made up of true believers, broken in their hearts with the mill of the divine Word, baptized with the water of the Holy Ghost, and with the fire of pure, unfeigned love made into one body.' *CWMS*, p. 145. See also *Ausbund*, hymn 55, stanza 23; hymn 92, stanza 23, and further examples in Walter Klaassen, *Anabaptism in Outline* (Scottdale, PA: Herald Press, 1981), ch. 9.

32. *LhBr*, pp. 453–4, stanza 6.

33. *LhBr*, p. 39, stanza 7.

34. *Ausbund* hymn 55, stanzas 6 and 7. Translation, with some modifications, taken from *Songs of the Ausbund*, vol. 1, p. 112. Stanza 22 of this hymn picks up the theme again: 'For by the bread he shows who has His Spirit. Such a person is His own, of His flesh and bone, a member of His body and His community.'

35. Two days before his martyrdom, Mattheus Bernaerts wrote to his two children: 'Thus did Christ Jesus institute the Supper with bread and wine, to be used in the Christian assembly, in the name of the Lord, for a token of brotherly love and unity, for a sign that we, through His merits, by faith in His holy name, have become partakers of Christ, the true bread from heaven, as Paul declares.' *MM*, p. 948.

36. As with baptism, the Supper could be celebrated falsely, by people who only appeared to have genuine faith and rebirth. Those who celebrated the Supper 'unworthily' would not harm the true Body, but would eat and drink to their own condemnation. Pilgram Marpeck wrote: 'Where the mouth alone receives the outward sign and the essence is missing in the heart, which has little or no regard to the essence, then it would certainly be better for him if he had never partaken of the sign. Therefore, Paul also says: "Let each man

examine himself and thus eat of the bread and drink of the wine" so that he may eat worthy of the Lord (1 Cor. 11:28).' *WPM*, p. 194. See *Ausbund*, hymn 92, stanzas 18 and 19.

37. *Ausbund* hymn 55, stanza 23. Translation, with some modifications, taken from *Songs of the Ausbund*, vol. 1, p. 116.

38. Pilgram Marpeck wrote: 'where the truth is in the heart as the essence (that is the significant thing), there the signs and figures as elements and creatures are no longer mere signifiers. They are . . . co-witnesses and essence with the inner essence.' Klaassen, Packull and Rempel, *Later Writings*, p. 107. The evidence of the eucharistic hymns and other writings of exhortation leads one to conclude that Marpeck was articulating a view widely held among Anabaptists, even if less clearly expressed.

39. *MM*, p. 781.

40. 'Ein kurtze einfaltige erkanntnuß' (*c.* 1573), Codex 628, Berner Burgerbibliothek, 13–14. Translation mine.

41. Marpeck wrote: 'Communion should be used or held often – not as a sign or figure but as a co-witness and essence with the inner essence of the heart. If a believer becomes careless and forgetful of the inner essence and memorial of Christ – his death and benefits; if he no longer knows how his heart should be disposed, for him it is mere bread and wine. In the Lord's Supper we use a figure and token of memory to recollect, challenge, amend, revivify, and edify our hearts.' Klaassen, Packull and Rempel, *Later Writings*, p. 107.

42. *CWMS*, pp. 146–7.

43. Footwashing had been practised in Benedictine monasteries, as well as being a part of Holy Week observances in the Catholic Church. See the *Rule* of St Benedict, chs. 35 and 53; Marpeck noted: 'One can still go to the cathedrals on [Maundy Thursday] and see this communion play acted out in all seriousness. Then the priests wash each other's feet.' *WPM*, p. 265. Marpeck judged that since 'spirit, love, and truth' were missing, such ritual footwashing was 'a monkeyshine'.

44. Hubmaier is said to have washed believers' feet in 1525, during the celebration of the Supper. However, he did not continue the practice in Moravia. Claus-Peter Clasen, *Anabaptism: A Social History, 1525–1618* (Ithaca: Cornell University Press, 1972), p. 118.

45. Original in Lydia Müller (ed), *Glaubenszeugnisse oberdeutscher Taufgesinnter* (Leipzig: Nachfolger, 1938), p. 78; translation from Daniel Liechty (trans. and ed.), *Early Anabaptist Spirituality: Selected Writings* (Mahwah, NJ: Paulist Press, 1994), p. 96.

46. Pilgram Marpeck was mining magistrate in Rattenberg during the time of Schiemer's imprisonment and was acquainted with all the details of the case. Schiemer was executed just two hundred yards from Marpeck's home in Rattenberg. On Schiemer and Marpeck, see Stephen Boyd, *Pilgram Marpeck* (Durham: Duke University Press, 1992), pp. 5–24, 30–6, cf. 76–80.

47. *WPM*, p. 51. See also Marpeck's 'Clear and Useful Instruction', *ibid.* pp. 79, 98.
48. *WPM*, pp. 318, 340. In his *Chronicle* of 1531, published in Strasbourg, Sebastian Franck notes that some Anabaptists 'claim the apostolic life' and 'go by the letter of Scripture, washing each other's feet', lending first-hand testimony to the occasional practice at that time. *SSGAA*, p. 235.
49. Riall, *Earliest Hymns*, p. 369.
50. *Ausbund* hymn 119, stanzas 6–10; translation from Riall, *Earliest Hymns*, pp. 371–2.
51. So Riall, *Earliest Hymns*, p. 376, n9.
52. See the *Mennonite Encyclopedia*, vol. II, 'Footwashing', pp. 347–51. (Hereafter *ME*.)
53. In his 'The New Birth and the New Creature', Dirk commends footwashing 'which the Lord Jesus Christ himself did and commanded his disciples earnestly to do and to follow his example'. *WDP*, p. 301.
54. *ibid.* p. 367.
55. *ibid.* p. 367–8.
56. Dordrecht repeated both of Dirk Philips' arguments: footwashing 'as a sign of true humiliation; but yet more particularly as a sign to remind us of the true washing – the washing and purification of the soul in the blood of Christ. John 13:4–17; 1 Tim. 5:10.' Howard John Loewen, *One Lord, One Church, One Hope, and One God. Mennonite Confessions of Faith* (Elkhart, IN: Institute of Mennonite Studies, 1985), p. 67.
57. *Ausbund* hymn 119, stanzas 16–18, *passim*. Translation (slightly modified) from Riall, *Earliest Hymns*, pp. 373–4.
58. Translation from C.A. Snyder, *Anabaptist History and Theology: Revised Student Edition* (Kitchener: Pandora Press, 1997), p. 370.
59. Pilgram Marpeck wrote: 'The true community and gathering of Christ cannot be identified with a place, nor can it be called a human name. Wherever such a gathering is, according to the Word of the Lord, there Christ is with the Father and the eternally abiding Holy Spirit [John 14:21]. They love Him who keep His word and commandment. To them, He and the Father will come and dwell. Therefore, whoever says that Christ is anywhere else than living on earth, as in heaven, in the power and clarity of the Spirit and in the heart of each faithful believer, he is a deceiver. Whoever does not find Christ dwelling in his own heart, eternally, will not find Him elsewhere. *WPM* pp. 455–6.

6. Anabaptist Spiritual Disciplines

1. Walter Klaassen, *Anabaptism: Neither Catholic nor Protestant*, 3rd edn (Kichener, ON: Pandora Press, 2001); Sjouke Voolstra, 'Hetzelfde, maar anders. Het verlangen naar volkomen vroomheid als drijfveer

van de Moderne Devotie en van de doperse reformatie', *De doorwerking van de Moderne Devotie. Windesheim 1387–1987, Voordrachten gehouden tijdens het Windesheim Symposium Zwolle/Windesheim 15–17 oktober 1987* [Uitgegeven P. Barge], ed. C. Graafland, A. Y. Yelsma, A. G. Weiler (Holdersum, 1988), 119–33; reference on 132.

2. James Stayer, 'Numbers in Anabaptist research', surveys the scholarship and concludes that Anabaptist martyrs probably numbered between 2,000 and 2,500, or approximately half of the total number of people (including Catholics and Protestants) killed for their faith in the sixteenth century. C. Arnold Snyder (ed.), *Commoners and Community: Essays in Honour of Werner Packull* (Kitchener, ON: Pandora Press, 2002), p. 59.

3. Song 67 in *Ausbund*. I have freely modified a translation taken from *Songs of the Ausbund* (Millersburg, OH: Ohio Amish Library, 1999), vol. 1, pp. 136–7.

4. Of course, a document written for cloistered Religious would also have included exhortations about celibacy, obedience to a rule, and stability in the cloister.

5. *BH*, p. 87.

6. Menno Simons wrote in his influential *Foundation Book*, 'Examine the Scriptures correctly and you will find that to the free children of God there is no liberty promised as to the flesh here on earth, even as Christ says, Ye shall be hated of all nations for my name's sake. Matt. 24:9. Again, if any man will come after me, let him deny himself, and take up his cross, and follow me. Matt. 16:24.' *CWMS*, p. 188.

7. *MM*, p. 728.

8. Timothy George, 'The spirituality of the radical Reformation' in Jill Raitt (ed.), *Christian Spirituality. High Middle Ages and Reformation* (New York: Crossroad, 1987), describes Anabaptism as 'a kind of uncloistered monasticism that presupposed a daily walk of holy obedience, prayer, and praise', p. 349.

9. Any monastic rule will provide a good example of this approach, as do very many medieval writings of edification. 'Let the animal man hear this. Up to the present he has been the willing slave of the body but now he is beginning to subject it to the spirit and fit himself to perceive the things of God. Let him determine to shake off the yoke of so foul a servitude and rid himself of the bad habits which the flesh has imposed upon him.' So said William of St Thierry early in the twelfth century, writing to beginners in *The Golden Epistle*, trans. Theodore Berkeley (Kalamazoo, MI: Cistercian Publications, 1971), p. 42.

10. See a brief review in Arnold Snyder, 'The Anabaptist Bible and the "Narrow Way:" Both Catholic and Protestant' in *Balanceren op de smalle weg*, ed. Lies Brussee-van der Zee, Annelies Verbeek, Piet

Visser and Ruth Winsemius (Zoetermeer: Boekencentrum, 2002), pp. 180–95.

11. For examples, see John Van Engen (trans.), *Devotio Moderna: Basic Writings* (New York: Paulist Press, 1988). It has been suggested that the true heirs of the *Devotio Moderna* are the Jesuits. On possible historical connections between Ignatius of Loyola and the *Devotio Moderna*, see R. R. Post, *The Modern Devotion: Confrontation with Reformation and Humanism* (Leiden: Brill, 1968), pp. 548–9.

12. Dennis Martin, 'Guided reading in Christian classics: a bibliography', *Conrad Grebel Review* (Winter 1991), 63.

13. In a classic expression of this process, the twelfth-century monk Guigo described the process of 'divine reading' as follows: 'One first *reads* it by putting it in one's mouth, then one crushes and chews it in *meditation*. As the first sensations hit one's tastebuds the meditation spills over intuitively into *prayer* which praises God and begs for a marvelous taste of the sweetness of *contemplation*.' Guigo II, *The Ladder of Monks and Twelve Meditations*, trans. with an Introduction by Edmund Colledge and James Walsh (Garden City, NY: Doubleday Image, 1978; reprinted Kalamazoo, MI: Cistercian Publications, 1981).

14. The manner in which the desert fathers carried out *lectio divina* suggests a practice more analogous to what we observe among the Anabaptists. In Christian antiquity, one did not read divine Scripture as a meditative *technique*, but rather it was Scripture itself that was the 'school of life'. Even the notion of reading in its modern sense was far from the practice of the desert Fathers, who *memorised* Scripture in order to have it running through their minds continually. They wished to live within Scripture constantly. Armand Veilleux OCSO, 'Lectio Divina as school of prayer among the Fathers of the Desert', presented at the Centre Saint-Louis-des-Français, Rome, November 1995. Available at: http://users.skynet.be//scourmont/Armand/wri/lectio_eng.htm

15. *Ausbund* hymn 19, stanzas 4 and 6. Translation modified from *Songs of the Ausbund*, vol. 1, p. 67.

16. *MM*, p. 1037.

17. *MM*, p. 1074.

18. *MM*, p. 536. In letters written to their children, imprisoned Anabaptists invariably included the admonition 'diligently read the Holy Scriptures', as Jan Wouterss wrote to his daughter in 1572. *MM*, p. 911.

19. This holds for letters and songs as well. Brad Gregory notes that Soetgen van den Houte's 'testament' from prison is 'a virtual flesh-and-blood concordance', which appears to have been recited from memory. Brad Gregory, 'Soetken van den Houte of Oudenaarde' in C. Arnold Snyder and Linda H. Hecht (eds.), *Profiles of Anabaptist Women: Sixteenth Century Radical Reformers* (Waterloo, ON: Wilfred

Laurier University Press, 1996), p. 370. See also Brad Gregory, *Salvation at Stake: Christian Martyrdom in Early Modern Europe* (Cambridge, MA: Harvard University Press, 1999), chs. 4 and 6.

20. *MM*, p. 775; the full story, pp. 774–85. Hans Schmidt reported on his interrogation in Württemberg: 'Then the special priest said, "The living devil disclosed that to you and if you do not forsake it, you are the devil's body and soul." I answered with Scripture verses, referring to the mote and the beam, to the fruit and the tree. God would not give anything evil to one asking him.' *SSGAA*, p. 371.

21. 'Protestant and especially Catholic authors regularly quoted patristic writers such as Augustine and Cyprian, whereas Anabaptists referred almost exclusively to the Bible.' Gregory, *Salvation at Stake*, p. 118.

22. Endres Keller was literate, but his Bible had been taken away from him in prison. Nevertheless, he cites an astounding amount of biblical text, from memory, in his lengthy written confession of faith. *SSGAA*, pp. 198–212.

23. *Concordantz vnd zeyger der namhafftigsten Sprüch aller Biblischen bücher alts vnd news Testaments, auffs kürtzest verfasset vnd zusammen gebracht. Sampt einem Register (c.* 1540); published in English translation as *SBC*. For critical information on print editions, see the 'Bibliographical Introduction' by Joe Springer, in *ibid*. The *Concordance* circulated freely in the Basel area and was confiscated as dangerous Anabaptist literature. See Hanspeter Jecker, *Ketzer-Rebellen-Heilige. Das Basler Täufertum von 1580-1700* (Liestal: Verlag des Kantons Basel-Landschaft, 1998), pp. 369–70, n107, pp. 539–41, 546, 562.

24. See the discussion in Stuart Murray, *Biblical Interpretation in the Anabaptist Tradition* (Kitchener, ON: Pandora Press, 2000), pp. 22–9. Miriam U. Chrisman, *Lay Culture, Learned Culture: Books and Social Change in Strasbourg, 1480–1599* (New Haven: Yale University Press, 1982), p. 282, concludes that after the Reformation, the average layperson in Strasbourg 'probably only heard the Bible read in their pastor's sermons'. Since the Bible was mediated through the clergy, most Protestant laity had little direct knowledge of the biblical text itself. The contrast with Anabaptist laity is striking.

25. '. . . the brethren read the Bible more often than any other book, and it influenced their way of speaking and writing . . . Indeed, we fail to understand the views and actions of the brethren unless we keep in mind that they were following the New Testament more strictly and literally than Luther or Calvin.' Claus-Peter Clasen, *Anabaptism: A Social History, 1525–1618* (Ithaca: Cornell University Press, 1972), p. 90.

26. For a particularly rare and detailed picture from the early period, see John Oyer, 'Anabaptist women leaders in Augsburg, August 1527 to

April 1528' in Snyder and Hecht (eds.), *Profiles,* pp. 82–105, espe-cially 'rules for operating an underground church', *ibid.* pp. 99–100.

27. 'In 1527 and 1528 the Anabaptists at Augsburg gathered in the houses of 33 fellow believers and in fourteen places outside the city walls. They continually changed their meeting place for fear of arrest. At Esslingen 26 of the 33 meetings in 1527 and 1528 were held in houses of burghers, and a few outside the city. The brethren at Esslingen also changed their meeting place, gathering in 27 different locations.' Clasen, *Anabaptism,* p. 66.

28. M. Krebs and H. G. Rott, *Quellen zur Geschichte der Täufer,* VII Band, Elsaß, I. Teil (Gütersloh: Gerd Mohn, 1959), p. 63; translation mine.

29. *ibid.*

30. Officials in Stuttgart, in 1557, described the Anabaptist view as follows: 'Earlier, when they still loved the world, with excessive eating and drinking etc., they were loved by the world. But now that they began to die to the world, they are persecuted. Therefore they are forced to come together in secret, just as the early church, and to comfort one another out of God's Word.' Gustav Bossert, *Quellen zur Geschichte der Wiedertäufer, I Band, Herzogtum Württemberg* (Leipzig: Nachfolger, 1930; New York: Johnson Reprint, 1971), p. 157; translation mine. Endris Fecklin was seen preaching to two tables full of people, a Bible in front of him from which he read to the assembled. *Ibid.*, p. 540.

31. Krebs and Rott, *Quellen zur Geschichte der Täufer,* p. 135. The Strasbourg records around 1530 document many small meetings in city houses. One witness reported that the Anabaptists met 'in the house next to the stone mason's,' in 'the tailor's house', and in the house of a smith 'by the butcher's gate'. Another reported suspicious comings and goings, and that sometimes twenty or thirty persons gathered together. See *ibid.* pp. 271, 273–5, 277–8, 231, *et passim.*

32. Noted in official documents prohibiting Anabaptist meetings, as in the following from 1571: 'For in such meetings many simple people are misled, and turned away from their proper church and political authorities.' Bossert, *Quellen zur Geschichte der Wiedertäufer,* p. 331.

33. Jecker, *Ketzer-Rebellen-Heilige,* pp. 182–90, *passim.* In Württemberg several widows are reported to have held Anabaptist meetings in their own houses. Bossert, *Quellen zur Geschichte der Wiedertäufer,* pp. 512, 515, 529, 546.

34. The account is cited verbatim in Abraham Hulshof, *Geshiedenis van de Doopsgezinden te Straatsburg van 1524 tot 1557* (Amsterdam: J. Clausen, 1905), pp. 208–11.

35. Clasen, *Anabaptism,* pp. 90–5, citation on p. 95.

36. Gall Diettmar of Fellbach reported in 1562 in Stuttgart that 'when they prayed, they knelt down'. Bossert, *Quellen zur Geschichte der Wiedertäufer,* p. 207.

37. A wide range of primary evidence is summarised in Clasen, *Anabaptism*, pp. 92–3.
38. Balthasar Hubmaier published a brief interpretation in 1526, in *BH*, pp. 241–4; early South German leaders who explained the Lord's Prayer were Eitelhans Langenmatel, Leonhard Schiemer, Hans Schlaffer and Hans Nadler. See *SSGAA, passim.*
39. See *SSGAA*, p. 141.
40. *ibid.* p. 238.
41. Bossert, *Quellen zur Geschichte der Wiedertäufer*, p. 208; cf. also pp. 211, 213.
42. *SSGAA*, p. 377.
43. *MM*, p. 1076.
44. *SSGAA*, p. 307.
45. *ibid.*, p. 339.
46. *ibid.*, pp. 352–3.
47. Adrian Corneliss wrote from prison: 'Lord, teach us to pray according to Thy will, that we may pray in spirit and in truth, that we may truly call Thee Father.' *MM.* p. 527. Balthasar Hubmaier described prayer as 'lifting up the mind to God in spirit and in truth'. *BH*, p. 347. This commonly expressed sentiment often accompanied opposition to formal liturgical worship in churches, which was often characterised as prayer 'with the mouth only'.
48. *MM*, p. 1076.
49. *ibid.* p. 709.
50. *SSGAA*, p. 199.
51. *MM*, p. 950.
52. *ibid.* p. 909; italics mine.
53. *ibid.* pp. 820–1.
54. Philip Wackernagel, *Das deutsche Kirchenlied*, vol. III (Leipzig: Teubner, 1870); Rudolf Wolkan, *Die Lieder der Wiedertäufer* (Berlin, 1903; reprint: Nieuwkoop: B. de Graaf, 1965); Helen Martens, *Hutterite Songs* (Kitchener: Pandora Press, 2002); Ursula Lieseberg, *Studien zum Märtyrerlied der Täufer im 16. Jahrhundert* (Frankfurt: Peter Lang, 1991).
55. Werner Packull, 'Anna Janz of Rotterdam' in Snyder and Hecht (eds.), *Profiles*, p. 341. It was said of Peter Ehrenpreis of Urbach that he won the favour of his neighbours by his piety and 'with his Anabaptist songs which he is accustomed to sing in his vineyards and elsewhere'. Cited in *ME*, II, p. 870.
56. Helen Martens, 'Women in the Hutterite Song Book (*Die Lieder der Hutterischen Brüder*)' in Snyder and Hecht (eds.), *Profiles*, p. 232.
57. *ibid.*, pp. 232, 235. See Martens, *Hutterite Songs*, pp. 43–6 for further examples.
58. Linda Huebert Hecht, 'Wives, female leaders, and two female martyrs from Hall' in Snyder and Hecht (eds.), *Profiles*, p. 191.
59. At the time of execution, Ursula of Essen, her husband Arent and

two other women 'had their mouths tied shut with pieces of wood to prevent their singing or speaking to the spectators, some of whom complained to the Spanish officials. All four were burned to death in huts of straw' (Maastricht, 1569). John Oyer and Robert Kreider, *Mirror of the Martyrs* (Intercourse, PA: Good Books, 1990), p. 41. There are numerous other cases of similar treatment.

60. See especially Martens, *Hutterite Songs*, for a detailed description of this process. It enabled the Hutterites to preserve recognisable sixteenth-century tunes, with no notation, over a period of four hundred years.

61. On the role of such songs in propagating reforming ideas, see the discussion and references in Helga Robinson-Hammerstein, 'The Lutheran Reformation and its music' in Helge Robinson-Hammerstein (ed.), *The Transmission of Ideas in the Lutheran Reformation* (Dublin: Irish Academic Press, 1989), pp. 141–71, esp. p. 161.

62. C. Arnold Snyder, 'Communication and the people: the case of Reformation St. Gall', *Mennonite Quarterly Review* 67 (April 1993), 165.

63. Natalie Zemon Davis, 'Printing and the people: early modern France' in *Literacy and Social Development in the West: A Reader*, ed. Harvey J. Graff (Cambridge: Cambridge University Press, 1981), pp. 69–95.

64. Martens, *Hutterite Songs*, p. 42.

65. The same thing was being done in other traditions. See Martens, *Hutterite Songs*.

66. *MM*, p. 647.

67. *ibid.* p. 738.

68. *ibid.* p. 531. Thanks to Alan Kreider for pointing out his and the preceding example of 'singing Scripture' from the *Martyrs Mirror*.

69. *WDP*, p. 345.

70. See *MM*, pp. 949, 976 respectively.

71. *BH*, p. 359.

7. Discipleship: Following after Christ

1. *WPM*, p. 423.

2. Menno Simons wrote: 'You have voluntarily buried in baptism all your avarice, uncleanness, pride, hatred and . . . you are arisen with Christ Jesus into newness of life (Rom. 6) . . . This new life is nothing but righteousness, unblamableness, love, mercy, humility (etc.).' 'A Kind Admonition on Church Discipline' (1541), *CWMS*, p. 410.

3. Heinold Fast (ed.), *Quellen zur Geschichte der Täufer in der Schweiz, 2. Band, Ostschweiz* (Zürich: Theologischer, 1973), pp. 561, 466. Andres, Hans and Adelheid Zimmermann, sometime in 1531 or 1532, held that 'a Christian should let a neighbor suffer no want, for this is what Christ taught'. *QGTS*, 1, pp. 333, 354.

4. Translation, slightly modified, taken from *Songs of the Ausbund* (Millersburg, OH: Ohio Amish Library, 1999), vol. 1, p. 287.

5. *CWMS*, p. 559. The same sentiments were expressed by Swiss Brethren at various times and places. For example, in Hesse in 1578: It is the duty of 'believing, re-born Christians' to keep their needy fellow members from want and poverty. Günther Franz (ed.), *Urkundliche Quellen zur Lessischen Reformationsgeschichte* (Marburg: N. G. Elwert'sche Verlagsbuchhandlung, 1951), no. 33, p. 435. (Hereafter TA, *Hesse*.)

6. TA, *Hesse*, p. 436.

7. *CWMS*, pp. 368–9.

8. Peter Rideman, *Account of Our Religion, Doctrine and Faith* (Hodder & Stoughton, 1950), pp. 126–7. See also Claus-Peter Clasen, *Anabaptism: A Social History, 1524–1618* (Ithaca and London, 1972), pp. 195–6.

9. TA, *Ostschweiz*, p. 467.

10. TA, *Hesse*, p. 437.

11. Menno wrote, with what turned out to be a lack of prescience: 'Yes, good reader, the whole world is so affected and involved in this accursed avarice, fraud, false practice, and unlawful means of support; in this false traffic and merchandise, with this finance, usury and personal advancement that I do not know how it could get much worse.' *CWMS*, p. 369.

12. *ibid.* p. 370.

13. C. J. Dyck, *Spiritual Life in Anabaptism* (Scottdale, PA: Herald Press, 1995), p. 124.

14. *MM*, p. 911.

15. Luke 12:32–34 was often cited in Anabaptist testimonies and writings. Peter Riedemann wrote: 'When the true and divine become one's treasure, the heart turns towards that treasure, emptying itself from everything else and regarding nothing any longer as its own but as belonging to all God's children.' John J. Friesen (trans. and ed.), *Peter Riedemann's Hutterite Confession of Faith* (Scottdale, PA: Herald Press, 1999), pp. 120–1.

16. *Chronicle*, p. 235.

17. The third article of the 'Five Articles of Faith' of the Hutterian Brethren was entitled 'True Surrender (*Gelassenheit*) and Christian community of goods'. The article collated and cited biblical references on the subject, in the usual Anabaptist fashion of a topical biblical concordance. When one includes marginal references, this article alone pointed to 74 scriptural passages. *Chronicle*, pp. 265–75.

18. Dyck, *Spiritual Life*, p. 121.

19. *ibid.* p. 121.

20. In the 'Strasbourg Discipline' of 1568, for example, the Swiss agreed that 'No brother shall engage in buying or building or other large (unnecessary) business dealing without the counsel, knowledge, and

consent of the brethren and bishops.' Harold S. Bender, 'The Discipline Adopted by the Strasburg Conference of 1568', *Mennonite Quarterly Review* (January 1927), 65.

21. *SSGAA*, pp. 266–7.
22. *MM*, p. 949.
23. *SSGAA*, pp. 203–4.
24. *CWMS*, p. 426.
25. *MM*, p. 511; italics mine.
26. *CWMS*, p. 92.
27. *MM*, p. 537.
28. *ibid.* p. 1079.
29. *SSGAA*, p. 267.
30. Translation, slightly modified, taken from *Songs of the Ausbund*, vol. 1, p. 88.
31. Thomas à Kempis, *Of the Imitation of Christ*, trans. Abbot Justin McCann (New York: Mentor-Omega, 1962), p. 17.
32. *The Theologia Germanica of Martin Luther*, trans. Bengt Hoffman (New York: Paulist Press, 1980), Ch. 38, p. 120.
33. *WPM*, p. 63.
34. Stanza 9 of *Ausbund* hymn 110 reads: 'Blessed are the peaceable, they are the children of God. The Holy Spirit lives in their pure hearts; it directs and guides them in God's Word alone.' Translation, slightly modified, taken from *Songs of the Ausbund*, vol. 1, p. 255.
35. *SSGAA*, pp. 304–5.
36. Cited in Walter Klaassen (trans. and ed.), *Anabaptism in Outline* (Scottdale, PA: Herald Press, 1981), pp. 273–4.
37. As just one example from literally hundreds, Joost Verkindert, martyred in 1570 in Antwerp, wrote to his wife: 'My chosen, comfort yourself in the Lord, and let us commit the matter to Him, and pray for those who afflict us with this; for, "Vengeance is mine, I will repay, saith the Lord." Rom. 12:19.', *MM*, p. 853.
38. *MM*, p. 1084.
39. *WPM*, p. 539.
40. *SSGAA*, p. 371.
41. *Legacy*, pp. 38, 72.
42. *MM*, pp. 914–15.

8. Martyrdom: The Baptism in Blood

1. Cited in Brad Gregory, *Salvation at Stake: Christian Martyrdom in Early Modern Europe* (Cambridge, MA: Harvard University Press, 1999), pp. 16–17.
2. *ibid.* p. 8.
3. *ibid.* p. 6; James Stayer, 'Numbers in Anabaptist Research' in C. Arnold Snyder (ed.), *Commoners and Community: Essays in Honour of Werner O. Packull* (Kitchener, ON: Pandora Press, 2002), p. 59.

4. Gregory, *Salvation*, p. 198.
5. The Swiss Brethren 'Simple Confession' listed those who followed the 'right path and way' as 'Adam, Abel, Abraham, Isaac, Jacob, Joseph, Moses, Joshua, Job, Ezekiel, Jeremiah, Isaiah, Micah, Amos, Daniel, Shadrach, Meshach and Abednego, the Mother with seven sons [in 2 Maccabees 7], Christ the son of God, the holy apostles and all the elect martyrs, servants, and followers of God and Christ. 'Ein kurtze einfaltige erkanntnuß . . .', Codex 628, Berner Burgerbibliothek, 361.
6. See especially Gregory, *Salvation*, chs. 2 and 4.
7. Cited in Gregory, *Salvation*, p. 50.
8. Nicely summarised by Walter Klaassen, '"Gelassenheit" and Creation', *The Conrad Grebel Review* (Winter 1991), pp. 23–35.
9. *MM*, p. 456.
10. *ibid.* p. 1028.
11. Translation from Helen Martens, *Hutterite Songs* (Kitchener: Pandora Press, 2002), p. 50.
12. John Van Engen (trans.), *Devotio Moderna: Basic Writings* (New York: Paulist Press, 1988), p. 87.
13. *MM*, p. 456.
14. *ibid.* pp. 642–3. Jacques Mesdagh wrote to his wife Susannah from prison in 1567: 'Paul expressly says: "All that will live godly in Christ Jesus shall suffer persecution." 2 Tim. 3:12. "For truth is fallen in the street, and equity cannot enter; yea, truth faileth; and he that departeth from evil maketh himself a prey." Isa. 59:14, 15. O my chosen sister, whom I love in God . . . we must here for a short time have tribulation and suffering for the name of Christ; for we must through much tribulation enter into the kingdom of God. Acts 14:22. And also Christ Himself says: "In the world ye shall have tribulation: but be of good cheer; I have overcome the world." John 16:33.' *MM*, p. 716.
15. Cornelius J. Dyck, *Spiritual Life in Anabaptism* (Scottdale, PA: Herald Press, 1995), p. 156.
16. Jacques Mesdagh wrote to his wife from prison: 'For if the holy men and prophets, and the apostles, had to suffer, yea, Christ Himself, who is one Head and Master, how much more ought we, who are poor, sinful and frail men to suffer, if we want to be found little members of His body; for the members are surely not better than the head.' *MM*, p. 717.
17. *Ausbund*, hymn 92, stanza 17. Translation, with minor changes, taken from Robert A. Riall, *Earliest Hymns of the Ausbund*, ed. Galen A. Peters (Kitchener, ON: Pandora Press, 2003), p. 120.
18. *CWMS*, p. 145.
19. *MM*, p. 807.
20. *Ausbund,* hymn 55, stanza 26. Translation, with some modifications, taken from *Songs of the Ausbund* (Millersburg, OH: Ohio Amish Library, 1999), vol. 1, p. 116.

21. *Ausbund*, hymn 92, stanzas 22 and 23, *passim*. Translation, with slight changes, from Riall after Riall, *Earliest Hymns*, p. 120.
22. *Ausbund*, hymn 92, stanza 25. Translation, with slight changes, Riall, *Earliest Hymns*, p. 122.
23. *MM*, pp. 554, 560.
24. *ibid*. p. 701.
25. Hermina Joldersma and Louis Grijp, '*Elisabeth's Manly Courage*': *Testimonials and Songs of Martyred Anabaptist Women in the Low Countries*' (Milwaukee: Marquette University Press, 2001), p. 87.
26. *MM*, pp. 872–3. Mayken Boosers had acquitted herself before many inquisitors; anticipating further interrogation, she wrote to her friends: 'I ask you that you will pray to the Lord for me, asking that he will guide my mouth to his praise and honor.' Joldersma and Grijp, '*Elisabeth's Manly Courage*', p. 179.
27. *MM*, pp. 901–2, *passim*.
28. *ibid*. p. 904.
29. Jan Gerrits wrote, while imprisoned at the Hague in 1564: 'While I thus spoke and they were getting ready to torture me, I felt neither fear nor apprehension; however, they handled me in a very severe and fierce manner . . . the order was: "Handle him without gloves: a drowned calf is a small risk." Behold, my dear brethren and sisters, how unmercifully they treated me. Nevertheless, the Lord was with me, blessed be His holy name; I had no control of myself, but the Lord directed my mouth, so that they could obtain nothing according to their will. See, my dear friends, how faithful the Lord is; him that trusts in Him He does not suffer to be confounded. Sir. 2:10.' *MM*, pp. 680–1.
30. *MM*, p. 840.
31. The song commemorating the martyrdom of Elisabeth van Leeuwarden reported her torture with thumb screws until she could bear the pain no longer, and cried out to God for help. God eased her pain to the point that she told her torturers to proceed, 'for as before I no longer feel pain'. Joldersma and Grijp, '*Elisabeth's Manly Courage*', p. 119. Abraham Picolet wrote: 'I find it to be true: he that trusts in the Lord alone has in his sufferings such joy of heart, that no one can know it, save he that experiences it.' *MM*, p. 823.
32. *MM*, p. 701.
33. John Howard Yoder, *The Legacy of Michael Sattler* (Scottdale, PA: Herald Press, 1973), p. 78. The historicity of Sattler's death signal is established by the reports of non-Anabaptist observers, who observed and reported the same thing. Was Sattler using the ancient Christian symbol of two fingers outstretched with the thumb against them? In the ancient church these were meant to symbolise, respectively, the dual nature of Christ and the Trinity.
34. The *Imitation of Christ* contained the following advice: 'Study so to live now that in the hour of death you may be able to rejoice rather

than be afraid. Learn now to die to the world, that then you may begin to live with Christ. Learn now to despise all things, that then you may go freely to Christ.' Thomas à Kempis, *Of the Imitation of Christ*, trans. Abbot Justin McCann (New York: Mentor-Omega, 1962), p. 45.

35. On martyrdom and the *Ars moriendi*, see Gregory, *Salvation*, pp. 52–5; citation on p. 55.
36. The phrase was applied to, among others, Elisabeth van Leeuwarden. See Joldersma and Grijp, '*Elisabeth's Manly Courage*', p. 121. The song recalling the martyrdom of six women of Antwerp says, 'In their faith strong, as men might be, though in the flesh, as one might think, Caught unawares they did feel fear.' *Ibid.* p. 143. See this collection for a good sampling of women's testimonies from the Netherlands, as well as an informative introduction. On Anabaptist women in general, see C. A. Snyder and L. H. Hecht, (eds.), *Profiles of Anabaptist Women* (Waterloo, ON: Wilfrid Laurier University Press, 1996).
37. Joldersma and Grijp, '*Elisabeth's Manly Courage*', p. 49.
38. For example, Friar Grouwel who attempted in vain to instruct Maria and Ursula van Beckum, is reported to have said, 'The devil speaks through your mouth, away with them to the fire.' *MM*, p. 467. Likewise in the case of Claesken Gaeledochter. See Joldersma and Grijp, '*Elisabeth's Manly Courage*', p. 79.
39. Translation from Joldersma and Grijp, '*Elisabeth's Manly Courage*', p. 137.
40. See the case of the six women of Antwerp, in Joldersma and Grijp, '*Elisabeth's Manly Courage*', p. 151, stanza 23: 'Four of them they drowned, In a tub of water, like they drown animals, Two they beheaded: these six dear kinsfolk, Were thus murdered in the dead of night.'
41. 'For Ignatius, the whole Christian life is an imitation of Christ, but this life reaches its culmination (for those called to it) in the perfect imitation of martyrdom.' Bernard McGinn, *The Foundations of Mysticism. Origins to the Fifth Century* (New York: Crossroad, 1994), p. 82.
42. McGinn, *The Foundations of Mysticism*, pp. 81–3.
43. *MM*, p. 439.
44. *ibid.* p. 429.
45. *ibid.* p. 773.
46. '. . . if our earthly house of this tabernacle were dissolved, we have a building of God, a house not made with hands, eternal in the heavens, and . . . we shall be clothed with it . . . O my dear wife, since we shall put off the flesh, and inherit such a dwelling, let us walk fearlessly in faith before God and His church, and purpose not to depart from the Lord.' *MM*, p. 713.
47. '. . . it is impossible to make any one believe what pain it is to bring

forth a child, except him who has experienced it; however, when it is born, then the pain is remembered no more. Thus it is also with me and my fellow prisoners; we are now in the throes of travail, many a heart grief fills us with anguish, and we must cry to God for help. And He comforts us, for He is a God of comfort, who can comfort all troubled hearts, as He also does. But I hope that we shall soon have brought forth; then we shall remember the anguish and distress no more . . . for He is faithful that promised it us, and will also keep it. We comfort one another much with the Lord's promises. John 16:21; Isa. 26:17; 2 Cor. 1:3, 4; Ps. 6:6; Isa. 25:8; 1 Thess. 5:24.' *MM*, p. 712.

48. Cited in Joldersma and Grijp, *'Elisabeth's Manly Courage'*, p. 99.
49. Cited in Joldersma and Grijp, *'Elisabeth's Manly Courage'*, p. 189.
50. Snyder and Hecht, *Profiles*, p. 52.
51. John H. Yoder (ed.), *Legacy*, p. 22.
52. Sattler wrote: 'Christ is despised in the world; so are also those who are His; He has no kingdom in the world, but that which is of this world is against His kingdom.' *Ibid*.